FROM THESE ROOTS

From These Roots

THE IDEAS THAT HAVE MADE
MODERN LITERATURE

By MARY (M. aguire) COLUM

COLUMBIA UNIVERSITY PRESS
NEW YORK

TO

my friend

DR. W. J. M. A. MALONEY

my editor

HENRY GODDARD LEACH

my husband

PADRAIC COLUM

CONTENTS

CONTENTS

PREFACE

THE nomenclatures attached to literary movements and methods have, as a rule, been given them with the fortuitousness of Adam and Eve naming the animals or the irrelevance of the German professor in the fable who retired to his study to evolve from his inner consciousness the characteristics of the elephant. Consequently these nomenclatures have too often but little connection with what they are supposed to describe. Names like Symbolism, Romanticism, Realism are frequently more of a help in misunderstanding literary movements and theories than in understanding them. For example, what is called the Symbolist Movement in poetry has nothing more to do with symbolism than has any other sort of poetry. The movement so called represented a number of groups previously known by various names, who had, however, two aims in common: the desire to take over into poetry the effects of music—*reprendre à la musique leur bien,* to quote Paul Valery—and the pursuit of an indirect method of expression. It is the too zealous pursuit of this last that has ruined much contemporary poetry for readers; it has led to the notion that literature can be expression without being communication. The idea of realism started with the intention of expressing the ordinary man in everyday surroundings, an intention unknown in the older literatures: in its heyday it was full of inspiration and made the fortune of the novel as a literary mode, but it is now dying of its own excesses.

This book is an attempt to describe and interpret the movements behind the various nomenclatures, to give the history of the development of literary tendencies and forces since modern literature began in the middle of the eighteenth century. In our world, ideas pass rapidly from one country to another, are adopted with adjustments in each new environment so that literary creations in any language are now dependent on and influenced by those in other languages. That is why I make bold to suggest that we should have in our colleges and universities a department of general literature run by people familiar with literatures in many languages. The old reliance on what was called "English" to supply all the instruction in literature is an idea that should be superseded if students are to get any real grasp of the meaning of literary expression. Side by side with this, some revolution should take place in the present method of writing literary history: this still remains at about the same stage as when it first began to be written. We are given commonly a narrative of the authors' lives, some account of their works interlarded with an array of dates in such a manner as to give an almost neurotic importance to chronology and comparatively little importance to the literature or to the stage of development in human expression which it represents.

The art of literature as distinct from the trade of writing is a rare product in any age; it is the interpretation in imaginative form of life and human relations. Sometimes this interpretation has taken an idealistic form; in modern literature under the domination of realism it veered more and more towards the materialistic. It can, however, be said that at any given period the expression is conditioned by certain controlling ideas of that period. These ideas in modern literature have often been dictated by discoveries in fields outside literature and it is these that have decided the patterns of literary performance. It is these patterns, these ideas that this book is concerned with. I have tried to reduce difficult and complex ideas to a clear, if not a simple, expression such as any reader interested in literature can comprehend. This book is not, as some readers of the first edition thought, a history of criticism or a series of essays: it is meant to be read continuously from the first to the last chapter and it is an account of the ideas that have gone to the making of modern literature. For the most part the writers who originated the ideas practised them in imaginative forms—great poets like Wordsworth, Coleridge, Baudelaire; great novelists like Balzac and Flaubert; a great critic who was also a dramatist, Lessing. All great originating writers are critics in the sense in which I understand criticism and which I explain in the first chapter. In conclusion there is something I should like to say: I do not believe that the new literature is meant, as has been so often stated, to be the expression of a disintegrating world. I think the world as it used to be has disintegrated under the discovery and expression of ideas that it had no power to cope with because they came on too suddenly. Of these ideas, the one I think among the most disintegrating is that which has had greatest influence on contemporary literature—the discovery of the importance of the subconscious. This in its very nature is bound to destroy many accepted ideas of human responsibility and eventually to bring about the revision of laws and ethical standards. Much of modern literature is an attempt to express in imaginative form the various modern discoveries in psychology. An instance is that most puzzling and exciting work, *Finnegans Wake,* which tries to reduce to literary and narrative form the immense implications of Jung's theory of racial memory and to make the resources of language equal to this expression.

When the first edition of *From These Roots* was published, the ideas and tendencies with which it deals seemed to be, in a group of writers, evolving into newer literary expression, but the explosion of the war has prevented or delayed this. It is possible, however, from a consideration of what has gone before to come to conclusions as to what the next stage in literature is likely to be: these conclusions, I hope, are implicit in this book.

MARY M. COLUM

Woods Hole
August, 1944

Chapter One

WHAT IS CRITICISM?

I

FOR AT LEAST one hundred and fifty years criticism has been increasingly operative on literature, yet, as a literary mode it is still in its infancy, though, as Anatole France predicted, it may end by swallowing up all the others. When George Sand wrote to Flaubert, on the death of Sainte-Beuve, that she believed criticism had come to an end, Flaubert, a man of enormously penetrating perceptions, answered, "I think, on the contrary, that it is at most only at its dawning. They are on a different tack from before, but nothing more. At the time of La Harpe they were grammarians; at the time of Sainte-Beuve and Taine they were historians. When will they be artists—really artists?" In these few words Flaubert, who, like Anatole France, was a fine critic himself though he expressed that talent chiefly in his correspondence, stated a truth not even now generally recognized. Literary criticism is now only at its dawning in spite of great and transforming critics like Taine and Sainte-Beuve, whom Flaubert erred in not recognizing as artists.

FROM THESE ROOTS

The older critics—that is, those who made a trade of criticism before Lessing came and gave it wings—were grammarians, rule-makers, analyzers, commentators, pedagogues, and it is these most people have in mind instead of the artist-critics like Lessing and Herder, Wordsworth and Coleridge, Taine and Sainte-Beuve— transformers of literature, all of them; men who made a new channel for the current of literature. It is still a notion fairly widespread that criticism of any kind is simply the action of one mind upon the work of another. This, in essence, would mean that criticism is a secondary sort of writing which does not invent or transform its material but is rather a kind of parasite on other minds and other forms of writing—a stepchild and handmaiden of the other arts and the other literary modes, as romances in their earlier forms were regarded. Any sort of literary genre in its lower forms is a parasite on other minds and modes. In its higher forms, criticism is as much creative literature as a fine novel, or a play or a poem; it is not the form or character which is the decisive factor in determining whether any kind of writing is creative literature or not—it is the quality of the mind behind it. Creative writing is simply writing produced by a creative mind regardless of the form or genre the writer uses for his expression: in fact, any fine critic can write finely in what the popular mind regards as the creative form: Lessing was a dramatist, Boileau, Herder, Sainte-Beuve and Matthew Arnold were poets. So many great literary critics have been great poets—Dryden, Coleridge, Poe, Goethe—that there is good ground for believing that there is a close relation between poetry and criticism. All poets have to be critics, and they can fitly be called great critics when the theories they evolve about their own work influence others, as Wordsworth's Preface to the *Lyrical Ballads* influenced generations of poets.

However, the creative mind is exceptional and there is no more reason for describing a successful piece of criticism as creative writing than for so describing a successful novel. But of all the rare forms of creative writing, creative criticism is the rarest, and those who have accomplished it to any extent might be counted on the fingers of one hand. One of the reasons why this is so is that the writing of criticism is very arduous and, in general, the rewards are sparse compared with the rewards for other forms of literature, and this in spite of the fact that the man or woman who writes criticism has less competition from the great dead and the great living than any other type of writer. Another reason for the rarity of fine criticism is the number of difficulties in the way of learning the job thoroughly. Other writers may be able to learn their trade alone, but critics, because they have to be familiar with writing of all kinds, are best developed when, during their formative periods, they are surrounded by writers, saturated in literature, rocked and dandled to its sounds and syllables from their earliest years, as composers have to be rocked and dandled to the sounds of music. Because the nature and province of criticism is still somewhat of a puzzle, particularly in the English-speaking world, an attempt to formulate a definition of it is not out of place, but is even the business of anybody engaging seriously in the craft.

2

The popular idea of criticism is that it is some form of abuse, or attack, or harsh judgment, and doubtless it was as some form of attack that criticism took its beginning. It is necessary also to ask the general reader to dissociate the term criticism as a literary mode from its meaning in practical life, where it commonly denotes a form of censure. With the lapse of time it may be concluded that there will be no more confusion between the meanings of the word than there is between the word "essay" as a literary form and the practical meaning of the word. At present, however, the confusion exists. Recently, in New York, a distinguished physician asked a patient how he earned his living: on being told that it was by writing criticism he warmly recommended him to abandon his job, for, said the doctor, criticism springs from a virus, an irritant in the mind which prevents a person from adapting himself to life. With this astonishing dictum the invalid, a simple-minded man who wrote reviews for a Sunday paper and who suffered from indigestion, seemed to concur, for he had never thought about his profession at all.

Criticism is in itself neither praise nor blame, neither attack nor judgment: as an intellectual force it represents a principle through which the world of ideas renews itself, which prunes and trims old ideas to satisfy new desires or aspirations. Purely literary criticism, which, of course, is only one branch of criticism, represents, in the work of its highest practitioners, that branch of literature whose most important office is the originating of the ideas, the discovery of the circumstances, the foreseeing of the lines that other branches of literature follow.

Besides its major rôles, criticism has many secondary ones, and, therefore, it may ordinarily be described as a literary force put at the service of another force. In relation to art, criticism is a literary force put at the service of art; social or sociological criticism is a literary force put at the service of society; literary criticism is a literary force put at the service of literature. As a force put at the service of literature, criticism can be exercised in various ways according to the nature of the talent that makes up the force. It may be literary history like Saintsbury's or Brunetière's, where the critic has to have the mind of an historian; it may be pure theorizing like Croce's or Alain's, where the critic has to have the mind of a metaphysician; it may be the sort of criticism that deals with the sources and genesis of a work of art, like that of Joseph Bedier, or Victor Bérard, where the critic has to be a specialized scholar, and of which a remarkable example in America is the work of John Livingston Lowes, whose book *The Road to Xanadu* is a production of genius in this class. Or criticism may be simply sensitive and brilliant and informing chatter about books, and to this class belong not only the witty, distinguished criticism of Anatole France and Lemaître and Oscar Wilde, but also the criticism of the best of our present-day columnists. It may be, and it most commonly is, a talent which expresses itself in explaining the work of authors past and present, and in passing judgment on them. Book reviewing, as commonly practised, is seldom criticism, being simply book news in which the writer gives some information about the book considered and passes some judgment on it. The book reviewer, to use Sainte-Beuve's phrase, is the secretary of the public and not necessarily a critic at all.

For, at its highest, literary criticism is the creation of profound, informing, and transforming ideas about literature and life—about life as well as literature, for no one can understand literature without a comprehension of life, which is the matter of literature. Hence the great primary critics have been those whose work had or has, not merely an effect on the understanding and assessing of writing, but a continuous influence on the creation of literature. According to this definition one would have

6

to begin any list of primary critics with Aristotle: however, as I am dealing with criticism in the modern world, where it has preceded great literary movements, I would list as the great creative critics Lessing and Herder, Wordsworth and Coleridge, Sainte-Beuve and Taine: these were the critics who changed and revitalized, in a way that critics had not done before, literature and the matter of literature. In any anthology of creative criticism one would have to include pieces by other writers—by Dryden, Matthew Arnold, Samuel Johnson, by Goethe, by Dante, and by the numerous writers of the Arts of Poetry since the beginning of literature—writers the main direction of whose work would not entitle them to a place with the transforming critics.

To the small number of the great critics there are the strongest reasons for adding the name of Madame de Staël, whose book *Literature in Relation to Social Institutions* is not only the basis of all the conceptions of literature put forward recently as Marxist, but is also one of the bases of the theories of Sainte-Beuve and Taine. She was a social rather than a literary critic and regarded literature as an expression of society—a theory, no matter how interesting in itself, which would, in practice, banish a great portion of the imaginative literature of the world, would banish nearly all lyric poetry and also such literatures as reflect a purely fantastic, imaginative, or psychic life. She influenced, not literature generally, as the great critics had done, but thinking *about* literature, and this makes her a passion with critics rather than with other kinds of writers.

Her importance—her very great importance—was in the fact that it was she who formed the bridge between the two great French critics, Taine and Sainte-Beuve, and the two great Germans, Lessing and Herder. It was she who discovered that German literature had been born of criticism and that it was Lessing who had given life to it.

3

Eighteenth-century Germany, the Germany into which Lessing brought his transforming ideas, was culturally sufficiently like the America we have known to make a parallel enlightening. A learned culture had been built up in the universities, at the courts, and among the literati in general, which was remote from the life actually lived and the language actually spoken, and its proponents, as in America, resisted the upthrust of other forces and the newer vitalities. In America in our time the last fight of the learned culture was made by Babbitt and More, who lost the fight as all such fights have to be lost. The leader of the learned culture who preceded Lessing in early eighteenth-century Germany might stand as typical of all the leaders that the fight against the newer, more confused forces brings forth.

This leader was a professor with various interests,

named Gottsched. His stock-in-trade was not exactly the same as that of the proponents of the learned culture in America, but his mind and theirs were of a like pattern. Like all such leaders—they are generally high-minded men—he believed that the Greeks were the one people who had produced a genuine literature and who knew the ways and means whereby it was done. He was one of a line of savants who had decided that the Greeks had every virtue, that Greek literature was powerfully moral, and that the characters in it represented the height of ethical achievement. To this standard notion was added the other notion that the continual reading of the Bible, with its accounts of the violent passions and emotions of barbarous, lusty men, naturally made people disciplined, restrained, and virtuous and likely to keep the Commandments. Gottsched, equipped with such convictions, reinforced with Leibnitzian rationalism and Lutheran ethics, looked through his learned spectacles at the Greeks and Latins, and especially Aristotle and the Aristotelian Poetics, and perceived that poetry was a branch of scholarship, a rational pursuit meant to add to the moral improvement of man; he perceived likewise that after the ancients, the people who knew most about poetry and drama were the French. To guide his fellow countrymen he made translations from Racine, and taking the old tag from Aristotle, which is so hard to interpret, about poetry being an imitation of nature, he proceeded to

9

write an Art of Poetry on his own account, in which he expounded the necessary rules for writing, showed the part that regularity, intelligence, reason, and common sense should play, and explained that the aim of poetry was to teach by giving pleasure. When a literary group in Switzerland, whom he had imagined to be his followers, wrote with extravagant admiration of the English poet, Milton, and went so far as to talk about the "wonderful" in poetry, it seeemed to Gottsched as if the end of all good taste, of all standards, was coming.

It was in the university where Gottsched professed philosophy according to Leibnitz, in his own university of Leipzig, that the very man was bred who undid him and all he stood for—Gotthold Ephraim Lessing. But the type is recurrent, and Gottscheds belong to every country with an undeveloped culture. This sort of professional critic and legislator of Parnassus is not likely to have much influence in a country with a long and highly developed literary tradition. But the Germans at this time were, to use a phrase of J. G. Robertson's, "as a literature-producing people of no consequence at all." Something similar might be said of Americans nearly up to our own time. The domination in Germany of a diluted classicism and the ascendancy of French culture corresponded to colonialism in America, with a similar theological background. In both countries there was a lack of focus of intellectual life: neither had a capital.

All peoples who have too few models of their own in

art and literature, and who are not familiar with the recorded expression of human experience, are likely to be pedantic in their writing or vacuously dull—this though at times they may show a streak of life and of genius. Sometimes a great political event will arouse such a people out of their tutelage to the pedants, and from dullness into some sort of life. Occasionally a sudden ferment of ideas will accomplish the miracle and start a real expression in literature. There had been in the past of Germany, as in the past of America, certain outstanding figures, but not many: Germany at the time of Gottsched was hardly a nation at all, and this forms a parallel with America. In Germany there had been a few poets, there had been theologians, and there had been the philosopher Leibnitz. Preceding our day in America, there had been a few poets, a few novelists, a few theologians, and, particularly, there had been the two Jameses—the one with his transforming psychology and the other with his transforming material and technique of the novel. There had been in both countries now and again an isolated masterpiece; there had been outstanding intellects, and there had been poets who were worth while, though, for the most part, in the literature produced, there had been dismal stretches of dullness: the minds of the writers, though sometimes filled with learning, had not awakened to complete awareness; they were not really deeply touched by life, for they met life at too few points. When their speculations were most transcendental they were hardest to get at: what is now read, in the one country, of Klopstock and Gellert, and in the other, of Emerson and Whittier, outside a small amount of exciting lyricism, is limited to a few specialists in literature.

It is patent that when literature is in this condition what especially is needed is something that will arouse people, or a section of them, to a state of self-criticism. First of all, there is the necessity for giving them sufficient racial and national pride to make them stop swallowing whole other cultures; then, if the country has the materials of literature, they have to be shown where these materials lie. If America had to make only in a limited degree the same fight against pedants that Lessing had to make in Germany, it had, on the other hand, developed very much less of the sort of life and the sort of human being that could be made into literature, for Germany had in its past a deeply rooted folklore and mythology which had given some of its richness to the commonest man in his every-day life. Therefore, in America, what was needed first of all was a vigorous social criticism in place of the refinement of literary criticism that was Lessing's contribution. And it is precisely in social criticism that America has excelled.

Lowell, fifty years ago, knowing perhaps only subconsciously what he meant, said, "We must have a criticism before we can have a literature." In America there is a new kind of society, a society built out of elements that have never previously come together, and a genuine literary expression of that society has to be preceded by a criticism of it. To produce works like *Main Street* and *An American Tragedy* a criticism is needed, but an even deeper criticism is needed before we can produce works like "Kubla Khan" or the "Ode to a Nightingale," or *Faust,* or *Les Fleurs du Mal.* Old homogeneous countries can evolve their literatures from their mythology and their folklore and their traditional life, but a new country which has neither folklore, nor mythology, nor much fertile tradition in life, has, first of all, to mold its society into shape and take stock of its values, before that society becomes material for literature. In the older countries, where literature was an evolution, the human values that were important in art were those always of powerful significance in actual life, but such values were not always significant in America. Too much psychical and physical energy had to go into conquering the soil and making it fit for habitation to leave overmuch of that sort of energy that goes into the making of a passionate or interesting personality, or into the developing of strong emotions and vigorous sensitivities and sensibilities.

In some of the frontier States, or even those last settled, one can encounter highly intelligent and even highly educated people of a blankness of spirit, a temperamental vacuity, which give the impression that one has met that wraith which some of the old philosophers used to talk about—a human being without a soul, one in whom the breath of the Creator, that breath that gives consciousness, has not entered. Their spirits and emotions are anemic through lack of that long interchange between man and the soil, that daily, almost unconscious contact with the recorded experience of man, which, in an old civilization, can make a rich, subtle, highly sensitized human being of even an illiterate peasant. For this reason, in spite of resemblances, the conditions critics had to cope with in America were not identical with, though in some respects similar to, those that Lessing had to cope with in Germany. He had to struggle to create a literature in a country where a literature of a kind already existed, and where, outside the foreign, learned culture, there was a folk-culture and a warm, rich life and language, native and of the people's own making. In spite of the fact that the learned, like Leibnitz and others, wrote in Latin or French, all this was to be found in Germany. But in America the language was the language of another people, the English, and, to begin with, the culture was transplanted seventeenth-century English, that later became a miscellany of all the cultures of Europe.

There was little art at first. The chief reason why new countries have little art is that the people do not want it—it is not that the potential artist is not born there, but that too few people feel the need of expression for that need to make an impression upon the artist's mind.

WHAT IS CRITICISM?

While life was a conquering physical adventure, as it had to be for long in America, people's energies were too much absorbed for them to demand anything from life except living. But there came a time when they began to wonder what there was besides. Out of this state there emerged with surprising suddenness a civilization in America different from anything the world had seen before, and, more surprising still, there emerged men who gave tongue to it—men whose spirits passed through the gates of utterance apparently without any of the preparation such spirits need in older countries. These artists, no matter in what form they expressed themselves—whether as novelists, like Sinclair Lewis, in *Main Street* and *Babbitt,* or Dreiser, in *An American Tragedy* and *Sister Carrie,* or as poets, like Frost, in *North of Boston,* or E. A. Robinson, in *The Man Against the Sky,* or Edgar Lee Masters, in *Spoon River Anthology,* or the amazing creators of the comic strips, with their satiric reproduction of every type in the country, or Mencken with his assault on the "booboisie"—were, every one of them, devastating social critics. The caricaturists of the daily papers, concerning themselves with the narrowness, aridity, and philistinism of American domesticity, a domesticity more enclosed inside family life than any in the Old World, made themselves part of the experience of the every-day men and women who take the subway or the commuter's train to their work. So that criticism in America not only affected the life of those interested in art and literature, but also the lives of people who read little except the newspapers. Whatever was overlooked by the literary men was savagely satirized by these caricaturists, by Briggs, Sidney Smith, and others. And whatever escaped the notice of the native critics the visiting critics made up for. Some of these outside critics, like Count Keyserling and André Siegfried, had many prcfound intuitions, but others were merely patronizing humbugs and chatterers.

No one who has made a study of American life, or who is familiar with the anemia, woolliness and narrowness of its intellectual life even as recently as twenty years ago, can fail to realize all that criticism has accomplished for it. So that we are justified in saying that American literature started, as Madame de Staël showed German literature to have started, with criticism—criticism that was the first wave of a strong, violent, productive life. However, not all the critics were equally effective: some of them were made arid by New England gentility; some had but short-lived vitality; some of those who set out to be literary critics especially were, like that typical champion of a learned culture, Gottsched, apostles of the notion that only the Greeks knew anything about literature, and that both literature and life should be conducted according to principles drawn from their work. Still, it must not be overlooked that their intervention was also valuable—they brought to people's attention the necessity for cultivation, for taste and scholarship. Their main fault was in thinking that these were the only ingredients that a literature needed. But what American literature and American civilization owe to the whole body of critics is tremendous; it is not easy to formulate; in fact, it cannot be formulated until it is looked at from the perspective of time.

It is also not easy to formulate for the reason that American critics started out without any theories except those they evolved as they went along or those they adopted wholesale from European writers. This adoption was inevitable, for both in life and in literature these were the ideas that had helped to make the world as we know it; they were the ideas behind modern literature, for, as distinct from the older literatures, modern literature was dependent on ideas which gave it a direction, and these had been evolved by a few men to whom the revelation came that, for a time, anyway, literature had to be about the ordinary man because civilization was developing around him, and modern literature and modern civilization were bound up with each other. It is with these ideas, the men who formulated them as a literary philosophy, and the men who applied them in literature, that this book is concerned.

Chapter Two

MODERN LITERATURE BEGINS: THE IDEAS OF LESSING AND HERDER

I

MODERN CRITICISM as a literary force began in Germany in the middle of the eighteenth century and began with Lessing, who laid the foundation on which all critics since have worked. In what way did this new instrument differ from what had previously been called criticism? It differed chiefly in this, that its major business was not rule-making or judgment-passing but the evaluation of the body of literature of the time. Literature in all countries was in a dreary condition: if in Germany real expression had not begun, in other countries it had lost the breath of life and was dying of anemia. A drying wind of reason, wit, rules, good sense, artificial language, had done its work; spontaneity, emotion, life, and lyricism were gone. The job the new critics had to tackle was that of changing literary taste, and they set themselves to it, first by showing up the weaknesses of literature as it stood, then by propounding new theories, and finally by persuasion, force, and example,

18

showing how the change could be accomplished and life brought back to literature. Each of them as he came along took over a stock of literary ideas from his predecessor and added a particular contribution of his own, for in criticism, as in all the other works of men, each originating mind adds to a sequence of already existing ideas: every writer who contributes ideas that revivify literature and that release the minds of other writers to fresh expression is a critic and generally a great one. Every great writer of any kind, even though the general direction of his work may not be criticism, is a critic: the critical mentality, and, one may add, the lyrical mentality, is a fundamental part of the outfit of every writer of the first rank. The most important writers of any period, whether poets, dramatists, or novelists, are very likely to be amongst its greatest critics in their own genre if they have the time or the energy to reduce their literary principles and theories to writing. The best critic of poetry in his own time, for example, was Goethe; the best critic of the novel in his own time was Flaubert. On the other hand, those writers the general direction of whose work is criticism express themselves likewise in other literary forms—in fact it is difficult to imagine how anybody can be a literary critic without that all-round comprehension of literature that comes from the practice of writing in many forms.

Aside from all this, there are certain definite tendencies in criticism and critics that must be taken note of:

one is that, at times of sweeping literary changes, the great transforming critics, consciously or unconsciously, work in pairs—thus we have Lessing and Herder, Wordsworth and Coleridge, Taine and Sainte-Beuve, where in each case one mind is the complement of the other. Then, running through what first-rate literary criticism we have, there will be found in evidence two kinds of minds: the poetical-critical mind and the philosophical-critical mind. Among the critics mentioned, Herder, Wordsworth, and Sainte-Beuve represent the poetical-critical mind, while the philosophical-critical mind was that of their co-workers, Lessing, Coleridge, Taine—for it should be noted that no matter how distinguished a poet Coleridge was, his criticism was philosophic rather than poetic. Finally, it must be repeated that the critical mind and the creative mind are not two distinct kinds of minds, but the same sort of mind developing through different outlets according to circumstances and the needs of the time.

Of the three pairs of critics mentioned above, all except Taine worked in several literary forms. Lessing's great interest was drama and controversy, so he wrote dramas, controversy, verse, and criticism; he was the first outstanding German dramatist and one of the greatest of controversialists. Herder's great literary interest was poetry, and he wrote poetry, history, and criticism. Sainte-Beuve's great literary interests were poetry, biography, history, and fiction, and he wrote all of them

as well as criticism. The great literary interest of Wordsworth and Coleridge was poetry, so they wrote poetry
and criticism. Wordsworth's criticism, to be sure, was
small in bulk, but it was tremendous in its import: it
has influenced nearly all poetry written since in Western
countries.

The literary ideas these critics put in circulation were
not always discoveries: sometimes they were the novel
application of old ideas. Lessing, in addition to his own
discoveries, gave a new application to the dramatic theories of Aristotle; he had made a study of the Greek text
of the Poetics and left the interpretation of it that is
now generally accepted by literary critics. The theory to
which Taine's name is most commonly attached, that
which explains all literary production by the influence
of race, milieu, and moment, was taken over from
Hegel, who expressed it in language almost word for
word with Taine. Hegel wrote in his *Aesthetik: "So
dann gehört jedes Kunstwerk seiner Zeit, seinem
Volke, seiner Umgebung."* "Every work of art belongs to
its time, its people, and its environment." A like formula
was gropingly applied by Herder almost a century before Taine had made an extensive explanation of this
part of his method, in his Introduction to his *History of
English Literature.*

Apart from the difficulty of disentangling what each
critic's special original contribution was, it is difficult,
and, I am inclined to believe, impossible, to formulate

with precision the literary discoveries of the great critics, for what they contributed was not so much a systematic philosophy of literature as a ferment of ideas. This phrase "a ferment of ideas," used by Lessing about his own *Laocoön,* is equally applicable to the work of all the critics considered in this chapter—to the *Biographia Literaria,* to Wordsworth's epoch-making Preface, to Herder's conception of poetry. In spite of Sainte-Beuve's effort to organize some of his ideas into the semblance of a system in his essay on Chateaubriand, and in spite of Taine's orderly *Philosophy of Art,* what these two critics also contributed was an exciting ferment of thought that aroused a ferment of thought in others. This is also true of all those important critics whose main reputation is in another literary medium, like Goethe, like Poe, like Flaubert, and, in our own day, like Yeats and Valéry and Eliot. These writers contribute a whirl of fertilizing ideas without which literature would become desiccated or even impotent as a vehicle of artistic expression.

2

In the case of Lessing, who, in the estimation of the present writer, was the most original and the most originating mind in modern criticism, though not the greatest, it happened that he aroused a whole nation to literary expression. Through the energy of his ideas and his practice he gave release to minds that without him would either never have found a voice or only piped a feeble note. Saintsbury said of him that the Germans owe him Goethe and the English, Coleridge. Goethe, who was never tired of telling what he owed to him, wrote, in *Dichtung und Wahrheit,* of the effect of Lessing's *Laocoön* on himself and his contemporaries, "As if by a lightning-flash, the consequences of his splendid thought lighted up the way before us, and all previous criticism was thrown away like a worn-out coat." Not only did his splendid thought light up the way for his own countrymen, his influence spread to all European literature. It is even true to say that not only the seeds of contemporary literary ideas, but the seeds of contemporary technical inventions in writing are to be found in Lessing's criticism, for the most recent developments in technique are an outcrop of his special notion of "action" in literary composition.

The two main principles with which his name in criticism is associated are the conception of literature as an expression of national or racial genius, and, secondly, the notion that each of the arts has a boundary beyond which it is best not to pass, and that the highest development of any art takes place inside its own boundary. The conception of literature as an expression of racial or national genius derives from the German philosophy of racism and is valid only to a degree: it does not cover the total range of literature in any country or in any period. However, in the heyday of its popularity it represented a high truth and was potent with inspiration until almost the year before last; it played an awakening rôle in many of the new European literatures—in Norwegian literature, in Russian literature, in Flemish literature and Irish literature. But in the world that in our time is coming into being, this conception has not the same power of influencing the creative imagination. In every country there is to be observed a cleavage between the intellectual and artistic life on the one side, and the racial and national tradition. Art, due in part to the purely prosaic influence of the ease and swiftness of transportation and transmission, is becoming international as well as national. The international conception is not crowding out national art, but is taking its own share of the field. Some of the newer writers are as national as writers ever were, but at the same time there are a number of others in every country who express in their work something outside of race and national genius.

The stressing of this idea, the racial and national idea, was a powerful force in exciting Lessing's readers; it was the first time in literary history that it had been put forward as a doctrine of literary production. And as any idea that has once been powerful may, in suitable soil, again be a source of power, it is worth while considering why it was powerful and why the soil was suitable. For one thing, Lessing put it forward both forcibly and convincingly, both in precept and practice; he was that figure who sometimes appears in literary history, the man with a new idea which, when it is expressed, goes straight to the minds and hearts of his readers as a form of nutriment for which they were longing. Before Lessing came and before his precept and example took effect, the Germans had been trying to make themselves over in imitation of the French and to give themselves French culture, as did the Russians later, and as the Roumanians have done in our time, and as the Irish and the Americans, until recently, tried to give themselves an English culture. Things had reached such a pass in Germany that all writing was an imitation of the French, and the educated classes spoke only French amongst themselves. The conquering king, Frederick the Great, made no secret of his contempt for the German language, and his own literary performances, such as they were, and they are not contemptible, were entirely in French. Now, this king was the ruler of the country in which Lessing in his young manhood tried to start a literature, and though Frederick despised the language as much as Lessing venerated it, and had the limited notions of a man of action of what made a country's greatness, yet if there had been no Frederick, Lessing's task would have been impossible. For although the great king never spoke the German language at all if he could help it, psychically he was one of the forces that made that language, and the literature in it, one of the greatest in modern Europe. It was this Germany that Frederick had created—invented, one might say—that Lessing willed to turn into the paths of literary expression.

When Lessing was a boy of eleven, Frederick ascended the throne of Prussia, and when, as a young man, after a false beginning, he turned to writing his first startling essays on literature, they were addressed to a people into whose blood the king had put life and iron. Twenty years before, they would have been addressed to a people whose minds had long gone stagnant under floods of theological argumentation and the despair of lost wars, invaded territory and wasted life, for during generations these had been the chief experiences of the German nation. For all outcropping of spiritual fruit there has to be a physical and material preparation. Nothing in literary history is more psychologically interesting than the influence of Frederick. We are not concerned here with the details of the wars and battles that he won, for we are only interested in certain of their effects. It had been the habit of other nations to hire as their fighting-men those foreign mercenaries who made a trade of war, but when Frederick took the field, with a large proportion of the powers of Europe against him, his forces were his own countrymen. When they, the long-beaten, found themselves conquerors in many battles, they began to reach a stage of consciousness that needed some other outlet than the battlefield. "The exploits of the great Frederick," wrote Goethe, in *Dichtung und Wahrheit,* "were the first living, genuine, heroic foundations of German poetry. All national poetry is empty, or risks becoming so, unless it rests on what is most profoundly human—on the destiny of peoples and their leaders, when they are identified with one another."

This was all true, but the great Frederick himself only believed in the future of Germany politically; he had no faith in it artistically. The poets who sang of his victories he treated with either scorn or indifference; for him his countrymen were intellectually slow and ponderous people who could never produce finely in art or literature. The best destiny he could think out for them was that they should become imitators of the French. For himself, he thought and spoke and wrote in French. He had an acquaintance of a kind with literature, got from books read between battles and drillings and from the society of the literary men he collected around him. The sort of literary knowledge he had bears a curious resemblance to that of Trotzky in our day: his interest in it was genuine; he could write fairly well himself, though he never understood the circumstances out of which literature came. This did not prevent him, however, from taking it upon himself to write criticism. Like Trotzky he wrote a work on literature remarkable for its directness, its common sense, its mixture of ignorance, superficial knowledge, and second-hand literary opinions. Naturally he wrote it in French. It was entitled *De la Littérature Alle-*

mande; therein he made an assault on the efforts of his countrymen to produce a literature, singling out in particular *Goetz von Berlichingen,* a work by a young nursling of Lessing's and Herder's, Johann Wolfgang Goethe, which he termed a vulgar imitation of Shakespeare. However, in this book of his he announced his belief that the great days of literature were to come, but that he himself would not live to see them. He did not know that these great days were upon him and that the makers of literature had sprung up all around him, a product of the seeds he himself had sown with his victories, and that the greatest of them all, indeed the greatest of the moderns, was that identical young man whose *Goetz von Berlichingen* he had so rashly attacked.

3

But if Frederick had no intuitions about the psychic life around him, there was another German ruler who had. Frederick's youthful fellow sovereign, the life-loving, poetry-loving Duke of Weimar, had not much territory to rule over and his name had cut no figure in the Gazettes, and he did not, perhaps, know a great deal about either conquering or ruling a kingdom, but he was a great aristocrat and he knew intuitively that art of aristocrats, the art of enriching life. And so he made the author of *Goetz von Berlichingen* his high priest, his chancellor, his boon companion. To Weimar also came Herder and Schiller and many others, until the little Duchy became a sort of Athens, alive with great intellects and great emotions. But all this outburst of creative life represented intellectual conquests by Lessing and Herder that were as marvellous as those of Frederick on the field of battle.

It was the fashion at that time for kings and rulers to have at their courts poets, littérateurs, men of genius. For life is dull for the politically great as well as for the financially great unless it is somehow lightened or made more meaningful and profound by contact with those who are in touch with the emotional and spiritual strivings of man. In spite of his bit of artistry, Frederick had no power of communication with the developing interior life of his people, for the writer he invited to his court was Voltaire. The King of Denmark might ask to Copenhagen, as a representative of culture, the German poet Klopstock, who wrote the *Messiah,* but Frederick would have no Germans. "I find myself in France here," wrote Voltaire after his arrival at Frederick's court; "they speak only our language; German is for soldiers and horses. I find that the cultivated people at Königsberg know my verses by heart."

Now this and similar was what Lessing had to cure his countrymen of—the contempt for their own language and culture and their mania for quoting the verses and dramas of the French poets, and in particular the poetry of Voltaire, which did not happen to be poetry at all, and his dramas, which did not happen to be dramas at all. When Voltaire arrived in Berlin, Goethe was a babe in arms; Herder, who later was to become Lessing's aide and disciple, was a little boy in petticoats, and Lessing himself was only twenty-two. But though Lessing earlier had, like everybody else, floundered around in imitations of the French, he soon outgrew this immaturity, and with the instinct of a man of genius, he perceived that if he was ever to rouse his countrymen to genuine literary expression, one of the first things to be fought was the influence of Voltaire. Voltaire had written in verse more than fifty plays; they had been enormously successful, as are the plays of Bernard Shaw in our own time and for much the same reason: they were brilliant; they were witty; they were amusing. But he had only slight power of creating character; his personages, like Shaw's, were mostly types on which he hung his philosophy; in general, his dramas were propaganda for his ideas—his mocking, brilliant, and sometimes noble ideas. His following all over Europe was an immense one, and to Frederick and his court and all educated Germany he represented the highest literary genius and the last word in intellectual sophistication. Lessing had to fight vigorously against all this, and he was well equipped for the battle: he was learned; he was witty; he was satirical; he could be profound; he could himself illustrate his own critical theories. In controversy he was a master. His literary attacks have been described as lacking in urbanity. But urbanity, which is a virtue in personal quarrels, has, it may be, no more place in a fight for intellectual convictions than it has in a statement of the theory of relativity; urbanity is a necessity in social intercourse, but truth, to quote Lessing himself, is a necessity of the soul.

4

In the realization of his theory that literature was an expression of national being, one of the first things Lessing had to cope with was the language of the literature he was trying to create. The language according to Frederick should be French, and according to Gottsched might be German, but only the German of savants, a language different from that of every-day life. Lessing, in spite of his passion for the Greeks, was, like Coleridge after him, like all the writers sprung from the blood of the old Teutons, by temperament more akin to the spirit of the Hebrew Bible than to that of the Greeks or Latins, or that of any people working in their tradition. He turned back to Luther's Bible, and to those long-despised sources from which Luther said he got the language that he used for his writing—"the mother in the house, the children in the street, the man in the market-place." The language, literature, and emotions of that other great Teutonic or part-Teutonic people, the English, had been profoundly influenced by the Bible, and Lessing now announced that the German mentality was subject to much the same influences as the English. All literatures influence each other, but a choice of influences had to be made and those chosen which were in accord with the national genius. But the only art the ordinary man among Lessing's fellow countrymen came in contact with was the artificial tragedy made in imitation of Racine and Corneille and staged by strolling players all over the country. This art, with its fantastic heroes and sceptered kings stalking across the boards and orating pages of rhetoric, was remote from any life the audiences knew.

It will be remembered that at this period, the middle eighteenth century, the novel was at its beginning: it had, as a matter of fact, appeared in English and French; in other literatures there were only odd picaresque romances that came out under Spanish influences. So that, for the average person interested in character, literature meant a play, generally a play in verse —when people spoke of literature they generally meant a composition in verse. It was for this reason that when Lessing started his literary reforms he began with the drama: with his versatile mind he was not only able to invent the principles of reform but to carry them into practice. The art the people came in contact with, he said, should reflect the people's life, and so he wrote a play, *Minna von Barnhelm,* that, for the first time in German literary history, brought German life on the stage. The audiences were delighted to see, on the boards, themselves and their problems, their life and their language, the contemporary history of their country. It was the first conscious and deliberate experiment in making literature national expression—an expression of the people. This has been done in other places since Lessing's day, and has its great popular success in countries where, for one reason or another, literary expression has been dominated by alien influences or is remote from the life of the people. One of the striking examples of its success in contemporary literature has been with that school of writers who formed what was called the Irish Renaissance, under the leadership of William Butler Yeats, Douglas Hyde, and Æ.

When the bulk of the people see their every-day life portrayed in literature there is a new stirring of vitality among them, even when they protest, as they frequently do, against the manner in which the artist has depicted them. However, as can easily be imagined, the portrayal of ordinary, every-day life may degenerate into a form of photographic realism from which all art and inspiration have been excluded. At this stage in our own day a theory the exact opposite of Lessing's, something that demands a purely fantastic or stylized expression, might have the best stimulus for the revivifying of literature. But a literary theory, if it has ever been really effective, never becomes moribund; it is always capable, when the need is felt, of taking a fresh form of life; a newer theory causes a re-arrangement of values, but that does not mean that the old one has been made completely obsolete.

About the same time that he produced *Minna von Barnhelm,* Lessing published his classic in criticism, *Laocoön.* This is one of those books like, in science, Darwin's *Origin of Species;* in criticism, Taine's *De l'Intelligence;* in psychology, Freud's *Interpretation of Dreams,* which turn men's minds in a new direction. Its subject was the boundary between literature or poetry and the plastic arts; its effect was the overthrowing of the rococo formalism, the conventionalism that had had a strangle hold on literature, and the release of the minds of his countrymen to literary expression. *Laocoön* was not only the first piece of real modern criticism—it was the first extensive piece of criticism since Aristotle. By showing that each art has its laws, its boundary beyond which it is possible to pass, but that each art achieves the best results inside its own boundary, that each art has a special function and that it cannot trespass on the functions of the other arts, he introduced into criticism a wholly new principle. *Laocoön* was not limited to the theme proposed: it was filled with exciting ideas about life, psychology, methods of writing.

5

There has always been a tendency in the minds of the art-conscious to confuse the various arts, to suppose that the effects of one art can be produced in another. Sometimes, it has been thought that the effects of a landscape as presented in a painting can be reproduced in words. From this notion sprang the long descriptions of places, or things, that have from time to time been the fashion in both poetry and prose. From this confusion, also, sprang the literary painting, the painting which tried to produce the effect of a story or a poem. And again, writers have believed that they could achieve in literature, especially in poetry, the effects of music, and the present-day attempt at these effects amongst certain modernistic writers is not so new as has been supposed: on the contrary, it is an ancient heresy. In his great attempt to define the boundaries of the arts, to show the limits of expression in each art, Lessing brought into criticism a wholly new principle, and if only this principle were put into general practice it would be a liberation for every art. The picture that tries to tell a story can never be anything but an illustration for a piece of literature; the literary passage that tries to produce the effect of a painting loses its natural verve; the poem that insists on being pure music is neither music nor poetry. Lessing meant the *Laocoön* to be only a first volume, the volume in which he delimited the provinces of poetry and the plastic arts; he had meant to write a second volume which would deal with the relations of music and literature and which would delimit the provinces of these

35

two arts, but he did not get down to it—perhaps through lack of sufficient knowledge or simply through lack of time: he lived only to be fifty-two. The fact is that whereas he delivered a lasting blow to the sort of literature that imitated painting and the sort of painting or sculpture that imitated literature, the notion that poetry can reproduce the effects of music still has a sturdy life in literary cliques. The boundary between poetry and music has never been defined—perhaps it really is too intangible to define. In the lifetime of Lessing himself there was born a man, Novalis, who by precept and example did considerable to confuse the boundary of poetry and music, and who provided rallying cries that were taken over into French by Verlaine, and, later and especially, by Mallarmé. Mallarmé not only adopted Novalis's theory that poetry was the more excellent in proportion as it produced the effects of music, but also his notion that poetry was the conversation of the soul with itself. From this we can see the evolution of the idea popular in certain modern coteries that literature expresses but need not communicate. In fact, it cannot be too often emphasized that the contemporary world has invented no new ideas with regard to literary expression.

To return to *Laocoön:* Lessing hung his ideas on the Laocoön in sculpture and the Laocoön in literature: the Laocoön of the Greek sculpture and the Laocoön of Virgil. He developed certain ideas of his predecessor, Winckelmann. It would have been against the laws of plastic beauty to show faces with muscles violently and permanently distorted; therefore, in the group of the sculptor, while we have Laocoön and his children entwined in a death grip by the serpent, in the midst of most frightful sufferings, we see on each face the expression of a soul at rest. This was, Lessing explained, because a statue or a picture can show us only a moment of time, whereas in poetry we have the development of an action. Virgil, therefore, could represent Laocoön as crying out with pain, not because he had a different conception of his character, but because he was working in a different art, a different medium. That is, plastic art deals with things coexistent in space—bodies; poetry (or literature in general) represents things sequent in time—actions. Plastic art is confined to immobility; poetry (literature in general) lives on movements and contrasts. In poetry, for example, Homer does not describe Helen's beauty, but shows how the sight of her affected the elders of Troy; he does not describe the completed shield of Achilles, but shows it to us in the making, and makes us, as it were, participators in its devising.

6

Without the aid of his younger contemporary, Herder, it might not have been so easy for Lessing to carry out his idea of literature as national expression. For

Herder had what Lessing lacked—the lyrical mind. Lessing was learned, witty, satirical, profound: he could analyze to the depths any type of literature except the lyrical, and this drawback made him somewhat lacking in the comprehension of every kind of poetry. He was never the equal of Herder in understanding the workings of the poetic mind. In spite of his spontaneity, in spite of the fact that he published a book of what he called lyrics, his mind was incapable of lyrical flights. This deficiency caused some of the younger critics of his later years to deny him the creative mind, though it is plain that he possessed one of the great creative minds of the eighteenth century—a mind that sowed ideas which have since cropped up in all sorts of places and have influenced the whole development of European literature. In his later days, in the hey-day of the great German lyric, the creative mind and the purely lyrical were confounded, as in our day the creative mind is popularly supposed to be the one which expresses itself in character creation or narrative making. Lessing could not be denied the power of character creation or of idea creation, but he was no lyric poet. Herder, on the other hand, no matter how one may estimate his own poetry, had the lyrical mentality, and because of this was naturally the poetic-critical mind as Lessing was the philosophical-critical mind. The aims of both critics were the same: to create a new German literature, to free the minds of their country-

men from the shackles of pseudo-classicism and the
rule-making criticism of pedants. Both had the same
belief that literature was the product of national
conditions, both had the same dislike of classical
French drama, the same passion for English literature
and for Shakespeare. But where Lessing was guided
by reason, Herder, who had a fiery, eager poet's mind,
was guided by flashes of intuition; it was his glory and
his defect that his mind worked in flashes. Where Lessing gave up his mind to the study of drama and the
development of literary and æsthetic ideas, Herder gave
his chiefly to the study of poetry, which he declared
"ought to be the most impetuous and self-assured
daughter of the human soul."

Lessing, for all his hatred of the rule-makers, had a
passion for Aristotle. In spite of his belief in what he
called "the inner rule" he thought that absolute canons
of art could be arrived at and that the way to reach
them was through a study of the Greeks. The rules expounded by Aristotle, he maintained, were as infalli-
ble as the elements of Euclid, and when he wished to
praise Shakespeare highly he said he was truer to the
Aristotelian principles than were the French classical dramatists. Herder, however, announced that the
Greeks, after all, were only the Greeks, and that they
had never been brought into the world to furnish artistic norms for all men to the end of time. The literature of the Greeks was like every other literature: a

product of national conditions which could not be duplicated in another country, in another age. That literature was the product of national conditions formed the chief matter of his agreement with Lessing. On other points they differed as much as did Sainte-Beuve and Taine. Herder did for poetry a service that Lessing was not capable of doing: he awakened the latent lyricism of the Germans. He announced that poetry was the mother tongue of mankind, that the first authors of every nation are its poets, that the earliest poetry in a nation's history, being the most spontaneous, is the greatest: that is, the poetry of Homer, of the Bible, and, he added, the newly discovered poetry of Ossian.

Herder wanted poetry to be said or sung, not read silently in a printed book. Homer, the first great poet, did not write; he sang. Of Homer he said, "Long centuries have knelt before him as before a god or a messenger of the gods." His conception of poetry as the mother tongue of mankind led him naturally to the study of the folk song; he brought out a collection of folk songs translated from many languages, in which he exhibited not only his own poetic gifts but his great power of penetration into the minds of primitive peoples. It was in his writing on primitive poetry that he showed his disagreement with Lessing and with Lessing's great friend, the soldier-poet Kleist, both of whom were inclined to regard poetry as composition.

"Do not be surprised," wrote Herder, in a paragraph that set many minds on fire, "do not be surprised that a young Lapp who does not know his letters, has never been to school and hardly has a god, sings better than Major Kleist. For the Lapp sang his song on the wing as he was gliding over the snow with his reindeer, impatient to see Lake Orra where his sweetheart lived, but Major Kleist made his song by imitation from a book."

The young Goethe, studying law and trying to Frenchify himself in the Alsatian town of Strassburg, met in that city this fiery literary revolutionary, just five years his senior, and this meeting was one of those lucky chances that befell Goethe all his long, lucky life. "Study the superstitions and the sagas of the forefathers," said Herder to him, and the saying passed not only into the soul of Goethe but, later, into the soul of Wagner. And Goethe, in studying the legends of the forefathers, attached himself particularly to the legend of Doctor Faustus, who sold his soul to the devil, and he made it into the history of the eternal struggle of the creative mind, and he made it also the history of the strivings of the modern man. Under Herder's influence he too became a collector of folk songs; he got the rhythm into his blood, the rhymes into his measures, and like Herder's Lapp he, too, began to sing his songs on the wing as he rode to see his sweetheart, and he got into them the earth and the sunshine, the clouds and the mountains, and the lyricism and spontaneity of the folk song.

> Wie herrlich leuchtet
> Mir die Natur!
> Wie glänzt die Sonne,
> Wie lacht die Flur!
> O Lieb', O Liebe
> So golden-schön
> Wie Morgenwolken
> Auf jenen Höh'n!

7

Herder's translations of the old spontaneous songs and poems aroused and quickened the lyrical genius of the poets around him. Among his other gifts was that curious power, sometimes noticeable in critics, of being able to form a conception of a whole work from a very small fragment of it—give him a line or two of an old song, a piece of a work of literature, and he knew the spirit, the structure of the whole. Strongly as he believed that literature, and especially poetry, was national and racial expression, it can be deduced from his work that there was one form of literature, at least, which from its very nature had to be international, and that was criticism. Literary ideas, no matter where they have had their rise, are equally the inheritance of all literatures that can avail themselves of them. Starting from this thought he became the initiator of the study of comparative literature, a necessary outgrowth of modern criticism. Even now the interdependence of literary and critical ideas is not sufficiently realized. Brunetière's *History of Criticism* is only a history of French criticism; he seems to think that only French criticism is of any import; Saintsbury, too, took very little stock in the interdependence of literary ideas: one would suppose that all the great modern critics were English, from his *History of Criticism* and his passages illustrative of critical theory and practice from Aristotle downwards, which he called *Loci Critici*.

Not only did Herder start the study of comparative literature, he was one of the initiators of the modern manner of studying history, and his *Philosophy of History* played a great rôle in the method of writing history. No doubt he was influenced in this work by the ideas of that strange seventeenth-century philosopher, Vico. However, while no one can pretend that any new idea comes into being without antecedents, the fact remains that Herder exerted the greatest influence in starting people's minds on a new conception of history. "History has been transformed," said Taine, writing nearly a hundred years afterwards, "within a hundred years in Germany [that is, since Herder's *Philosophy of History*], within sixty years in France, and that by a study of their literatures." That is to say, the transformation was brought about by the application of Herder's thought. It is true that he was never able to outline his ideas with precision as Lessing could and did: his intuitions were often expressed in loose, cloudy, flowery language. Yet in its own loose way his mind sowed the seeds of as many ideas as did Lessing's. All those later critical theories explaining literature by the time and place, or accounting for it as an expression of society, are to be found in germ in Herder's work. His influence on the philosophers was marked; some of Hegel's æsthetics being simply certain ideas of Herder's, pondered over, systematized, and philosophically stated—notably, the idea of the race, milieu, and moment referred to previously, and which was taken over by Taine. Both Herder and Lessing powerfully influenced a series of German philosophers, beginning with Hegel and Fichte—Fichte's famous *Addresses to the German Nation* being simply a metaphysical and political expression of the literary theories of these two great critics.

In Lessing, who gave his mind especially to the study of form, we have in germ very many of the most modern developments of literary forms—the abolishing of transitions, the revelation of physical traits of people or landscape or things by showing them in action. After two hundred years, sentences from *Laocoön* are still literary sign-posts taking one away from swamps and jungles. Nothing has been said about emotional extravagance in art better than Lessing's—"In the whole gamut of emotion there is no moment less advantageous than its topmost note." For, as he said, "Beyond the top there is nothing more and nothing is left to arouse the imagination." It may equally be said, however, that there is nothing below the lowest note, and that the common habit of the moderns of expressing emotion on its lowest note makes an unfair demand upon the imagination. And who better than Lessing has noted the necessity for the extension of the boundaries of art beyond the notions of the Greeks, to include not only the naturally beautiful but the whole of nature and humanity, of which the beautiful is only a part? For, as he remarked, an ugliness of nature can be transformed into a beauty of art. And how clear and emphatic are his objections to the use of propaganda in art! "I should like the name Works of Art to be reserved for those alone in which the artist could show himself actually as artist. All the rest, in which too evident traces of religious dogma appear, are unworthy of the name. Art here has not wrought on her own account but has been auxiliary to religion." In Lessing's day, it should be noted, religious propaganda was the one most generally encountered in art, as in our day the propaganda most likely to be encountered would be political and social. "The frigid delineations of physical objects," to which Lessing objected, were effectively banished from poetry in his own day, but it is only in our own time that they are being banished from the prose narrative. In addition to attacking

French neo-classicism Lessing made a study of the Greek text of Aristotle's *Poetics* and gave the interpretation that is now generally accepted.

While stressing the originality and power of both Herder and Lessing, it is not to be denied that they were deeply influenced by certain of their predecessors —Lessing by Winckelmann's studies of the Greek plastic arts, and Herder by Hamann's discourses on English and on primitive poetry. In spite of their opposition to French influences they were themselves influenced by Rousseau and Diderot—Lessing noticeably by Diderot—and Herder was easily won over to the doctrine of the goodness of the natural man. Where they found ideas that fitted in with theirs or could be used to help along the creation of the new literature they had in mind, they took them over and formed their own construction on them. This is what all the important critics have done: those who came after Lessing and Herder in their turn used the ideas of these first modern critics as a foundation for their own contribution. For these two were the founders of a new school of literature, and that means the revealers of a new side of life; they emphasized a different side of man from the one which for so long had been exploited in literature: that product of the Enlightenment, the uniformitarian man, went into the background. A great renewal of life and literature had suddenly begun.

Chapter Three

THE ENGLISH CONTRIBUTION: COLERIDGE AND WORDSWORTH

I

THE CONCEPT of literature as racial and national became so universalized, not only during their lifetime but all through the nineteenth century down to the Great War, that it is not easy for us to comprehend the sweeping extent of Lessing's and Herder's reforms and the nature of the struggle against seventeenth and eighteenth-century Enlightenment and Uniformity. There are in humanity a set of deeply rooted desires towards uniformity and standardization that in suitable soils and periods can be developed to an alarming extent. These tendencies towards pattern and standardization are sometimes confused with discipline, sometimes confused with high ethical and political aspirations, and while they have been responsible for much that is great and stately, they are also responsible for those regimentations of ideas that, if carried far enough, are ruinous to all forms of vigorous life and art.

But seldom is any idea carried too far, for ideas, like creatures when their usefulness is past, are shelved or die, or, rather, they die to that extent that some other idea generated by them is started on its career and in its turn influences humanity. The standardization, the uniformity that Lessing and Herder successfully combated, gave way in their turn to a set of ideas that have ruled men's minds down to our time. How all-embracing was the uniformity of that period sometimes called the eighteenth century, but in reality partly the seventeenth and partly the eighteenth, how this uniformity was operative in movements of the period which at first sight seem totally dissimilar in temper and orientation, has been shown by Arthur O. Lovejoy in a paper called *The Parallel of Deism and Classicism*. Uniformitarianism, to use Lovejoy's term, was the first and fundamental principle of the Enlightenment. When the outstanding men of the period talked about "nature," whether it was Spinoza, or Fénelon, or Voltaire, or Rousseau, the common element of the meaning of the word as it was understood by all of them was uniformity. All the history of civilized mankind for them had been a long tale of departure from the uniformity and simplicity of nature. In theory the æsthetic of neo-classicism was fundamentally an æsthetic of uniformitarianism. "The fact is writ large," to quote Professor Lovejoy, "in all the most famous expositions of neo-classical doctrine." The objection to the *differentness* of men was also extended to the *differentness* of races and nations. The rebellion against this uniformitarianism has been the motive principle in literature and art generally, from the time of Lessing down to our own time.

In the Enlightenment the object of the reformer, religious, moral or social, as well as of the literary critic, was to standardize men—their beliefs, their likings, their activities, and their institutions. But there was in the Enlightenment, as in everything else, an admixture of many opposed ideas, and some of these contained the seeds of racism, nationalism, and romanticism. Lessing himself, forecasting modern developments in psychology, said that there does not exist a single unmixed feeling in nature. Nor, may it be said, does there exist a single unmixed idea: each idea contains the seeds of its opposite or of what can be developed into its opposite. In both Lessing and Herder themselves there were the vestiges of many of the ideas they were out to combat. Lessing thought that by logic one always arrived at true conceptions, and while out against the rulemakers he was all for the Aristotelian rules, though Aristotle as a critic represented the opposite kind from Lessing, being the critic who coming after a great period in literature draws from masterpieces handed on to him the laws for creating others. Lessing, on the other hand, was the sort of critic who foresees and directs great movements in literature—the sort of critic

that is considered in these chapters. If he had vestiges of the rule-makers in him, Herder, in spite of his attachment to folk songs and primitive poetry, had strong vestiges of eighteenth-century pedantry.

2

The more remote heirs of the thought of Lessing and Herder were the great French critics, Sainte-Beuve and Taine; the nearest heirs were Wordsworth and Coleridge, who, between them, did in England exactly what Herder and Lessing had done in Germany—changed the course of literature by making people realize that another phase of human experience and of the mind of man had to be expressed.

These two, Wordsworth and Coleridge, are, I hold, the greatest minds in English criticism—both nearly the same age, both younger contemporaries of the great German critics. They worked even more closely together than did their older contemporaries. As is well known, they brought out jointly the volume *Lyrical Ballads* illustrating their literary ideas. It has been commonly said of them, and especially of Wordsworth, that their literary principles represented an æsthetic statement of the Rights of Man as proclaimed by the French Revolution: this, I think, is a great mistake. There is no doubt that their minds were influenced by this social upheaval, but it was a transitory influence. Their æsthetic principles were very similar to those of

Lessing and Herder, but on many points they represented a development of the German ideas. Lessing wanted ordinary life and the ordinary man expressed in the drama; Wordsworth wanted him expressed in poetry. Lessing wanted the speech of drama reformed so as to be the actual speech of men; he wanted to have the eighteenth-century poetic diction and rhodomontade banished and to have every-day life and speech upon the stage. These are the same literary principles that Wordsworth advances in his Preface, developed several degrees further and applied, not to the drama, but to lyric and narrative poetry. It has been said that originally the seeds of these ideas were supplied to Wordsworth by Coleridge, and very likely they were. But the fact remains that it was Wordsworth and not Coleridge who developed them, reduced them to vigorous and simple language, and who wrote the famous Preface—the one solitary example, in English literature, of a poetic manifesto that started a school of poetry, which school, it should be added, lasted down to our own time. Both Coleridge and Wordsworth had the same notion of what constituted poetry as Herder had and the same recognition of the necessity for turning to old songs and ballads. Many of Herder's ideas are explicit in the famous Preface—his passion for the primitive, for folk poetry, all poetry that was the expression of natural passions.

These four critics, Lessing, Herder, Wordsworth, and

Coleridge, had an identical object in mind: to destroy the deliberate style of the neo-classicists, to abolish artificial and "poetic diction," to extend the boundaries of literature so that it could express familiar life and the ordinary man's passions and desires; they had the same desire to get rid of "gaudiness and inane phraseology," to awaken an interest in Shakespeare and in all spontaneous and lyric writing. This lyricism was, it should be noted again, less a passion with Lessing, who had no great comprehension of lyric poetry, than with the other three. The two great English critics had no such struggle against the ravages and extravagances of neo-classicism and uniformity as had the two Germans; English literature had been classicist and uniformitarian for a brief period only. On the other hand, the English writers had not the same virgin field to work in: Germany had produced practically no literature; England had already produced one of the great literatures of the world, and though Wordsworth and Coleridge might and did start literature on a new track, they could never surpass the great age. The lyricism and spontaneity of that age they could restore; they could, in the estimation of some of their admirers, equal the great figures; they could and did extend the bounds of expression; they could and did explore the path to new material. All this, to be sure, amounted to a great reform—a reform which started English literature on a new course. With Lessing and Herder, on the other hand, the great age of German literature, the age of modern literature, began.

As is well known, the Preface was not prefixed to the first edition of *Lyrical Ballads,* but to the second, and was written after the return of Wordsworth and Coleridge from Germany, where Coleridge already had fallen not only under the spell of Lessing and Herder, but also of Schelling, one of the philosophers influenced by the new critics. That the Preface was really not a preface at all but was written long after the poems and was partly a rationalization, an apologia, for work already done, makes no difference; that the ideas themselves were, to some extent, already current in Germany, makes no difference in the value of the great manifesto. Wordsworth took to himself the literary ideas that were most akin to his mind, he added new elements to the thoughts of others, and these new ingredients had a virility and a power of life that in their turn gave out the seeds of future ideas. In the *Lyrical Ballads* the two poets, according to Coleridge's account, had two aims in mind: Wordsworth in his subjects and verse was to give "the charm of novelty to things of every day," and Coleridge was to deal with "persons and characters supernatural, or at least, romantic." Wordsworth was to make the familiar wonderful and Coleridge to make the wonderful familiar. Coleridge attempted his part of the enterprise in the "Rime of the Ancient Mariner," and among Wordsworth's attempts to make the familiar wonderful were "Tintern Abbey," "The Idiot Boy," "The Reverie of Poor Susan," "Simon Lee." In the second edition, the edition with the Preface, he added poems he had written in Germany—"Lucy Gray," "Ruth," "Three Years She Grew," "Michael," and others. Thus, some of the greatest of Wordsworth's poems belonged to the *Lyrical Ballads* period.

If we take the Preface as a piece of independent criticism and not, as it is generally taken, a standard to measure whether the poetry does or does not illustrate the principles laid down, the conclusion must be that it is one of the most powerful and influential critical statements of the last hundred and fifty years and Wordsworth one of the greatest of critics. Its influence, as Coleridge tells us in his *Biographia Literaria,* began almost immediately. "Not only," said Coleridge, "in the verses of those who had professed their admiration of his genius, but even of those who had distinguished themselves by hostility to his theory and depreciation of his writings, are the impressions of his principles plainly visible."

3

Let us now consider the salient points of the Preface. The most familiar of these is the one relating to language, which he returned to again and again, expressing it in slightly different ways. This was that the language of poetry should, as far as possible, be a selection of the language really used by men. When he expresses this idea with a slight variation he tells us that his purpose was to imitate, and, as far as possible, to adopt, the very language of men. He rejected the sort of language that had come to be called "poetic diction" because it was used only in poetry. In addition, he rejected what was associated with poetic diction—personifications of abstract ideas, which he called "an ordinary device to elevate the style and to raise it above prose."

This theory of language is, in some of its facets, a very old one: we have Luther's version of it in his statement that he took the language he used in his version of the Bible from "the mother in the house, the children in the street, the man in the market-place," and Dante's consideration of "the illustrious vernacular" and "the vulgar tongue which, without any rules at all, we get by imitating our nurses," and which he called "noble" because it is in common human employment and is not academic or literary. Wordsworth stated his theory of language with the passion of one who had discovered it anew. Round it he hung a conception of poetry that speedily made its way into the minds of readers and writers, and it is this general conception of his, rather than his much-debated theory of language, about which there is really nothing to debate, that has made him such a force—in fact, his theory of language is but a natural consequence of his general conception. Poetry was not to be metaphysical

Essays on Man or on Criticism, or dissertations on the Pleasures of Hope or the Progress of the Mind or the Vanity of Human Wishes; it was to be about "the essential passions of the heart." And these passions, in Wordsworth's mind, found a better soil to mature unrestrainedly "in humble and rustic life" because "in that condition of life our elementary feelings co-exist in a state of greater simplicity, and consequently may be more accurately contemplated and more forcibly communicated." The subject of poetry, therefore, was to be "the incidents and situations of common life," but at the same time the poet was "to throw over them the coloring of the imagination, whereby ordinary things should be presented to the mind in an unusual aspect."

To make the incidents and situations of common life the subject of poetry was, at this period, a literary principle of vast revolutionary import. Wordsworth wanted, what all the literary revolutionists wanted, an extension of the boundaries of literary expression; he designed a more extensive expression of life as it is really lived. For literature, it cannot be too often said, has expressed only a limited amount of the experiences of men, and one of the ways for revealing in words a wider area of life is first of all to envisage something that has been left out of literary expression, and then, if necessary, to invent new technical devices for expressing this. Any one literary principle has many antecedents, and the fact is that Wordsworth repeated a demand that Lessing had made—with Lessing it was for drama, with Wordsworth for lyrical and narrative poetry. The short appendix to the *Lyrical Ballads,* published two years after the publication of the Preface, dealt again with the language of poetry and reproduced the Herder conception of poetry and language, and in similar words, but Wordsworth made it more precise and intense, and gave it a new coloring, and added new elements from his own mind.

In addition to what Coleridge called his "literary principles," Wordsworth devoted his Preface not only to the subject and language of poetry but to a consideration of what poetry is, of what a poet is, and to what degree he differs from the ordinary man. He did not mind repeating himself and reiterating his major ideas, for literary principles always need to be repeated in the same or similar words until they make themselves a part of the reader's mind and imagination. "All good poetry," he said, "was the spontaneous overflow of powerful feelings." And, at the same time, he went on to explain that while this is true, "poems to which any value can be attached were never produced on any variety of subjects but by a man, who, being possessed of more than usual organic sensibility, had also thought long and deeply." He said, in effect, that the spontaneity and powerful feelings were directed and modified by thoughts—thoughts, he said, which are indeed the representatives of past feelings. This statement is in itself a clue to the mind of Wordsworth, whose thoughts all sprang from past feelings—sometimes, as some of his critics have declared, from dead feelings, feelings that had no more life. Continuing to develop his theory, he maintained that poetry takes its origin from "emotion recollected in tranquillity; the emotion is contemplated till, by a species of reaction, the tranquillity gradually disappears and an emotion kindred to that which was before the subject of contemplation is gradually produced." In this way he gives us what is in actual fact an account of the workings of his own creative personality, of what happened in his mind before he wrote a poem, during the writing of it, and what he conceived to be the result when finished. He turned the powerful critical side of his genius to an analysis of his own mind, and while it is, perhaps, true, that he was too much inclined to regard his own as the norm of the poet's mind, the fact remains that his revelations apply to the workings of a great many poets' minds. Substantially the same account has been given of their creative processes by many others since, including our contemporaries Paul Valéry and Robert Frost.

Some of the definitions and descriptions of poetry which are in the Preface are, in effect, the same as Coleridge's, who, in spite of minor disagreements with Wordsworth about the language of poetry, was in agreement with him as to its nature. "Poetry is the image of man and nature," said Wordsworth, "its object is truth . . . carried alive into the heart by passion. . . . Poetry is the breath and finer spirit of all knowledge." Compare these with Coleridge's "Poetry is the fragrancy of all human knowledge, human thoughts, human passions, emotions, language. . . . No man was ever yet a great poet without being, at the same time, a profound philosopher." If their poetry differed, their literary principles were almost the same, and one must remember that with Wordsworth and Coleridge, as with Lessing and Herder, as with Boileau, as with Dante, as with Aristotle, the word Poetry stood for practically everything in imaginative literature.

Wordsworth's description of a poet could stand for that of any creative writer of any type. "What is a poet?" he asks. "He is a man speaking to men, a man, it is true, endowed with more lively sensibilities, more enthusiasm and tenderness, who has a greater knowledge of human nature and a more comprehensive soul than are supposed to be common among mankind. . . . One who rejoices more than other men in the spirit of life that is in him. . . . To these qualities he has added a disposition to be affected more than other men by absent things as if they were present. He is chiefly distinguished from other men by a greater promptness to think and to feel without immediate external excitement, and a greater power in expressing such thoughts and feelings." What are these thoughts and feelings that the poet expresses? Are they something peculiar and personal to himself? No, they are the passions, thoughts, and feelings of men, for poets do not write for poets alone, but for men. From these general literary principles of Wordsworth's was derived that special one about the language of poetry being a selection of the language spoken by men, which, though it has aroused more discussion than all the others, was really but a minor part of his whole poetic creed. It was not even an essential part as practised by himself, for of all his literary and poetical principles it was the one he most often left out in actual writing. Others following him carried out this particular one much more readily than they did his great and major ones. There have been many poets who have spoken forcibly to men in their own language without really having very much to communicate to them, while great poets, men speaking to men, have spoken clearly and lastingly without using at all the ordinary language of men.

All writers in a new literary era or a new literary movement have to cope with the problem of language. It is one that comes up when the language of writing becomes worn out or becomes too exclusively literary, or has not been revivified from the actual speech of men. The problem arises again if this actual speech has become but conventional symbol and not a real medium of emotions and thoughts. Wordsworth's principles penetrated more widely and more rapidly than his poetry, and often to places where his poetry never penetrated at all. His poetry, great as it was, was like Milton's in that it was too peculiarly English to have a ready following in other countries. The admirers of his poetry abroad, like his admirers at home, were inclined to exalt him for what they believed to be the philosophy that they extracted from his work, especially from his long poems.

The French exiles who returned from England to France with volumes of English poetry in their baggage brought, amongst others, the poetry of Wordsworth, but they more especially brought the Preface, the doctrine of which was rapidly disseminated. Sainte-Beuve made his own of it: in France it became the poetical doctrine associated with his name. Something similar happened at a later date in the case of the poetic doctrines of Poe. We know that Baudelaire was influenced by Poe, though, as he tells us, he had never read a line of him until after the *Fleurs du Mal* was written: it happened simply that Poe's ideas had infiltrated into many coteries. In Wordsworth's lifetime people quarrelled about the Preface who never read the poetry, or who read it only to see how he put his principles into effect. The audience for the Preface has been an enormous one; the audience for the great poems has been much more limited, for the Preface, his manifesto, satisfied the greater need at the time, the need for a new æsthetic doctrine, the need for rejuvenating and transforming ideas, in all the mature European literatures. It was a masterpiece of literary criticism.

In that secondary form of criticism, the criticism of judgment, Wordsworth was equally outstanding. His estimate of Gray, of Johnson, of Cowper, though it occupies only a few succinct pages, is a masterly example of the art of judging poetry, and especially of the art of judging the poetry of an age that was going out by a practitioner of the poetry of an age that was coming in. The manner in which he picks out the lines that have the quickness of life in them and discards the lines that belong merely to an outmoded convention, reinforcing his intuition with his carefully worked-out literary principles, is an unforgettable example of the application of insight and principle to the evaluation of poetry. One's decisions upon poetry, he held, conduced to the improvement of one's own taste, "for an accurate taste in poetry is an acquired talent which can only be produced by thought and a long-continued intercourse with the best models of composition." Coleridge, on the side of the criticism of judgment, made mistakes in estimating his contemporaries that it would be difficult to imagine Wordsworth committing, such as, for example, the rhapsodies on the sonnets of Bowles and the work of Southey, which we find in the *Biographia:* no one can doubt that it is Coleridge's praise that has kept Southey's name alive in the anthologies. On the other hand, Wordsworth's mind was narrower; he had not that diversity of intellectual interests—psychology, philosophy, politics—that helped Coleridge to evolve all those principles for estimating literature and analyzing the creative mind, and which have gone to make him the first English writer to give criticism a metaphysical framework.

4

The age of Coleridge and Wordsworth was one of extraordinary interest in literature, in England. An early training in it was more possible then than now, as we can see from Coleridge's own account of the manner in which he was taught as a schoolboy to compare various works of literature. One of the reasons why the *Biographia Literaria* is one of the greatest books on literature in any language is that it was written for an age, in a country, that was at the time capable of appraising the ideas it presented and of discussing them with excited interest, of attacking some and accepting others. This book of his, Coleridge said, represented "a statement of his principles in politics, religion, and philosophy, and an application of the rules deduced from philosophical principles to poetry and criticism." The result was, not only the biography of his mind, of his religion and his philosophy, not only a statement of his own politics, but of the politics of the time, in which he as literary and political editor of *The Morning Post* had played an active part. In this rôle he was an ardent admirer of Burke; he launched vigorous onslaughts upon the administration of the day, and showed the same hostility to "French principles and ambition" that he showed to French literature, though I am inclined to believe that he caught his dislike of the literature from Lessing and Herder, the influence of whose ideas is very apparent in the *Biographia.*

Fox went so far as to accuse *The Morning Post,* and the ideas circulated through it by Coleridge, of causing the war with Napoleon. In short, the part he played, not only in literature but in journalism, in politics, gives no ground for the charges against him of bamboozling his mind with idlenesses, with dreaming, with laudanum. It is true that he idled, that he dreamt, that he took laudanum, that he was a metaphysician in a country that had but little use for metaphysicians, but through all of these impracticalities, or through some of them, he made of his mind a marvellous and subtle instrument. John Livingston Lowes's great piece of criticism, *The Road to Xanadu,* in which are charted the mind of Coleridge and the influences which went to the making of it, has done much to remove the effect of those foolish aspersions that marked him as a man who never finished anything and who dreamed his life away. Carlyle is sometimes judged responsible for this characterization of Coleridge, but as a matter of fact these charges were all brought against him early in his life-time, and, as he records in the *Biographia,* caused him serious injury. "By what I effected," he said himself, "am I to be judged by my fellow men. What I could have done is a question for my own conscience." What he did effect is imposing: in mere bulk his work both in prose and verse is large. It would have been to the gain of literature if he had worked less diligently, if he had not tried to make a living by writing, but had, like Wordsworth, procured a sinecure to provide for himself and his family. Out of Coleridge's work, when winnowed, there come enough poems of the highest quality to fill a fair-sized volume, and a volume of criticism that belongs to the half-dozen or so great works of the kind ever written. These two collections belong to the first order of genius: in his work of the secondary order there are a dozen or so more volumes of all kinds, some of poetry, some translations, some dealing with politics, fine arts, philosophy. In the poems, as Saintsbury has remarked, "the poetry of the nineteenth century is almost wholly suggested and, to a very great extent, contained after the fashion of the oak and the acorn," though this, of course, is equally true of Wordsworth, of both of them together.

Certain of his admirers regard Coleridge as greatest in his poetry, others as greatest in his criticism. But the truth is he is great in everything he has touched—poetry, criticism, psychology, philosophy. He was the first

English writer to evolve an æsthetic, and as a critic, as has been said before, his work belongs to the philosophic-critical group. Of the two conditions on which great literature depends—the action of significant mind on significant material—he, more than any of the six chief critics discussed here, comprehended that mind and all the elements that compose it. I am willing even to hazard the statement that he comprehended it better than any critic who wrote before or since. The philosophers who dealt with æsthetics too seldom understood sufficiently the conditions under which literature is actually produced—not only the external conditions of place and time, but the subjective conditions peculiar to the writer—to realize the several elements that go into literary creation. Coleridge knew them and everything connected with the production of literature; he charted the mind, marked it with signposts, illuminated it with definitions, and turned a blaze of light on all the summits. He explained, for all the writers who came after him, the difference between genius and talent, imagination and fancy, prose and poetry, art and nature, consciousness and mysticism. When he distinguished genius and imagination from talent and fancy he did not maintain that genius should be without talent or imagination without fancy: on the contrary, he said that genius needed talent properly to manifest itself. Lessing would have said that genius needed the critical mentality properly to manifest itself, and in his investigation of the literary mind he concluded that all men of genius were naturally critics, but that the converse was not equally true—the critic was not always a genius, for the critical talent in some degree could exist without any other sort of talent in literature.

5

On what did Coleridge ground his literary principles? Over and over again he tells us, in somewhat varying language: on the nature of man, on the nature of the whole being of man. There were some points, to be sure, in this nature, some common points, some common emotions, that a great poet, of necessity, shared to some extent with all his fellows, and these common points Wordsworth understood better than Coleridge, for he had explored very thoroughly the bit of life given him to experience or that he chose to experience. It was in the comprehension of the uncommon emotions, the uncommon flights of the mind without which there can be no literature, that Coleridge went beyond Wordsworth and beyond the others. He understood these, not merely in individuals, in men of great genius like Shakespeare or Chaucer or Dante, he understood these in whole ages of time. He was able to put his understanding into short, clear definitions such as his definitions of imagination, genius, and fancy, into his discoveries that genius and intellect, imagination and judgment were all equally powerful in the writers of the first order such as Shakespeare, Chaucer, and Fielding. He was able to show the especial points of difference between the literature of the Greeks in the pagan age and the literature of the moderns in the Christian age, in a way that metamorphosized thinking on the subject. The Greeks and the moderns really represented opposed ideas—"The Greeks receiving the names of their gods from Egypt soon deprived them of what was universal; they changed the ideas into finites, and these finites into anthromorphi or forms of men. Hence their religion, their poetry—nay, their very pictures—became statuesque; with them the form was the end." He showed that the effect of Christianity had been the reverse of all this. In a Christian age, finites, even the human form, must, in order to satisfy the mind, be brought into connection with, and be, in fact, symbolic of the infinite. The two great effects of Christianity on poetry, he deduced to be a combination of poetry with doctrine and a combination of poetry with sentiment —the latter combination being brought about by turning the mind inward on its own essence instead of letting it act only on its outward circumstances and communities. In short, literature became more subjective, and "it is this subjectivity which principally and most fundamentally distinguishes all the classic from all the modern poetry."

In these conclusions of Coleridge we have his explanation of the difference between the classical spirit and that which came to be called the romantic; we have, in fact, the beginning of that discussion about classical and romantic literature, and about the very terms themselves, which Goethe said were the invention of Schiller and himself. This discussion renews itself every time the expression of the mind in literature takes on a new phase, and always finds support in academic circles. It figured for a brief space a couple of years ago during the temporary excitement over the New Humanism, the rule-making critics writing then, as always, on the assumption that classical literature was something that a writer could produce if he put himself into a proper state of mind, learnt the technique, read Aristotle and the Greeks, changed his conduct.

Coleridge forestalled Spengler and recent historians of culture in showing that the two types of literature, classical and modern, represented essentially different forms of civilization—two differing ages, two differing cultures. Greek literature represented one form of religious experience and aspiration; the modern European, down to our own time, represented another. From our time a new era begins, and while it is impossible to affirm anything about the future, it can be said of the bulk of current literature that the religious mentality and religious aspiration in any shape or form are generally absent.

He anticipated many modern conclusions and discoveries, particularly those dealing with the association of ideas and with the conscious and the unconscious. He divided "all human knowledge into those on this side and those on the other side of the spontaneous consciousness," and as the Romans talked of Cis- and Trans-alpine Gaul, he talked of "the *citra et trans conscientiam communem.*" Of this knowledge on the other side of consciousness he made the distinction between that which was controlled by the intellect, and which he called philosophy, and the second, which he condemned as "flights of lawless speculation which, abandoned by all distinct consciousness, because transgressing the bounds and purposes of our intellectual faculties, are justly condemned as *transcendent.*" A similar distinction between these two kinds of thinking is made by the psychoanalyst, C. J. Jung, who terms them "directed thinking" and "fantasy thinking"; "the first, working for communication with speech elements, is troublesome and exhausting, the latter, on the contrary, goes on without trouble, working spontaneously with reminiscences." Coleridge, however, did not foresee that these "flights of lawless speculation, abandoned by all distinct consciousness," would become, a century later, an element in literature of great import and an element that is in literature to stay, though it will assuredly be forced to become less lawless, more subject to form, and therefore less monotonous than it is today.

The majority of people, Coleridge thought, could not and did not penetrate far *trans conscientiam;* "the first range of hills that encircle the scanty vale of human life is the horizon for the majority of its inhabitants. On *its* ridges the common sun is born and departs; from *them* the stars arise and, touching *them,* they vanish. By the many, even this range, the natural limit and bulwark of the vale, is but imperfectly known. Its highest ascents are too often hidden by mists and clouds from uncultivated swamps, which few have the courage or curiosity to penetrate." It may be noted here that one of the differences between our own era and those eras that Coleridge divided into pagan Greek and modern Christian is this obstinate attempt to penetrate beyond consciousness into regions uncontrolled by the intellect, to surmount not only "the first range of hills that encircle the scanty vale of human life," but any other possible ranges that may be beyond them. The chapter of the *Biographia* from which are taken the above quotations, the marvellous Chapter Twelve, entitled "A Chapter of Requests," which contains his famous explanation of the "subjective" and "objective," so irritating to many of his countrymen, is one that can be more readily comprehended in the light of modern discoveries in psychology than it was in his own day.

"All knowledge," he said, "rests on the coincidence of an object with a subject. . . . The sum of all that is merely objective we will call nature . . . the sum of all that is subjective we may comprehend in the name of the self, of intelligence. . . . During the act of knowledge itself the objective and the subjective are so instantly united that we cannot determine to which of the two priority belongs." "Self-consciousness," he declared (and we would use the term consciousness), "is not a kind of being but a kind of knowing."

The truth concerning Coleridge's struggle with the subjective and objective, with self-consciousness and beyond-consciousness, with transcendent and transcendental, was that he was trying to arrive by speculation at a conception of the conscious and unconscious or subconscious which was not possible to reach by mere speculation. In other words, he was trying to explain the unconscious life of the mind, the existence of which we have only come to understand since the experiments and investigations of Charcot, William James, Breuer, Janet, Freud, Jung, and the other psychoanalysts, all of which will be dealt with in a later chapter.

It was not only his speculations on the subjective and objective and beyond-consciousness—*extra-consciantiam*—that were considered "formless digressions" but also his speculations on philosophy, on Kant, on Fichte, on Schelling, and on those whom he called the unlearned mystics whose writing "contributed to keep alive the heart in the head." To those whose only conception of the function of criticism was the action of one mind on the work of another the important chapters in the *Biographia* were those on Wordsworth's poetry—these are the ones commonly treated in the histories of literature and generally the only ones students read; the other chapters are considered as a digression. But if any, it is the chapters on Wordsworth that may be said to be the digression, for in the book as a whole he is always consistently carrying out the intentions that have their statement on the first page—"A statement of my principles in Politics, Religion, and Philosophy, and an application of the rules, deduced from philosophical principles, to poetry and criticism." However, he was as careful as Herder to point out the limits of all rules, and in a sentence that forms a striking parallel to Herder's on the same subject, he shows the great mistake made by writers like Pope and the eighteenth-century classicists in condemning Shakespeare for not following the Greek dramatists. These writers mistook for the essentials of the Greek stage "certain rules which the wise poets imposed on themselves in order to render all the remaining parts of the drama consistent with those that had been forced on them by circumstances independent of their will." The circumstances in the time of Shakespeare, which it was equally out of his power to alter, were different; consequently, all these comparisons of Shakespeare with the Greeks, in which he was judged by the rules that accidental circumstances imposed on them, were simply futile. "Critics are apt to forget," he said, "that rules are but a means to an end, and where the ends are different, the rules must likewise be so." "The ultimate end of criticism," he maintained, "is much more to establish the principle of writing than to furnish rules how to pass judgment on what has been written by others." As Arthur Symons, himself in his day one of the most interesting of modern critics, said of him, "In this he is defining that form of criticism in which he is supreme among critics."

When Coleridge himself comes to the judgment of certain great writers it is no longer the mere reasonings and conclusions commonly associated with the criticism of judgment, it is an intuition into the processes of the writers' minds; it is that rarest of all rare powers in literature, the ability to penetrate into the genesis of a man's genius, which, along with the power of creating new literary ideas, is the mark of that unique figure, the creative critic. In spite of the cumbersomeness of his prose style he had the faculty of making concise generalizations which are truly memorable. For example, the following as a definition of poetic genius would, if learned by heart, save many writers from imagining they were poets and many critics from being deluded about what poetry is. "The sense of musical delight with the power of producing it . . . together with the power of reducing multitude into unity of effect, and modifying a series of thoughts by some one predominant thought or feeling." And who more concisely than he has noted certain of the curses that afflict literature from the inside, in every age? There are the writers "who mistake an intense desire to possess the reputation of poetic genius for the actual powers and tendencies which constitute it," and, "those popular writers who have raised themselves into temporary fame and reputation with the public at large by that most powerful of all adulation, the appeal to the bad and malignant passions of mankind." "Of all trades," he lamented, "literature at present demands the least talent or information—men who first become scribblers from idleness and ignorance next become libellers from envy and malevolence." And we have this insight into fanaticism and superstition, which, he says, spring from "a debility and dimness of imaginative power, and a consequent necessity of reliance on the immediate impressions of the senses; having a deficient portion of internal and proper warmth, minds of this class seek in the crowd for a warmth in common. Cold and phlegmatic in their own nature, like damp hay they heat and inflame by co-acervation." The vigor, and even violence, of these remarks was aroused by the irresponsibility of criticism in his day, a transition period in literature, and for that reason abounding in "arbitrary and sometimes petulant verdicts." In the great critical reviews like the *Edinburgh* and the *Quarterly,* the reviewers seemed to be possessed, not so much of any literary principles as of a personal resentment against the authors they were dealing with. This aroused Coleridge to the point of even suggesting the formation of a sort of society of critics or an academy—a "number of learned men in the various branches of science and literature," who would "pledge themselves inwardly, as well as ostensibly, to administer judgment according to a constitution and code of laws . . . grounding this code on the twofold basis of universal morals and philosophic reason, independent of all foreseen application to particular works and authors."

Easily as one can see why Coleridge and the other poets of the new movement, harassed by ignorant and sometimes malignant reviewers, would demand an organization of critics who would base their judgments on literary knowledge, it is difficult now to see how such a proposal could be carried out. What he meant by "universal morals and philosophic reason" is now hard to get at, nor can we very well figure how he could expect "Kubla Khan" or the "Ancient Mariner" or "Christabel" to be judged and explained according to such a code. It shows something of that tendency stressed by Taine as being especially English, the tendency to moralize that came in with the Puritan domination of England. Taine describes English writers as engaged in giving a moral background to everything; he represents their public as saying to them, "Be moral. We have practical minds and we would not have literature corrupt practical life. We believe in family life and we would not have literature paint the passions that attack family life. We are Protestant and we have preserved something of the severity of our fathers against enjoyment and passions." The literary taste of the nation certainly imposed moral intentions, and Taine shows the difference between Balzac, who was interested in all passions, all life, neither praising nor blaming, who regarded men and women as interesting in themselves, and Dickens and Thackeray, who, instead of penetrating the depths of a character, preferred to weep over it or rail at it or satirize it. We remember that Coleridge commended Southey because as a writer "he has uniformly made his talents subservient to the best interests of humanity, of public virtue and domestic piety." A like concern with moral intention obtrudes itself here and there in Wordsworth's Preface.

Chapter Four

DE STAËL BRINGS THE NEW IDEAS
TO FRANCE

Now AT THE end of the eighteenth century or at the beginning of the nineteenth a new sort of literature based on certain new freedoms was well on its way. And this new literature took its beginning not out of the French Revolution, but at the moment when Lessing recognized and forcibly expressed the fact that every-day man and every-day life had not been revealed in literature, and that it was the business of the new writers to deal with the every-day man and the every-day life. Great literature in the past had, of course, sprung from life, out of man's mind, but had very seldom been about ordinary life or ordinary man: it had been about life stylized, emotions stylized, human relations and human aspirations stylized, and characters stylized into types. It had, of course, always touched life and the passions of life at some point, but life as lived by the generality it had treated only incidentally. Even English literature, the most human of all literatures up to this time, had seldom dealt with ordinary men and women. Shakespeare had revealed all the passions but not all men; his characters were mainly kings and heroes and conquerors, great lovers, strange women, people outside the ruck of humanity. The common man, in Shakespeare, was likely to be a grave-digger or a clown; general life was as rarely touched upon as it was in Sophocles, or Æschylus, or Dante.

But from this period on, from the latter part of the eighteenth century, what was meant by progress in literature was to be progress towards the revelation in language, in poetry and prose, of the mass of men, of their lives and experiences. From this time on, too, the history of literature was to become the history of the adventures of ideas and doctrines through the imagination of men. Complex philosophical ideas and doctrines were to have a tremendous motive power both in life and in literature: civilization took on a new movement, literature took on a new movement. While it would be ridiculous to try to explain any separate work of literature by this or that idea, this or that doctrine, yet the large movements of the mind, the literary schools, the new techniques, were all the outcome of ideas and doctrines.

The revolution in literature was in being in both Germany and England before it spread to France, and this though some of the most fruitful seeds had originally come from that country. But in France literature had been more stylized than in any other country; it was a major interest to a greater percentage of the population, so that a larger movement was involved in the change; more hard-and-fast ideas had to be loosened; wider sections of society had to be affected. The influences, however, that finally set it going became concentrated in a woman, Madame de Staël; many ramified tendencies, social, political, literary, philosophical—French, German, and English—came to a focus in her work: she represented the strong currents of the eighteenth century that were passing away, as well as the new currents of the nineteenth century that were just setting in. From the side of the eighteenth century her mind had been formed by the Encyclopedia and the Encyclopedists, above all by Diderot, Voltaire, Rousseau and Helvetius—in fact, it may be said that the general tendencies of their thought became fused in her enfranchised and strongly intuitive intellect so that something new and prophetic of the new forces came out of it.

On the negative side these general tendencies were a desire to break away from the authority of tradition, from old forms of government, old social stratification, from the classical school in literature and from organized religion. On the positive side they stood for a belief in reason, in progress, in the continuous development of the mind and of the arts. They stood for joy in the delights of the senses, in the present time and in the passing moment. From Diderot and Rousseau, especially, among the Encyclopedists, came the questioning of the value of European civilization and the doctrine of the primacy of strong feelings. From Rousseau came the plea for the exaltation of the heart over the intellect, for a trust in instincts and natural passions, and for the freedom of the individual; the whole inclination on one side was towards praise of life and what Wordsworth called "the natural passions of the heart." On the other side, perhaps as an outcome of this, there was a strong trend towards materialism and towards a belief in the almighty power of the fact, which later became systematized in the criticism of Taine, and which eventually had the result of affecting minds with a profound pessimism. From Helvetius came the theory which, in the nineteenth century and our own day, was to have a powerful effect on every art and which was, at the same time, responsible for many vagaries—the theory that the mind grows with the passions and that one becomes stupid when one ceases to be passionate.

Out of these influences together came the conviction that the way to progress was to shake off the authority of the past, and this notion has grown in prestige and takes on a new importance every time there is in the world a considerable change of any kind. All these trends and doctrines, some more securely than others, found a place in the mind of de Staël and urged her towards the evolution of those theories that made her work such a vitalizing force in the general thought of her own time and later. This brilliant and sophisticated cosmopolite was somewhat older than the two English poets and critics and had a vast experience, not only of the social world but of the intellectual world in all its facets.

2

Though born in Paris, Germaine de Staël was not a Frenchwoman but a Genevan married to a Swede, the daughter of Necker, the finance minister of Louis XVI, and included among her ancestry German, French, and Irish strains, which gave her a more natural sympathy with cosmopolitan and especially with German ideas than was customary in France at the time. She paid a visit to England just after the publication of the *Lyrical Ballads* had definitely turned English literature on a new path; she visited Germany a couple of years after Coleridge and Wordsworth had been there, and when the new German literature was rising to its ripest development, when the change in taste effected by Lessing and Herder was bearing its noblest fruit. She had early, as her book *De la Littérature* showed, been strongly stirred by English and German literature; her first work had appealed to both Schiller and Goethe, and Goethe had translated portions of it for publication in the periodical that the two poets were running in the interest of the new school. When she went to Germany, therefore, de Staël's mind was prepared to fall completely under the sway of ideas with which she had always sympathized. In fact, it was after this visit, and as a result of it, that her mind really began to bloom. To her the criticism of Lessing and Herder, the poetry and dramas of Goethe and Schiller, represented the literature of the future, and as such she put them forward to her countrymen.

In her book *De la Littérature* she had already criticized the shackled condition of French drama and poetry, which she declared had lost vigor under the domination of the salons; their endeavor to conform to the spirit of good society had placed grace and taste before originality and power. In addition, French tragedy had for the most part confined itself to the same subjects as the Greek and to the same laws of composition, though lending to the personages French sentiments, customs, and gallantries. Like Lessing she demanded that the dramatists give up treating of kings and gods and get down either to subjects from their own history, as did the English dramatists and Schiller, or to subjects from every-day life, as did Lessing. Not only the limitations of the subject but the unities and the verse-form, the Alexandrine, had been an obstacle to getting actual life on the stage. A master like Racine had, she was willing to admit, conquered all these obstacles, but while decrying any idea that she was attacking the great French tragic dramatists, she declared the time had come for a different type of literature.

French literature had stood in the same place too long, and this chiefly because of continual imitation of the masterpieces, both its own and the ancient Greek and Roman. Nothing in life ought to be stationary, and when art does not *change* it becomes petrified. Life had *changed;* the Revolution had altered the foundations of society, and now on the threshold of the nineteenth century, she perceived that a new sort of life was coming into being, and this new sort of life needed a new sort of literature. She offered to her countrymen as the type of this innovation the literature that was being produced in Germany, with its originality, its individuality, its free form, its philosophic depth, its independence of social conventions: this was what she called the literature of the North, modern literature, in contra-distinction to the literature of the South, classical literature.

In *De la Littérature* she had talked of what she called the two distinct literatures that Europe had produced, that which came from the South and that which came from the North. The Greek, the Latin, the Italian, the Spanish, and the French of the century of Louis XIV belonged, she stated, to the literature of the South; the English, the German, the Teutonic literature generally, the Scandinavian, the Icelandic, the Celtic, belonged to the literature of the North. The differences between these literatures she explained, according to the central theory of her book, by the climate, the nature of the soil, the political and social conditions—in short, according to her doctrine that literature was an expression of society. She indicated a new basis for criticism, a new principle by which literature was to be evaluated, when she wrote an explanation of her purpose. "I propose to examine the influence of religion, customs, and laws on literature, and also to examine the influence of literature on religion, customs, and laws. It seems to me that the moral and political causes which affect literature have never been sufficiently analyzed. . . . Religion and laws decide almost entirely the resemblance or difference between the minds of nations. . . . The climate accounts for some differences, but the general education of the leading classes of society is always the result of political institutions. The government being the center of the greater portion of the interests of men, customs and ideas follow the course of the interests." This view of literature proved to have rousing effects and brought to her, not only in her lifetime but even to a greater degree since, many disciples. It represented a fresh discovery, a fresh portion of truth, and like all such discoveries affected a release of minds of differing tendencies—politicians, historians, and poets, critics like Schlegel, historians like Prosper de Barante.

Immediately after de Staël came Sainte-Beuve and the whole group of the *Globe* newspaper, who based their criticism on her theories. In our own day all the theories by which she related literature to society and made it an expression of society have been taken over by that school of critics who call themselves Marxists, but with a more narrow interpretation of the possibilities of man and the perfectibility of the human spirit, and with the substitution of the economic man for the Rousseauan natural man. In fact, she is the originator of a school of social criticism which, especially in America, has had a noteworthy influence on life and literature. Her thesis that literature is an expression of society is also the thesis of every social and sociological critic since her time.

As a social critic Madame de Staël was the most stirring and the most original of the train of those who are her descendants. Like all social critics she had serious limitations on the purely literary and æsthetic side, which have to be taken into account in all applications of her theories, particularly her early theories as expressed in *De la Littérature*. She understood best the sort of writing that was the expression of society and thought that all literature was neither more nor less than this. In spite of her ardent espousal of the poetic theories of Herder she appears to have got little out of poetry except its intellectual and emotional content, a weakness of all social critics since her time, including the Americans. The poetic utterance itself, the apprehension of the form, all that really made the process of poetry different from the process of poetic, or imaginative, or lyrical prose, she seemed either constitutionally incapable of grasping, or, it may be, she was determined to measure all writing by the eighteenth-century standards of reason and logic.

3

And so it happened that, much as Goethe and Schiller admired her, we have evidence that they did not think she really understood their poetry. Her theory of literature as an expression of society works very well when applied to memoirs, diaries, certain kinds of drama and fiction; it was to work very well when applied to the new form of writing that was coming in and which, to some extent, she practised herself—the novel. Applied to literature of other types, the highly imaginative or the deeply philosophic, or to most types of poetry, it creaks ominously. To state its defects, however, is not to deny the great influence of the challenge that it gave, or to limit the enduring influence her own explanation of it has had on literary thought. It stirred new writers to the study of the actual life around them with the object of expressing this life and this society in literature, it started off whole movements in technique, especially in prose. But like all literary doctrines its limitations became clearly visible when applied wholesale to literature by too literal minds, which happened almost immediately. Her theory, like Lessing's, explains some traits in all kinds of literature including the ancient Greek; it explained almost completely that new form of literature that was coming in—the novel —as well as the new drama of contemporary life; she herself showed that it could be applied with revealing results even to the sort of drama that was going out, the classical theatre of Racine.

But, after all, the work that was to have the most thrilling influence on her immediate successors was her book on Germany for which all her early work was a preparation and which represented the highest flight of her mind. The thought of Lessing roused her as it had roused Coleridge, but that side of her mind which had been formed by Rousseau and Diderot was most strongly drawn to Herder. Those two ideas of Herder's that especially fascinated his followers, the one about the significance of primitive poetry, including the notion that poetry came from the primitive side of the imagination (though she had little understanding of what primitive imagination was), and the other about the difference between the literature of the North and the literature of the South, between the literature of the moderns and the literature of the ancients, took possession of her mind. Coleridge had also seized on this notion of Herder's and had attached it to a metaphysical idea, by asserting that the Greeks changed ideas into finites and these finites into anthromorphi or forms of men. He also explained it more simply by a comparison of Paganism with Christianity, of Greek architecture with Gothic architecture, and of the *Antigone* of Sophocles with the *Hamlet* of Shakespeare. But de Staël was to illuminate it with a more direct light.

After her sojourn in Germany she proceeded to identify the literatures she had previously divided into those of the North and those of the South, with Romantic and Classical literature. The expressions "Romantic" and "Classic," though put into currency by de Staël, appear to have been first used in his lectures by William Schlegel, who became a great friend of hers. Goethe, in his *Conversations with Eckermann,* said that it was he and Schiller who were the originators of these terms. "This division of poetry into Classic and Romantic comes originally from Schiller and me. It was my principle in poetry always to work objectively; Schiller, on the contrary, wrote nothing that was not subjective. The Schlegels got hold of the idea, developed it, and little by little it has spread throughout the world." Now the idea that lay behind the terms, as we have seen, was first put forward by Herder and later worked over by Coleridge. But it was de Staël who took the terms out of the realm of speculative ideas and attached to them something ardent and related to life.

"The name Romantic," she said, "has been newly introduced in Germany to designate the poetry which was born of chivalry and Christianity. If one admits nothing except Paganism and Christianity, one can say that the North and the South, chivalry on the one side, and the Greeks and Romans on the other, divide the empire of literature between them. One sometimes uses the word Classic as a synonym of perfection; for myself, I use the term in another meaning—considering Classical poetry as that of the ancients and Romantic poetry as that which proceeds in some way from chivalrous traditions. This division relates equally to two periods of the world—that which preceded Christianity and that which followed it." In addition, she went back to her old claim that the modern Latin nations, of which the French were the most cultivated, leaned towards the Classical and imitation of the Greek and Latin, whereas the Teutons, of which the English were the most illustrious representatives, produced Romantic literature. This diversity of taste, this divergence of literary orientation, she believed, sprang not from accidental causes but from primitive sources of imagination and thought. With this latter sentence, according to certain critics who followed her, she changed the object of criticism by relating literature to the states of civilization of which it is, in her idea, the natural product.

Her comparison of the simplicity of Greek civilization, where men carried the action of the soul outwards, personifying nature and ideas, with the modern tendency towards continually turning the mind inwards, influenced people to take this complex modernity of mind more and more into account; so this had the effect of increasing the mood of introspection and subjectivism. Romantic literature, she believed, was the only type of literature natural to this modern mood, because it alone had, according to her conception, the potentiality of growth and renewal.

Through her power to foresee the trend that civilization and literature were taking, she was able to define in advance the character of the prose and poetry that were to be dominant in Europe for the next century. The qualities she saw in this new literature, "the sorrowful sentiment of the incompleteness of human destiny, melancholy, reverie, mysticism, the sense of the enigma of life," became the qualities pursued by the new writers. She pointed out the main defects of French literature: that in type, form, and content it belonged to a civilization that had become obsolete; that besides being a reflection of the Greek, it had been developed too much according to the demands of good society. The brilliant company that had congregated in the salons required above all a form of writing that could be easily read and understood. Profundity, the power of meditation, of brooding on life, all had been sacrificed to grace and good taste, qualities which ended in sterility, lack of fervor and monotony.

Literature, as she maintained, can stand only as much grace, taste, and refinement as is compatible with genius. Not only was the artist shackled by the precepts of good taste that made originality and individuality undesirable, but he was shackled also by the Aristotelian unities, by the rigid verse forms, and by the convention of taking the same themes as the Greek and Roman dramatists. Break away from all these conventions, she advised; give up depicting kings and heroes on the stage, and easily delineated qualities like jealousy, ambition, and the like, and depict the complex characteristics of the modern man. The great classical drama was not enjoyed by the common people as were the dramas of Shakespeare and Schiller; they were too remote from any life the ordinary man experienced, understood, or could imagine. Contemporary German writers had produced a literature that shook the imaginations and emotions of men, a strong, violent, and original literature, because, unlike the French, they were not absorbed in the life of society and had not to consider the taste and tone of society. In explaining all this, she made careful studies of the work of Lessing, Herder, Klopstock, Goethe, and Schiller: she had encountered their work and some of them personally at the moment when literary expression and artistic productiveness had reached their height in Germany. The qualities that marked their work she wanted brought, not only into French but into all contemporary literatures, for her great desire was for a common European literary art, national and at the same time international.

What she actually succeeded in bringing about was

a fusion of the qualities of the Teutonic and the Latin literatures, a fusion not entirely relished by some of her French critics: she has indeed been accused by them of diverting the national literature from its native direction. But, like Lessing, she affected profoundly the minds of the writers who came after her, and this in spite of a curious moralizing tone in her criticism, which belonged to her Genevan background rather than to the country she was addressing. Her emancipated literary ideas were frequently interlarded with such assertions as, that it was not in the power of a poet to draw forth a tragic effect from an incident which admitted the smallest tendency to an immoral principle, or that "literary criticism is not infrequently, indeed, a sort of treatise on morality," and she was sure that "perfect virtue" is the *beau idéal* of the intellectual world.

The main defect, however, in her criticism is her attitude to poetry. Schiller, indeed, went so far as to say "of what we call poetry, she has no perception." Yet, as a good disciple of Herder, she asserted the primacy of lyric poetry—that song on the wing that he said all real poetry was, and that all early poetry had been. She re-stated Herder's remarks about poetry, perhaps without really comprehending them; she even put forward the strange statement, very strange in a champion of lyricism, "poetry is, of all the arts, that which belongs closest to reason." Still, in spite of such limitations, she, more than any of the other critics up to her time, made ideas and literatures seem the common possession of all men and of all countries; she led the European spirit across national frontiers, even though she was not able to lead it across class frontiers. The new writers took as guide-posts watchwords and talismanic phrases drawn from her books. Hugo and Lamartine devoured all she had written: she gave the former the intellectual background necessary to shape the elemental force that was his genius. As Brunetière has pointed out, there is nothing in Hugo's famous preface to *Cromwell,* around which so much of the Romantic Movement eddied, that did not come from her book on Germany. There is, indeed, almost nothing in any of his literary ideas of which she is not the parent. He, like Walter Scott, went straight for inspiration to those Middle Ages, to the Troubadours, to Chivalry, out of which, as she declared, modern romantic literature had proceeded. Sainte-Beuve, the friend and critic of Hugo— they were both about the same age, having been born in the dawn of the nineteenth century—was so deeply influenced by de Staël and her name comes so frequently into his criticism, that she has been called the heroine of his *Lundis.*

4

The great affair of all the critics whose work has been discussed in these chapters had been to change the course of literature in their respective countries, to change its orientation; for long the sap had been drying up, and the writers were ceasing to provide spiritual nutriment. Each modern literature from this time on had to take graftings from the others, for countries were becoming intellectually interdependent, and the old frontiers, the old national prejudices, the old literary prejudices, had to be broken down. To turn into literature new springs of such strength that the old bed was re-channelled—that was what they all had labored for.

The French was the last of the great European literatures to change its course, to attune itself to the rhythm of the new civilization, the new attitude towards life. The German had come first, the English next, and then the French. But the ideas that came in the train of the change in French literature brought with them more developments than came from the change in any of the others: developments in poetry, in the novel, in biography, in psychology and, especially, in that study which was the inevitable outcome of the work of the new critics, the study of comparative literature.

Several conclusions emerged from the changes in the great literatures. First of all, as has been said above, it became obvious that literary ideas were interdependent, they spread from country to country. It became clear that modern literature, unlike early literature, no longer developed unconsciously around certain inherited tales, fables, and traditions, and without guides or charts. The unconscious stage was passed. Now it was plain that a few men with a dream and an idea could turn literature on to a new path, could deliberately say, "This side of life or man has not yet been expressed; this or this tendency, this or this attitude to life, which was not in the ancient world, has not yet been revealed —let us find a way to do it." They could say, too, "Language, from over-use, through its employment by everybody in every-day life, has become worn and dull—let us put life and iron into it."

In effect, all these critics said the same thing; the services to literature of all of them were of the same kind; they revealed a new attitude towards civilization, towards the development of man; they extended the bounds of what could be expressed in literature; they brought in new subjects; they revivified language; they tried to make literature the possession and the instrument of the ordinary man. Herder and Lessing, Goethe and Schiller, Coleridge and Wordsworth, Hugo and Lamartine, brought in emotions, passions, characters, that until then had been ignored or even scorned as material. They started new rhythms in language; they changed, as it were, the very sound of it; they made it respond to the new ideas that were surging in. There is a sentence in Zola's *Lettre à la Jeunesse* in which he sums up what Hugo had achieved, and this summing-up applies to all these innovators. "He renewed the language; the classical language was dying of anemia; he put into circulation a vocabulary that had been scorned; he wrote verses that had the sheen of gold and the sonority of bronze."

Chapter Five

THE IDEAS ON THE MARCH:
SAINTE-BEUVE AND TAINE

I

AT THE OUTSET of the movement towards the renewal of literature and the extension of its boundaries, the men who evolved the theories were also those who put them into practice. As time went on, there arose the necessity for a label that would differentiate the new kind of writing from the older productions: there became annexed to it somehow the label "Romantic." It was the label that Madame de Staël had taken over from the Germans as suitable for distinguishing what she called the literature of the North from the literature of the South, and the literature of the ancients from that which came out of modern minds given another orientation by the Christian religion and the traditions of Chivalry. Acrimonious discussion rose round the use of the term "Romantic," which was really a misnomer and has thrown innumerable difficulties in the way of understanding the trend of literary expression all through the nineteenth century and up to our own day. But owing to the innate passion of men for attaching a name to a thing once it comes into existence, regardless of whether the naming is suitable or not, the label "Romantic," in spite of all protests, quickly effected an entrance into people's imaginations; not only the early innovators but the whole change that swept in with the new era came to be described as "The Romantic Movement." Yet even those to whose work the label seemed most appropriate—Victor Hugo, for instance—objected to it. Others thought that a loose label like "Modernism" was better fitted to describe the new trend. The Germans, even, who were originally responsible for the designation, had for the most part been content with calling their own production "the newest literature." It was not easy for the innovators themselves to comprehend exactly what was happening, but now, looking back on it, we can perceive that it all was simply a strong impulse towards bringing into literature a larger variety of human experience, more and more of humanity, and greater complexity of emotion.

Madame de Staël had said that the distinguishing mark of the new literature was the sorrowful sentiment of the incompleteness of human destiny and the complexity of the modern man. Coleridge had declared that it was "subjectivity" which principally and most fundamentally distinguished all modern from all classic poetry. As divergent notions of literary technique and literary expression developed, varied and sometimes fantastic labels were devised, especially in France, to define the various stages of the new literary doctrines. Some of the most practical of these, such as "Realism" and "Naturalism" in prose, or "Symbolism" in poetry, are still vital enough, or are, at least, handy and convenient critical terms. The word "Romantic" itself, however, is now so hazy in its significance that it has no possibilities of conveying any clear-cut meaning in regard to the whole literary trend; in our every-day vocabulary the expression has followed the fate of the word "genteel," and is now somewhat derogatory in meaning.

With the literature that grew out of the new doctrines came a whole new attitude to life, a new trend of civilization, based partly on the evolution of history, partly on the evolution of expression. The minor movements that came out of the main one were from time to time regarded as reactions against it, when, as a matter of fact, they were specific developments of it. Actually, there was no reaction against the movement as a whole until our own time, and this, at the moment, is in some degree a reaction and in some degree, as will be shown later, a fresh development of the main doctrines.

2

When Sainte-Beuve, the next of the great minds that kept ideas on the march, appeared on the scene as a young critic of the *Globe* newspaper and as a member of the Poets' Club, the *cénacle* that surrounded Hugo, the earlier shape of the movement, in all countries where it was in being, was beginning to change. It kept growing and growing and, at times, some of the forms of its development, as of the opposition to it, became a trifle ridiculous. The limits of absurdity in the opposition were reached in France when seven writers of the older school petitioned the King, Charles X, to banish the new romanticism from the Comédie Française.

Many of the major figures of the movement in various countries were alive and producing at the same time: Herder was still living when Wordsworth and Coleridge visited Germany and when Madame de Staël wrote her book on literature; Goethe and Schiller were in their prime when Sainte-Beuve and Victor Hugo were born. Wordsworth, one of the chief instigators of the change, lived through many different phases of it to become Queen Victoria's poet-laureate; he lived long after his creative period had come to a close; he survived to find himself regarded as out of fashion, but at the same time he saw, or could have seen, all his ideas bear fruit—sometimes an unpredictable sort of fruit—and, oddly enough, rather more on the Continent than in England. The greatest carrier of his ideas to the Continent was, of course, Sainte-Beuve, who was not only intimately acquainted with the poetry of Wordsworth, but with that of the whole Lake School.

He had a passion for translating Wordsworth, Southey, and Coleridge, for translating and quoting them, which was to affect French poetry all through the nineteenth century. Not only did he attach himself as a critic to the Wordsworthian doctrine of poetry, but in his own verse he put the doctrine into practice. A good portion of Sainte-Beuve's own poetry was an attempt to write of humble life, and the humblest things in life, in terms of the Wordsworthian ideal. He presented little stories in verse, little dramas of nature, simple pictures of real life, and these started in France at least two schools of poetry the developments of which will be dealt with later.

After writing three collections of poems, Sainte-Beuve abandoned not only poetry but all other sorts of writing except criticism, into which he put all his variety of talents. He was the first figure in literature to become the critic-specialist, the all-round literary expert. One may have one's preference as between these two vastly influential critics, Sainte-Beuve and his successor Taine, but it is not easy to decide which of them was the greater critic, for their influences on literature were from differing angles: the two were contrasting mental types; to go back to the distinction previously made, Sainte-Beuve was the poet-critic, Taine, the philosopher-critic. We have Sainte-Beuve's own dictum that the critic ought to be part poet: *Il est mieux qu'il y ait dans le critique un poète: un poète a le sentiment*

plus vif des beautés, et il hésite moins à les maintenir.
The poet in Sainte-Beuve gave a perpetual fresh life
to his criticism; for him, the artist-critic, a book is the
expression of an individual, the fruit of his mind and
personality. The leading principle of his method, the
identity of the man with his work, *tel arbre, tel fruit,*
was a translation into terms of criticism of one of the
great guiding motives of the new dispensation—the
primacy of the individual, the importance of the personal, the ego, in literature.

Very early in his career, at the height of his friendship with Hugo, at the time of his first enlistment with
Romanticism, Sainte-Beuve began to evolve his distinc-
tive method of criticism. Originally it was sketched out
in his portrait of Corneille in the *Globe* newspaper to
which he was attached as literary critic. Sainte-Beuve
was quite aware that in epochs when literature was
less personal, or even impersonal, his method would
not have had such fruitful results, for, as he said himself, in the case of the older writers, anyway, very little
data about their personal lives existed, so that their
biographers devoted their thought to their work, and
little or none at all to the man behind the work. In
this, the first bare outline, Sainte-Beuve declared that
a writer must be studied, not merely in his work, but
in his private and domestic relations as well. As to his
product, it was important to get a revelation of him
at its source, that is, at the moment when he brought

out his first significant work. When you have unravelled the circumstances which led to this work, when you have discovered that region where his genius first took up its abode and thrived, then you understand your writer.

This essay on Corneille, however, showed only Sainte-Beuve's groping after his method: it was as late as thirty years afterwards, when he had experimented with it all his life and worked it out to perfection, that he described it fully in his essay on Chateaubriand. Here it appears so clearly and is described so succinctly that it is almost as if tabulated into rules. A literary product is not separable from the one who produces it; it is difficult to judge it without a knowledge of the man who wrote it; therefore, real criticism of the work of the ancients is not possible because there are not sufficient data about their lives. . . . To know a work, to study it, you must first know its author, you must study him; after this, comes the study of the type of mind to which he belongs, for there are families of minds, Sainte-Beuve thought, as there are families of plants and animals. But with men, of course, he added, one could never draw an exact conclusion. Literature for him was the product of certain great and superior minds which it was the duty of the critic to understand and explain. It was well, therefore, to begin with the race and native country of this man of superior mind, to study him physiologically in his ancestors and in his descendants. His family, his brothers, sisters,

children, should be carefully considered; special attention should be paid to the mother as the more direct
parent. This study of his blood relations will often
reveal important lineaments of the writer's personality,
which were masked, in the man himself, and which are
extremely important to know about.

After his family, the next important subject in the
study of a writer should be the group of which he first
formed a part. A group, par excellence, would be such
a one as surrounded Racine or Molière, or, in English
literature, the Wordsworth group or the Shelley group,
or, in America, the Emerson Concord group, or, in Germany, the Goethe-Schiller Weimar group. By examining, from all known data, the quality of the minds of
the group, one gets another light on the mind one is
endeavoring to reveal. It might be noted here that
Sainte-Beuve himself, when at the age of twenty-four
he gave the first outline of his method, was a member
of a group, the group of critics on *The Globe*, who devoted themselves largely to disseminating the ideas
of Madame de Staël. It is the group, to continue Sainte-
Beuve's account of his method, the fellowship, the
active exchange of ideas, which enables a man of talent
or genius to find himself and develop. His earlier idea
of the importance of grasping the man at the moment
of his first important work he stressed all through his
career as a critic. In addition, he said, there is always
in the life of every writer a period to be studied with

equal care—it is when the promise of the first real work either never fructifies or when it surpasses the earlier promise. Then, again, the critic must likewise take note of the moment when the great talent begins to waver, to grow old or to weaken. This does not necessarily mean that it is age that brings the weakening of the talent: on the contrary, Sainte-Beuve believed that few talents survive to old age at all. Fifteen years, he maintained, was the length of the average literary life, the average period during which a man was at the height of his power. Sainte-Beuve himself seemed to be at the height of his power for over thirty years. Yet his own criticism of himself was "I lost early, not my fire, but my wings." But the reader, in Sainte-Beuve's last as well as in his first work, is apt always to hear the beating of wings.

In the general estimation of a man and his work, Sainte-Beuve believed no question too insignificant, no sort of information too unimportant, even information which has no apparent connection, or but the slightest, with his actual production. The questions he lists that should be asked by a biographer and a critic about his subject are: What were his religious views? What was his attitude towards women? Towards money? Was he rich? Was he poor? Was he affected by scenery? What was his daily manner of living? What was his vice? His weakness—for every man has one? What were his physical characteristics, and were these translated into his writing? The answers to all these are important unless the book the subject has written is a treatise on geometry. Finally, who were a man's friends? His enemies? His disciples? His admirers? Nothing shows better the nature of a talent than the point at which the revolt against a writer begins, for in nearly every author's life there comes a period when his own, or a younger generation, begins to find him inadequate. Now we can arrive at a comprehension of Sainte-Beuve's most characteristic definition of criticism, the one, of all those descriptions of its function, scattered through his work, which most clearly defines his own kind of criticism: "Real criticism, as I define it, consists in studying each person, that is, each author, each talent, according to the conditions of his nature, in order to make a vivid and pregnant description of him so that he can later be classified and put in his proper place in the hierarchy of art."

The word "classified" in this definition is one of those recurring and guiding words that serve as a key to Sainte-Beuve's thought. It was his ambition to make what he called a "natural history of minds" and to classify them in families. "I am a naturalist of minds," he remarked of himself; "what I should like to establish is a natural history of literature. Some day," he said, "there will come a great observer, a natural classifier of minds; meanwhile the work of the most humble of us is to prepare the elements and to describe the individ-

uals, relating them to their true type—that is what I
am trying to do more and more. . . . The genuine and
natural families of minds are not so numerous. . . .
When one has observed and worked over sufficient examples, one recognizes how many diverse kinds of
minds, of organizations, are related to certain types,
come under certain leading heads. Any noted contemporary whom one has well observed and understood
will explain and evoke a whole series of figures of the
past, from the moment the real resemblance between
them becomes manifest and certain family characteristics have compelled your attention. It is exactly as a
botanist works with plants or a zoölogist with animals.
. . . An individual carefully observed is related prompt-
ly to the species, which one has only noted in a general
way, and throws light on it." However, he did not believe that human beings could be classified with the
same exactness as animals and plants.

In addition to these leading ideas, he had all sorts of
ancillary notions—how one age grows out of a previous age; the relation of a man to his age; how any man,
even the greatest, is partly plunged into the prejudices
of his time, though great men, unlike the common run,
are not imprisoned in their time. And there is that sentence of his, pondered over by so many novelists, including Proust and Joyce, about the mobility, the
changefulness of men and life and the mind, which are
always in flux. "Every day I change; my tastes of yes-

terday are no longer my tastes of today; my friendships themselves wither up and are renewed; before the final death of the mobile being that bears my name, how many men have already died within me?" Then there was his notion of the master faculty, now chiefly identified with Taine, the notion that in every man, and in particular in every genius, there is one quality of mind —*la qualité principale—le trait dominant*—which dominates all the others. But with regard to this, too, he was certain that no great result could be obtained until psychological knowledge was more advanced. Himself a great natural and intuitive psychologist (he had received, he said, the fatal gift of reading the secret of souls), he worked without any of the data that modern psychological research has placed at the disposal of our contemporaries who have taken over his method. Nevertheless, he remains the only complete master of the method.

And the only perfect workings-out of it are still his. That method has its most revealing results in his *Port-Royal* and his *Chateaubriand;* the one, the critical history of a group, and the other, the critical history of an individual. In his *Port-Royal* he refers again and again to the points of his method, remarking that he is applying it to the group as he would to an individual, following the succession of happenings, the developments, step by step, on all sides—theological, philosophical, literary, and in the individual careers—not only of the great men of the group, Pascal, Racine, Arnauld, Jansenius, but even of the minor figures associated with it.

In *Chateaubriand* we have an example of the method at its best, when applied to an individual, and likewise an example of the very type of writer to whom the method could be most revealingly applied. Chateaubriand was precisely one of those writers whose work could be explained by his life, his ancestry, his family, his personal relations, and by the answers to all those questions which Sainte-Beuve had listed as significant to ask. In the case of Sainte-Beuve's imitators, the results depended on the nature of their abilities, on their particular temperament, experience, and psychological insight. It must likewise be said that the successful working out of the formula depended greatly on the user's ability to adopt a critical attitude towards his own personality and on his power to keep it from intruding on the study of his subject. The procedure gives a great deal too much leeway, to an uncritical or personal-minded writer, to work off his own complexes, experiences, or temperamental twists, on his subject. Its inventor never intended it to be used in the manner of a hostile judge or prosecuting attorney, which has been the manner of so many biographers who are his disciples—often unknowingly his disciples, because his ideas, like those of all real initiators, have become part of the common stock.

In contemporary writing the best examples of the

method are seen where the subject is a public figure about whose private life and ancestry intimate details are easily discoverable, as, for instance, in Lytton Strachey's *Queen Victoria,* or Stefan Zweig's *Marie Antoinette* or *Mary Queen of Scotland*. But where the subject is an artist, the biography frequently turns out to throw more light on the writer of it than on the subject. For example, in John Middleton Murry's *D. H. Lawrence* and in Van Wyck Brooks's *Mark Twain,* the result is a work as exciting as any novel, with interesting psychological and historical judgments, but with a private-minded interpretation of the subject's work and personality. A dubious use of the method is exhibited in André Maurois's book on Shelley, called *Ariel,* where the author concentrates on Shelley's private life and leaves out of account altogether Shelley's poetry—the *raison d'être* of any biography of him. The most deliberate application of it is that by Gamaliel Bradford in his portraits or psychographs. In this case the great drawback in the results came first of all from the second-rate mind of the writer, and secondly, from the fact that he works out the problems in the lives of his characters from data given by books, without any of that fullness of life which made Sainte-Beuve himself the only real master of his own method, and without any of his power of relating them to living families of minds. Yet in spite of the defects of the method and the difficulties of fully applying it, it revolutionized biography, for of course Sainte-Beuve is the father of modern biography and very largely also of the modern autobiographical novel. No one now starts out to write the life of any personage without first of all asking concerning his subject all those questions and seeking that information which Sainte-Beuve sets out as of first importance.

3

The effect of his method was to bring into literature new types of writers: Sainte-Beuve opened the gates of literary expression for a lot of men and women who heretofore had no way of expressing themselves, or who had done so only in elementary ways. There was, for example, the intuitive psychologist, the character reader, who in the past had set forth his talent in humble ways like astrology and palm reading; there was the prosecuting attorney, who might have to expend his gifts in a law court or in displays of oratory; now he could bring a human being before the bar in a book, examine him, present him to the public, and pass judgment on him; there were, besides, all those who could create neither character nor ideas but who could exercise an analyzing and psychological talent on persons who had actually lived. In this way it was possible for mediocre minds without any great sense of life to attain a passable success in writing, and indeed it was this type that the Sainte-Beuve procedure frequently equipped with a method and a scalpel for dissecting the great. Our contemporaries have had an extra weapon placed in their hands, a sort of scientific weapon that the modern discoveries in psychology provided. In short, ever since Sainte-Beuve the sharply investigating biography has become a common feature of the literary landscape, though the bulk of this sort of writing must be described as of passing interest only. For the great biographer, like the great critic, is a very rare figure in literature; only once have the two been united in the same man—Sainte-Beuve.

What made him a master on both counts was his vast knowledge of both life and literature, his profound psychological insight, his all-round gifts as a writer, his great love for the interior lives of men—a love that often made him as interested in the second-rate as in the first-rate mind. Supporting all his natural gifts was his training, and as part of this training his medical studies. "It was to medicine," he said, "that I owed the spirit of philosophy, the love of exactitude, the physiological reality, whatever of good method has passed into my writing." In addition to his gifts of imagination and interest, and his extraordinary training, there was his reverence for the superior man, his respect for the great individual who added to the achievements of the race. But a whole array of the new biographers who imitated him concentrated less on what made their subjects great and superior than on those qualities that made it possible for other people to patronize them. It would have been of little interest to the public at large to be given an account of the mental discipline, the searing meditation and emotions, that went into the making of the *Divine Comedy* or the *Fleurs du Mal* or *Faust*. But the love-affairs of great men, their futilities, their petty degradations, their inferiority as citizens to their fellow citizens, some concealed or reserved incident in their lives, something that could make other men pleasantly familiar with them or condescending to them—these were what too many of the Sainte-Beuve imitators seized upon.

Many of the great Victorian writers have been made comic to the point of buffoonery through a biographer's placing a wrong emphasis on some trait. Thus, their discipline has been made to appear hypocrisy, their loves childish or sordid. Those temporizings, those adaptations which all men, and especially men of genius, have to make with their surroundings and with conventions originally made for the greatest good of the greatest number, have been presented as cowardly subterfuges. And this has been done by unduly stressing the answer to some one of Sainte-Beuve's questions, when he meant all of them to be part of the general pattern, and subsidiary to it. It has been said of some of these biographers that they wormed their way into the subject, and the figure of speech is excellent, for in many cases they left the subject worm-eaten and with little remaining of one who had been a great figure in life: they ate him away as parasites would.

In spite of the fact that it revolutionized criticism, the method had its defects, and the first to admit it would have been its initiator. While he stuck closely enough to it, he never let it master him. "I have never ceased to follow it," he said, "or to vary it according to the subject." But his own mind was too complex, he was too great a man of genius, to believe that the mind can always be gauged by any measuring rod invented by man. He drew back before a too logical application of it. With all his allegiance to his idea, it represented to him simply the best plan for working that he could devise, and like all plans for working, he was aware that it had drawbacks even though he did not himself fully realize what they might lead to. As a matter of truth, his famous method applied to some writers could explain almost everything; applied to others, it explained but little. Applied to certain men of great genius like Shakespeare or Keats or Racine, even if there had existed enough information about them to supply all the answers to Sainte-Beuve's questions, it was likely to explain nothing except a few minor phenomena. Applied to others like Rousseau or Chateaubriand or Byron, concerning whom the known information is extensive and to whom dramatic events happened, it could explain and interpret so much that we can comprehend why Sainte-Beuve himself believed that it could explain nearly everything—a belief that he shares with every originator of a critical or psychological method.

As to his well-known dictum, *tel arbre, tel fruit,* there does not seem to have entered into his calculations the notion that the fruit is sometimes not like the tree, and that the book is sometimes different from the man who wrote it. An action is generally like the one who performs it: it comes out of the life he lives: but a book, a picture, a poem, a statue, a symphony, can be a dream, a journey into a land where the author has never set foot, an escape into emotions he has no outlet for in life. A writer often expends in a book quite other energies than those he uses in every-day life. In fact, his daily life and experiences may prevent him from tapping again the energy he has already used or exhausted once and for all. It is only in the case of a certain type of writer that it can be assumed that his life explains his work, or that his work reveals the sort of life he lived. In some cases, the creative life seems to have so little relation to the every-day life that the answer to the Sainte-Beuve questionnaire would be sure to fall short of any great revelation concerning the work. The great myth-makers like Shakespeare and Balzac, perhaps indeed most great artists of any kind, had an every-day personality and a creative personality, and as creators they could make worlds and people them with beings, human and otherwise, that they never encountered in life.

The truth about Sainte-Beuve's method, as about all methods and systems that aim at explaining men, their works and days, is that, employed with mere literalness and without the corrective of genius and disinterested intuition, it most successfully explains the second-rate: no method is completely adequate to the first-rate. Even when used by Sainte-Beuve himself, it worked out most interestingly and fruitfully in the case of those in whom the imponderables of genius and creative power were not too vast. However, when all is said and done, the fact remains that the process thoughtfully elaborated can explain something of every writer and nearly everything of some. There have been a few ingenious additions to the method, notably the one employed by a French biographer, Bazalgette, based on the notion of key words in phrases, where the subject was presented by the biographer in sentences and phrases abstracted from his own writing. But, on the whole, the additions have meant nothing worth while, though they have been borrowed by imitators of imitators of the master.

One of the curious influences exercised by the method was the conclusion by Sainte-Beuve's contemporaries, and those who came after him, that if a writer's life explains his work, then a writer might deliberately live the sort of life that might be supposed to be inspiring for his writing—cultivate the passions, the emotions, the senses; try all sorts of experiences, all sorts of intoxications and *paradis artificiels,* including those brought on by drugs. And so there came into existence the type of artist who abandoned himself to tasting life to the lees. Sainte-Beuve had explained the dryness and impersonality of Boileau's style and of his art *poétique* by the dryness of his life, and it seemed as if the new school, Baudelaire, De Musset, Verlaine, were determined at all costs not to have a dry life.

It was Sainte-Beuve's theories of poetry, and his own poetry, as much as his general criticism (relating the writer to his work), that deeply affected the new writers, and, in turn, their successors until our own day. He had two theories of poetry, which, like his theories of criticism, had far-flung effects. His own special theory, which he put into practice in his verse, was the one he developed from Wordsworth and from the famous Preface. He believed that he himself belonged to the same family of minds as the Lake School, and his ambition as a poet was to be the French Wordsworth, to be the poet of nature, of the hearth, of domestic things, of humble and ordinary life. His muse, he said, was no grand lady, no brilliant odalisque or young and vermillioned Peri, but a poor, coughing girl, living in a cabin, washing her clothes in a stream and keeping her old blind father whose reason was gone. The people who populated his poetry, his little stories in verse, were, he explained, not the grand and romantic heroes and heroines of Byron and Chateaubriand, with aristocratic lineages and splendid castles; they were the poor people of the *faubourgs,* the suburbs, and the countryside, who had no choice in their woes as did Childe Harold or Manfred or René; their woes were those that every-day life thrust upon them. He used his hospital experiences in these poems, and we have realistic accounts of the illnesses and miseries of the humble. Believing profoundly, himself, in the poetry of ordinary life, of the common man and woman, he gave currency to such poetry. The reign, he said, of the older poets is over; their work is incapable of satisfying the new needs of the imagination and of the heart; poetry must be about the lives of the men and women we meet. To Wordsworth's famous rustic as the subject of poetry, he added the small-town man and the suburban, crushed with work and illness. Some of his poetic work was regarded as morbid, and both in its morbidity and in its subjects, as well as in the every-day language employed, it was the antecedent of the work of Baudelaire and of La Forgue and of their imitators in all lands.

If this first theory of his was evolved or taken over from Wordsworth, the second came from Hugo, Byron, Chateaubriand, from all the Romantics, in fact. It was this, that poetry was the expression of the individuality of the poet, of his ego, of his personality, of his personal emotions and experiences—in short, the expression of the man himself. He could not find this personality, this necessary personal emotion, in Boileau, or in others of the French classical school, but he claimed to find it in the older French poets. He once went so far as to seek, for the new literature, an ancestry in the poets of the Pléiade, whose lyricism seemed to have something in common with the modern Romantics. This conclusion of his was meant to do something to take away from the imputation that all these new literary ideas were a foreign importation, taken over from Germany and England, and alien to the French spirit.

As a great writer, as a contributor of revolutionizing literary ideas, as an influence of wide significance covering more than a century, Sainte-Beuve is a personage of the greatest importance in modern literary history. He was the first literary critic who brought to criticism the most complex variety of literary gifts; he could and did excel in many kinds of writing, but a power of creating ideas and of analyzing minds and works urged him to turn all his gifts to criticism. His influence still goes on; to many he is the greatest purely literary critic that has ever appeared, and with this conclusion it is hard to disagree.

4

The critic who attempted to carry on Sainte-Beuve's ideas, who developed them in his own way and added his own distinct and remarkable contribution, was Hippolyte Taine. As an influence on all literary output since their time, the effect of the ideas of these two men is still extraordinary; no new ideas have sprung up strong enough to displace theirs or even to seem a development of them, though Sainte-Beuve is nearly seventy years dead and Taine nearly sixty. Sainte-Beuve's influence is still active in criticism, in poetry, in biography, and in the autobiographical novel; Taine's in the realistic novel, in history, and in social criticism. All except a minority of living writers pursue a path marked out for them by Sainte-Beuve and Taine. Though the literature of emotion and of rhapsodic imagination gives to the majority more eager and lasting delight, yet it is the literature of ideas which, in the modern world, has the profoundest effect on the originating of other forms of literature.

The forces of literature may be compared to an army composed of divisions, general staff, an advance guard, and right and left wings. It is the main duty of criticism to foresee which way the army ought to take so that it may proceed to the best advantage; it is its duty to know when it is time to make new roads and build new bridges. The objective of the forces is the achievement of the complete expression of man in language: very little of this objective has yet been achieved; the total experience of the most ordinary man, woman, or child has never yet been expressed in literature. We do not even know how it can be done, or if it can be done. If complete expression can be achieved, such expression will take men a long way on the hard road to complete consciousness. We make a little advance in expression from one century to another; our advance in literature has not been towards making a greater literature than the ancients achieved, but towards one that gives a more comprehensive expression to humanity. No modern literature, that is, no literature based on the ideas started by Lessing and developed by all these critics, can get on without that directing force, that idea-creating force, that he called criticism. The older literatures, literature at its dawn, when its business was to create a few powerful masterpieces broadly expressive of a few outstanding emotions, or symbolic of a few adventures, could do without it. A literature like the English in the past got on without much of this sort of leadership, or at least without the leadership organized. But a literature like the German could not have come into being without it, and there was hardly a period in French literature when it was not a powerful directing force.

Where Taine, who liked to think of himself as Sainte-Beuve's successor, differed in purely literary ideas from his predecessor, is, as the latter himself said, very hard to discover. But the intellectual structure of their minds was totally different: as Sainte-Beuve would say, they belonged to different families of minds: one was the poet-critic, the other the philosopher-critic. Taine's philosophy was a materialistic determinism which, as he worked it out in literature, had points in common with the manner in which Marx applied the dialectic of materialism to history. Literature, the mind of the author, the master-faculty, were determined by three forces: the race, milieu, and moment. He himself said that "every man and every book can be summed up in three pages, and these three pages can be summed up in three lines." His method can, in fact, be summarized, if not completely stated, in a line or two, in more or less the original formula from Hegel's *Aesthetics,* plus the chief details of the Sainte-Beuve method.

But if one supposes that all of Taine could be included in this, one would come to very wrong conclusions. The combination gave him a working base. After passing the Hegel formula and the Sainte-Beuve formula through his mind, he developed them in this way: a work of art is not isolated; it belongs to the total work of the artist who is its author, and is definitely related to and linked with his other works. The artist himself is not isolated; he belongs to an ensemble greater than himself, which is the school or family of artists of the same country, of the same period, to which he belongs.

Shakespeare, Taine notes, seemed a wonder fallen from the sky, a meteor from another world. Actually, he was one of a group of great dramatists, Webster, Ford, Massinger, Marlowe, Ben Jonson, Fletcher, who wrote in the same style and spirit; their plays had the same sort of characters. Likewise, in the domain of painting, Rubens seemed a unique personage, but he really was one of a group whose talents were similar to his—Van Dyck, Jordaens, Van Thulden, Van Roose, and others who painted in the same spirit, and who, with all their differences, still keep the air of belonging to the same family.

These great artists belonged, in turn, to a vaster ensemble, which was the world around them, the public. The state of mind, manners, and habits of the time are the same for the public as for the artists, but it is the artist's voice alone that we hear across the centuries. Below this clear, penetrating voice there is the low hum, the multiple voice of the people singing in unison around him. This is true of all periods and of all the arts. The men who made the Parthenon and the Olympian Jupiter were, like the other Athenians, educated in the Palaestra; like them they had wrestled, exercised, voted, and deliberated in the public square; they had the same habits, the same ideas, the same interests; they were men of the same race, the same education, the same language; they were like their public in all the important parts of their lives: therefore, to understand any work of art with exactitude we must picture to ourselves the general state of the manners, public spirit, and mind of the time to which it belongs. If we look at the principal epochs of history, we find that the arts appear, then disappear, at the same time as certain states of mind and manners to which they are attached. The greatest artists are men who possess in the highest degree the faculties, the sentiments, and the passions that the public surrounding them possesses in some degree. The products of the mind, like those of nature, can be explained only by their environment. As there is a physical temperature which determines the appearance of such and such a species of plant, so there is a spiritual or psychic temperature which, by its variations, determines the appearance of such or such a species of art.

All these points of his method Taine maintained as laws, and he worked out their application with a perfection of logic which makes them convincing, to the reason at least. It was the business of a critic, he said, to concern himself with the laws, not to impose precepts on the artist. Anyhow, he explained, there are only two precepts: the first is, to be born with genius; the second is, to work hard so as to be a master of one's art.

As to the famous scientific system with which he applied his method, it can all be discovered in his *De l'Intelligence,* that first important contribution to modern psychology, which Pierre Janet has described as his *livre de chevet*. There could be no real criticism, no real history, no real study of anything relating to the mind of man without scientific psychology. "The basis of history," he said, "ought to be scientific psychology. What historians do with the past, great novelists and dramatists do with the present." But on what was this scientific psychology to be based? In the preface to the book, Taine announced that "the matter of all knowledge was little facts, well chosen, important, significant, amply circumstantiated, and minutely noted." The great thing to know was how these little facts could be combined and the effects of the combination. For instance, he conceived of personality as made up of little facts which formed the phenomena of consciousness, and nature as formed of little facts which made up the phenomena of motion. Even poetry he described as the art of transforming general ideas into *petits faits sensibles*.

Of his own critical procedure he stated: "The modern method, which I try to follow, consists in considering the works of man as facts and products of which it is necessary to mark the character and seek the causes." And as for the man responsible for the works, "One can consider man as an animal of superior species who produces philosophies and poems somewhat as the silkworm makes cocoons and the bee cells." But this animal, man, has been described by Comte—who, after Hegel and Sainte-Beuve, was the great influence on Taine's mind—as "a continuation of nature, a being like the other guests of the universe called animals." Taine, continuing this conception and applying the formula taken from Hegel, declared that this animal, man, was subject to conditions of race, climate and milieu. "Discover, therefore, the conditions of race, climate and milieu, education, customs, in which he lived, and you can deduce with a certainty the nature of his talent and of his work, and the diverse conditions that establish the master-faculty, both the causes and the consequences at the same time. Art, therefore, is a product which can be explained like any other product, if we have the data to go on, all the little facts. In fact, vice and virtue are products like sugar and vitriol."

Of the little facts that make up personality, there is a system of inner impressions and operations that form an artist, a musician, a religious man. Each has his own special structure; in each the connection of ideas and emotions is different. But the structure of all of them has some dominating trait, some essential characteristic, as would be shown in natural history. This essential, in natural history, carries with it all the others, and its presence determines or regulates the constitution of the entire animal. In man, this force, the great motive power to which all others are subordinate, he called the master-faculty. This central force, this determining force, is also, on its part, conditioned by the race—by the

characteristics transmitted by the blood; by the milieu—
that is, by the ensemble of circumstances and influences
to which the individual is subjected; by the moment—
that is, by the drive of the past on the present. If you
uncover the master-faculty in a man, then you have
uncovered the man himself, and you can define his
mind through its most fundamental trait.

The master-faculty, the dominant trait, Taine sought
for, not only in individuals, but in whole epochs of
civilization. "In periods and centuries likewise," he said,
"there is a dominant trait which determines each of the
parts. For in each period, first of all, there is a surface
characteristic, surface manners which last two or three
years; the variations of fashion or dress reveal this sort
of spirit; below that lies a layer of more solid characteristics, lasting twenty, thirty or forty years, half an epoch
in history; below that again, is another layer of characteristics, lasting the entire epoch, which remains itself
through all the changes and renewals of the people—
this is the dominant characteristic."

The dominant characteristic, and the influence of the
race, milieu and moment in an individual, he worked
out in detail, and what he would call scientifically, in
the case of La Fontaine the fabulist. As a naturalist,
working on a natural history of minds, he proceeds to
examine La Fontaine. As bees make cells, he had said,
man makes philosophies and poems. Imagine, therefore,
that in the presence of the fables of La Fontaine you are

before one of these hives. We shall want to know how, given a garden and bees, a hive is produced. What are the intervening operations? and what general forces act on each step of the operation? Given France and La Fontaine, what were the general forces that determined the nature of the *Fables*? Behind the fact of the *Fables* there is the fact of the man who produced them; he was a Frenchman of Gallic race, a Gaulois speaking to other Gaulois, with the innate and hereditary dispositions common to all of them. He had, in fact, these dispositions to an exaggerated degree—that is, he was not very strict as to morals; his dignity was only passable; he was exempt from the grand passions and inclined to pleasure; he was middle-class, well-connected, living the gay life of a provincial bourgeois before the Revolution; he gambled; he loved wine and the pleasures of the table; he read books and made verses; he never took marriage seriously, neither his own nor that of his friends; he had affairs with women of all kinds and degrees; his feeling for them was neither passionate nor gross; he was inclined neither to strong emotions nor to brute enjoyments; he simply wanted happiness and pleasure—a good time generally, and so he avoided the disagreeable and the irksome as much as possible. This is the hereditary Gaulois. Then he was a poet; he had in a high degree the two great traits of a poet, "the faculty of forgetting the real world and that of living in an ideal world, the gift of not seeing matter-of-fact things and that of following the life of his dreams." . . . "He gave to himself the harmony that his verses bring to us. . . . His mind moved among a multitude of sentiments, fine and gay and tender; he traversed the range of human sentiments, occasionally among the most elevated, generally among the gentlest." "I think," Taine writes, "that of all Frenchmen, it is he who has been most truly a poet." So much for the man and the racial background; now for the milieu. He was born in Champagne, in that area of France which is most thoroughly French, which has conquered and molded all the others. Everything there is temperate; the climate is neither warm nor cold; there are neither excesses nor contrasts; the mountains are ranges of hills and the woods clumps of thickets; everything is on a small scale, with a tendency towards delicacy and refinement rather than strength—narrow rivers wind between clumps of alder trees; a row of lonely poplars in a grayish field; a fragile birch tree trembling in a glade of firs; a flash of a stream through hampering duckweed; the delicate colors of distant woods—this was the scenery that formed La Fontaine; this was the soil and the climate that fashioned him and the race he came from; this was the scenery that appeared in the *Fables,* for he had taken the imprint of this soil and sky. Now, for the moment. It was the period of the Grand Monarch, Louis the Fourteenth, when France was the greatest country in Europe, with the most magnificent court life and a galaxy of the greatest writers, which included La Fontaine's fellow Champagnois, the great Racine. The animals of the *Fables* were the people of the Court, as Racine's Greeks and Romans were so often the ladies and gentlemen of the Court; the characteristic types of the period also appeared in the skins of animals. In addition to the courtiers and the noblesse, there appeared the monk, the bourgeois, the provincial squire, the merchant, the peasant—every one was there; the *Fables* had the profusion of an Iliad; "they form our epic," Taine declares, "our only epic." The King was the Lion; the chief courtier, the Fox, the hypocrite of the Court, as the Cat was the hypocrite of religion; elephants, bears and the larger clumsy beasts symbolized the country squires and squireens; the Master Rat was the Burgomaster; the Ant was the small bourgeois, and so on; there was a whole gallery of characters, a whole array of events and emotions.

5

As Sainte-Beuve's study of Chateaubriand is the clearest and most characteristic example of his method applied to an individual, so Taine's *La Fontaine* is the perfect example of his. Both these critics chose from their native literature the writers who suited their investigations in every detail. The answers to Sainte-Beuve's questions explain Chateaubriand; Taine's investigations worked out with most excellent results in the case of La

Fontaine, whose life and work exemplified his formula and could illustrate his dictum: "Recover the conditions of the country, climate, race, milieu, education, habits in which a man has lived, and you will deduce unquestionably the nature of his talent and his work, and from the diverse conditions of his life you will establish the master-faculty with its causes and consequences."

Although, in *La Fontaine,* Taine worked out the master-faculty as a part of the study, he made it his main study in his work on Livy, the Roman historian. As was usual with Taine, in his preface he stated the problem he proposed to answer: Can a man of genius or of outstanding ability be described in a formula? Are the faculties of a man like the organs of a plant, interdependent on one another? Are they all governed by a single law? Is there in us a master-faculty whose uniform action is communicated differently to our different mechanisms and which impresses on our machine a necessary system of predetermined movements? He replies by an example, and the example worked out by him is the historian Livy.

"The difficulty for me in an investigation," Taine said, "is to find some characteristic and dominant trait from which everything may be deduced geometrically; in a word, to discover the formula of the thing. It seems to me that the formula for Livy is as follows: an orator who becomes an historian." This, then, was Livy's master-faculty, the gift of oratory, and from this spring both the merits and the faults of his work as an historian; it accounts for the beauty and the eloquence of his style; it accounts for his indifference to material that might have been available from the study of the remains of early Rome. But Livy was not interested in perusing ancient treaties or bronze tablets, or the moldy writings in old temples. Within the limits of his temperament he was accurate, and had authorities for every statement he made, but the dominant traits of his mind make him chiefly interested in such facts as were material for eloquent utterances. Anything that would have the effect of making his style dry he avoided; what he liked to write about were battles, decrees of the Senate, quarrels in the Forum. Dramatic action was what interested him; he was more interested in the story of Virginia than in new legislation; he did not care, in his search for facts, to wade through the enormous pile of superstitious puerilities that made the earliest records of Rome; he did not dig into family archives or check up sham genealogies. With the orator's concern for moving us and convincing us, he treats facts as mediums for oratory; he was always representing the characters in his history as making speeches, delivering harangues, exhorting armies. When he faced the facts of history he tried to bring back to life the long-dead passions and emotions that had animated them.

Taine shows us, in fact, a Livy who is one of the fathers of romanticized and dramatized history. In this study of Livy, the most often repeated words are his favorite "facts" and "laws"—the word "fact" sometimes occurring five times on a page. Facts are the material of all knowledge, and when you have enough facts, he seems to be always telling us, you can make a law; even from a single general fact you can deduce a law, as Newton deduced the law of gravity from the falling apple.

In these two early books we have the basic points of Taine's method in its application to individuals; we have also the first emphasizing of other ideas in his system: the primacy of the fact and the document, and the importance of the master-faculty. In his *La Fontaine and His Fables,* Taine had said, in effect, "Here is the work; let us re-create the conditions of race, climate, country, milieu, in which La Fontaine lived, and see how his work is conditioned by them." In his *Livy,* as we have seen, he posed and answered the question, Can a man of genius be circumscribed in a formula? Is there such a thing as a master-faculty that imposes itself on all the others? His formula for Livy was: an orator becomes an historian; Livy's master-faculty, therefore, was oratory; this was the dominating trait in his *History,* and he sought naturally such facts as were the best material for this to work on. So much for the application of Taine's method to individuals.

6

But as you can construct the spiritual and psychological history of an individual writer from his work, so you can construct the spiritual and psychological history of a people from its literary production. And as Sainte-Beuve applied his method to a whole group, the Port-Royal group, Taine proceeded to apply his, in its entirety, to the whole literature of a people. But for his experiment he had, first of all, to find a great and complete literature which had kept its life and vitality through the vicissitudes of its people's history. Of this type of literature, he believed there were only three great and complete examples: the English, the French, and the Greek, and of these three, Greek literature and civilization were over. Of the living literatures, he did not feel that the Italian and Spanish were complete, because, as he believed, they had ended in the seventeenth century. He did not accept the German as complete, because of the gaps in its production and because, in fact, as a great literature it was only beginning. But the English had been continuous; its difference from French literature made a special appeal to a Frenchman; being living, it was subject to direct examination and could be studied more easily than a dead literature or a dead civilization. Taine, therefore, set out to deduce from their literary production the moral and psychological history of the English people.

For the purpose of this study he thought that a people's literature supplied more fruitful facts and documents than its legal or religious codes; for politics are made alive in speeches, and religion in sermons, and both speeches and sermons belong to literature. He set out to arrange the literary product in periods, to study the climate and the soil; to show how the race was formed, to show the effect of the Norman conquest, on which he laid great stress. He traced the development of the language; he studied the dominating characteristic of each period, the dominating characteristic of the outstanding writers, their psychological mainsprings, their connection with the surrounding society and with their epoch. The result was a psychological and sociological study of English literature that cast a powerful light on English civilization.

If he did not explicitly say that the *raison d'être* of literature was an expression of society, his attitude was that it so largely had that result that he was justified in studying it to discover the dominant traits of the civilization, the psychological history of the people and their social trends. In his study of epochs he was extraordinarily illuminating, but when he found himself confronted with great single figures like Shakespeare, Swift, or Wordsworth, his refusal to see literature as anything but predetermined by forces, his refusal to face the fact or the mystery of individual genius, led him to some strange conclusions. Like Madame de

Staël, he comprehended best such literature as was really an expression of society. He incorporated in his critical system all the discoveries of his predecessors, not only de Staël's theory of literature as an expression of society, but Lessing's theory of it as an expression of national genius; he likewise included Herder's theories of history, applying them to literary history, and he took over Sainte-Beuve's procedure of seeking the man behind the work.

On the other side, he was blind to the genius of Wordsworth and Coleridge in creating ideas that gave a new direction to literature. Coleridge he barely mentions, and that in passing; Wordsworth he considered inferior to Cowper, and was frankly bored by his poetry; he did not see, as Sainte-Beuve saw, that imbedded in it lay the beginnings of a new trend in literary expression, the expression of a new trend in civilization even, a new trend in human history. What he saw in Wordsworth was a philosophical moralist; he saw but little of the poet and nothing of the critic whose ideas had such a transforming effect on poetry. Wordsworth's molds, he said, are of bad, common clay, cracked, unable to hold the noble metal that they ought to contain. Like those admirers of Wordsworth about whom Matthew Arnold complains, he was looking for a philosophy instead of for poetry, and for moralizings instead of æsthetic ideals.

Equally strange were his conclusions about Swift,

whom he considered an example *par excellence* of the positive mind, and whom he represents as "inspired and consumed by the excess of his English qualities," with the intensity of desire "which is the main feature of the race." He also describes him as showing "pre-eminently the character and mind of his nation." In reality, Swift was an Anglo-Irishman, possessed of the Anglo-Irish mentality in one of its most typical manifestations, endowed with wit, satire, combativeness, strong emotion, social indignation and political insight; Swift was intensely affected by the country in which he was born and by the unsettlement of his milieu; also, his peculiar kind of literary talent has not been uncommon in Irish literature. But Taine regarded him as an example of the positive mind, the mind which, he says, wishes to attain, not to eternal beauty, but to present success. Swift does not address men in general, but certain men; he does not speak to reasoners, but to a party; he does not care to teach a truth, but to make an impression; his aim is not to enlighten the mind, but to stir feelings and prejudices. As is usual with Taine, his whole study of Swift, wrong-headed as it is, in detail, is full of the wisest and profoundest critical generalizations, and contains all of the arguments as to why special pleading and propaganda in themselves cannot be literature. It is only that his arguments, applied to Swift, do not even present a half-truth.

His study of Shakespeare has sometimes been described as the least successful in his *History*, but, as a matter of truth, in its general effect and largely even in its detailed criticism of the characters and the plays, it is, in spite of some strange conclusions, one of the most illuminating studies of Shakespeare and of the English mind of the period that has ever been written. Taine brings his force and passion, all his critical imagination, all he had learned of life and psychology, to bear on Shakespeare. His psychologizings make credible and human the author of the plays and the sonnets, and that by presenting him as a man of extreme humanness, ardent in thought, bewildered in love, mighty in feeling, equally overcome by man's greatness, his piteousness and his twisted nature. The other artists of the age had the same kind of mind, the same idea of life, but in Shakespeare it was stronger and in more prominent relief.

Great works of art, Taine tells us, can be interpreted only by the most advanced psychological systems; Shakespeare himself can be comprehended only by the aid of science, and so, by his own psychological system and his own science, he tries to interpret him. What was the master-faculty in Shakespeare's case? Taine finally decides that it is an impassioned imagination freed from the shackles of reason and morality, though we can observe him wavering around the idea of describing it as love and passion. In going through the plays and observing the ease and subtlety with which

Shakespeare can depict not only the highest grade of the creative imagination and the reasoning mind but also all the grades of the unreasoning mind and the disordered imagination, in observing his power in depicting *idées fixes,* hallucinations, the caprices of the mind, Taine imagines Shakespeare writing a treatise on psychology and he concludes that if Shakespeare had framed a psychological system he would have said with the French psychiatrist, Esquirol: Man is a nervous machine governed by mood, disposed to hallucinations, carried away by unbridled passions, essentially unreasoning, a mixture of animal and poet, having, instead of mind, rapture, instead of virtue, sensibility, with imagination for prompter and guide, led at random by the most determinate and complex circumstances to sorrow, crime, madness and death.

7

Taine's own major interest, like Sainte-Beuve's, was psychology, and he piled up all the facts that he could collect, about the mind of man and its development from the cradle to the grave, including all that was available in his time from doctors and students of insanity.

His *De l'Intelligence* is really the first modern treatise on psychology, the first account of the structure of the mind based on experiment and observation, on facts that could be examined and related. It is, therefore, a work in experimental psychology; in some ways it is the most important of all his works: he himself considered that it contained the roots of his ideas, for he had reflected over it for twenty years. Taine worked on all the facts made available through the discoveries of physicians and physiologists, by studies of *idées fixes,* illusions, psychic hallucinations, troubles of memory. He studied the developing speech of children, dreams and the phantasies of opium-eaters, and the talk of people affected by mental maladies. As for psychological research, consciousness, our principal instrument, he showed is no longer of any more value than the naked eye is in optics; the range of consciousness is not great; its illusions are numerous; the greater part of ourselves remains beyond our grasp. The visible personality (*Le moi*) is incomparably smaller than the hidden personality. William James, ten years later, put this observation in a striking image when he compared personality to the iceberg, the unconscious being the greater part which is submerged and out of sight.

Amongst Taine's studies, too, were the question of the existence of more than one personality in the same individual, automatic writing, spiritism. All special states of intelligence, he considered, should be the subject of monographs; every painter, poet, novelist, of exceptional lucidity, ought to be interrogated and observed by a psychologist-friend; one should learn from the artist the way in which figures form themselves in his mind; his manner of mentally visualizing imaginary objects and the order in which they come before him, whether by involuntary fits and starts or in regular procedure. He thought, for example, that if Poe, Balzac, Hugo, and other men of genius, had been questioned and had left memoranda, we should have had information of the greatest value. The observations extant about persons suffering from mental maladies, the limited amount of transcripts or stenographic accounts of their conversation that were available, he made use of. He considered that the reach of consciousness was so limited that it needed the extension of whatever microscope or telescope a study of the abnormal could provide. He regarded himself as doing in psychology only some pioneer work. But it would surprise a good many readers to find that a psychological method which they consider especially to be the fruit of the twentieth century belongs in reality to the middle nineteenth.

Chapter Six

THE COMING OF THE REALISTS

I

THESE, THEN, were the different literary ideas and doctrines that provided the philosophy and the working inspiration for modern literature, that is, for the literature that began when Lessing proceeded to break down the old æsthetic. For modern literature really had its beginning when Lessing perceived that the boundaries of literature would have to be extended far beyond what the Greeks and the Middle Ages thought was beautiful and what the seventeenth and eighteenth centuries regarded as good taste in literary accomplishment. The whole of nature and humanity, of which the beautiful was only a part, had to be expressed.

That the ordinary man had to be given in literature was a well-organized idea before the rights of the ordinary man in politics came to be recognized. Undoubtedly the men who played a rôle as the precursors of the political idea—Rousseau, Diderot—influenced Lessing, but there is no reason to suppose that he would not have propounded the idea without them. For a new world was coming in, and of this new world the idea-makers were the movers and shakers; some of the old dreams that had kept civilization together were dying; the art, the literature, the social ideas that had dominated the world were changing. The old dreams, in fact, were dying too quickly, long before sufficient new ones to take their place had been envisioned. Still, in the beginning of the change, anyway, and even up to the death of Taine, the last great idea-maker in literature, it seemed as if it were bliss "within that dawn to be alive, and to be young were very heaven." The new epoch had need of a new literature and there were plenty of writers to make it: there were Goethe and Schiller; Wordsworth and Coleridge; Keats and Shelley; Byron and Chateaubriand and Pushkin; Scott and Balzac; there was a great chorus of voices in every country. The new literature represented a conquest, though the extent of the conquest, as happens in a new age, was exaggerated. But walls were down, and there were fewer and fewer barriers against experience; ideas and emotions could take flight in expression, no longer bound down by the rule-makers. The notion, too, was abroad that the life that was a great adventure was at hand. When Taine came and gathered all the ideas into one receptacle there seemed to be no limit to the adventures that the mind might seek. He brought the conviction that there were to be no more mysteries, that science and a proper study of facts would explain all things.

THE COMING OF THE REALISTS

It must not be taken for granted, however, that the old notion of the beautiful, that *only* the beautiful should be expressed in art and literature, was finished. What happened was that the new ideas caused a re-arrangement of values. The very fact that the whole new movement to extend expression had been called the Romantic Movement showed the persistence of the older æsthetic ideals. What was actually the "beautiful" side of the movement, its romantic side in its earlier manifestations, was what gave it its name. But the lasting core of the change, the inner dominating idea, was that which stood for the expression of everything in life, everything that touched men, whether this was beautiful or ugly, beneficent or evil, whether it repre-sented noble human passions or base ones, sordid hu-man experiences or grand ones.

In the first flush of the movement, with its devotion to the blue rose, to grand, wrecking passions, and with a lyric production the greatest the world has ever wit-nessed, what was really new was more or less covered, only groping its way; it was hidden for long by the label. Yet romanticism had always been in literature, and the lyric was the oldest form of literary expression; both romanticism and lyricism had been in Greek literature and in Roman literature; the greatest of all English poets and dramatists had been romantic through and through, as was indeed all but a minor part of English literature. But romanticism and lyricism did not express the bulk of humanity, and to express the bulk of humanity was really what these reformers started out to do: romanticism was only one side of the shield or one stage of the progress or one part of the whole objective. The real goal of the movement—the expression of every man and every side of him—made headway only in proportion as the technique for accomplishing this was discovered. Even Wordsworth himself, who had written the poetic manifesto and who had made a determined attempt to express the common man in an art alien to him—the art of poetry—and in a language considered alien to that art, the language of every-day speech, was himself more deeply enmeshed in the romantic side of the movement than in the every-day-life side of it. His was the mind, it will be remembered, that, in addition to constructing the poetic manifesto for the revolutionary age, had also discovered that "it was bliss within that dawn to be alive." Imaginations, emotions and longings took a great leap, regardless of where they landed, and they generally landed at a long distance from ordinary life.

In England, the lyrical and romantic side was carried to its highest point by a group of younger contemporaries of Coleridge and Wordsworth, Byron, Shelley, Keats, all of whom represented the new passion for freedom and the hatred of injustice, and manifested it in different ways. Both Byron and Shelley showed that passion which might be said to be common to international romanticism, the desire to construct the interior life on the idea of freedom of emotion. Byron in England, Chateaubriand in France, evolved the type of the proud, free, unhappy, heroic aristocrat, half sincere, half poseur, devoted to lost causes, chivalrous and un-self-seeking, "present on the day of danger, absent on the day of rewards"—a type which captivated the imagination down to the Great War and was a model for imitation in life and in fiction. Byron made literature out of his sins and misfortunes, was a believer in freedom, and at the same time was convinced that grand, free, generous emotions, courage and magnanimity were the birthright of the aristocracy alone, as indeed was Chateaubriand. At heart, Byron believed Wordsworth to be a prosy rustic and, like Matthew Arnold, he regarded Keats as a druggist's apprentice, great poet though he might be. Byron was one of the representatives of international romanticism, as was Goethe in his *Werther* and in his *Faust,* as was Chateaubriand in his *René,* as was Victor Hugo in his dramas and lyrics. With his dashing, aristocratic vulgarity, in his poetry and in his dramas, he represented something that was really new in English literature. Great lyricists, like Shelley and Keats, had been in English before. The lyric was peculiarly suited to the English mind and there were not wanting those who insisted that the lyricists of the new age be described as a continuation of the Elizabethans. Byron, with his *Manfred,* his *Cain,* however, was different. There was something in him that the new Europe understood. His energy, his sense of adventure, his realism, his scorn were all more comprehensible to the ordinary man than the shuddering lyricism of Shelley, than the winged idealism of "Laon and Cythna" and "Epipsychidion," or the emotion, at once passionate and luminous, of Keats. There were no winging skylark song, no charmed magic casements or foam of perilous seas, or faerylands forlorn, in Byron. But his loves and his lusts, his scorn, his aristocratic dash, the activity of his life, his chivalrous defense of the Greeks, all made him easy to understand. Shelley and Keats did not live long enough to make themselves understood in their own lifetime, though they were, as a matter of fact, more in the ancient tradition of English poetry than was Byron. Their ancestry went far back, whereas whatever of Byron did not belong to the spirit of his age went no farther back than the eighteenth century.

Byron and Goethe in poetry, Scott in the novel, were, in the movement's early days, the most familiarly known figures in Europe. As we look back on the modern mind in literature, the first really great and universal one was Goethe's: in his work were focussed all the trends that went with the new order—lyricism, nationalism, mysticism, symbolism, criticism, scientific investigation; he worked in every literary form—lyric, drama, novel, autobiography, criticism, not to speak of his scientific essays; he wrote subjectively, romantically, at one part of his career, and objectively, classically, at another. His mind was one of those comprehensive ones that are really above the tendencies of the time, though they include them. The biases of any movement are generally best observed in its men of secondary genius, the first being above all tendencies and influences. Goethe, infected as he was by Lessing's ideas, yet made very little attempt to translate the every-day man into writing; he essayed to write novels that are, however, treasure-houses of poetic imagination rather than revelations of the common mind. But the time spirit was moving steadily towards bringing this mind into literature, and it became evident that with the development of the novel this was going to become easier to achieve.

2

Novels of any kind, it has been said, were, before Balzac, happy accidents, but when he came, he worked out a conscious scheme both for subject matter and technique; the novel was to be a study of society, a sort of testament, of historic and documentary value. The historic and documentary value had, before him, to some extent, been achieved by Scott, to whom it had brought European homage. In our day it is perhaps difficult to understand the vast admiration given to Scott in his own time, but the fact is that he was one of those writers, representative of a new age, who seem extremely important to their contemporaries. Goethe even was sufficiently dazzled by the contemporary spirit to say of him "a great mind unequalled anywhere." And to Balzac he was the standard-bearer in the art of the novel, who elevated it, as he said, to the philosophical value of history, who united in one form narrative, drama, dialogue, portrait, landscape, description; who brought in, side by side, the epic elements of the marvellous and of the real. To people whose literary diet had been classical tragedy and high-flown romances, the novels of Scott seemed to portray recognizable life with some relation to the lives of men. Nevertheless, the man who really tried to bridge the pass between romance and realism, between the romantic and the every-day, between the dream and the reality, was Balzac himself.

Greatly influenced by Scott, Balzac, who had begun with sensational romances, worked out in detail a project for putting life, as common experience, into literature, under the general title of the *Comédie Humaine, The Human Comedy,* as against *The Divine Comedy* of Dante, the common life as against the life of vision. He determined to make himself the historian of French society as he saw it. As he himself said, French society would be the historian, he would be only the secretary, and he would thus achieve the history overlooked by so many historians—that of manners. Having made up his mind as to what he wanted to do, he worked out a plan and an æsthetic that represented a halfway house between the ideas of the first romantics and of the later realists. In his theoretic outlook on society, akin to that of Taine, on whose mind he exercised a marked influence, Balzac decided that men and women should be studied for literary purposes as a naturalist studies animals or plants; in fact, he declared, there is only one animal; the Creator used one and the same pattern for all creatures, and all the differences in animals come from the milieux to which they have to adapt themselves. With a mixture of that simple and astounded admiration for the new science of zoölogy, and for the work of Buffon and other naturalists, which affected so many French writers of the time, and with a combination of naïveté and powerful critical intuition, Balzac set about explaining what he wanted to do and rationalizing what he had already done.

There were different species of men, Balzac announced, as there were different species of animals, and he proposed to write a work which should do for society what Buffon had done for zoölogy—exhibit the different types of men that make up society, as Buffon had exhibited the animals. Thus, for the first time, what was known as "Naturalism" came in as a literary ideal. The *Comédie Humaine,* he said, would deal with men, women and things—that is to say, with persons and with the whole environment they created for themselves. What might be called the pre-romantic ideas of the movement, such as de Staël's notion of literature as an expression of society, and Lessing's that a beauty of art was not the same as a beauty of nature, made a strong appeal to Balzac. Examining society, he estimated that there were at any period about four or five thousand people who represented the whole of it, and these four or five thousand he proposed, in his capacity as secretary of society, to get into his work. While he put forward many theories that later became part of the canon of realism, he himself should not be described as a realist, for he created a world of his own rather than made a description of the one around him. To the critics who accused him of not being true to life according to the new literary notions that were just coming in, or of not representing life as it is, he replied that real life is either too dramatic or dramatic in ways that would not seem probable in literature; the novelist should go beyond nature, improve on its crudities, transfigure his characters and make of them types.

Balzac really had no interest in painting directly from life or in depicting every-day people; in fact, when he was taken to task for not doing so, he protested that to write about ordinary people whose life was without drama would make his work unreadable. He tells how he kept his sketch of the character of César Birotteau for six years, despairing of ever being able to make an interesting figure out of a mediocre little shopkeeper with his common misfortunes, his stupidity, until it suddenly dawned on him that he could transfigure him by making him the image of probity, that is, by elevating him to a type. Like Taine, he believed in the master-faculty, or rather in a master-passion, or a master-quality, and his chief personages are all moved by a dominating passion, so that they become typical and representative of that passion, as characters in the older classical literature were typical and representative. His Père Grandet as a miser is as typical as Molièrc's Harpagon; the daughters of Père Goriot are the types of filial ingratitude; Cousine Bette the type of jealousy. In his pursuit of this master-quality he was led into exaggerating personages and milieux to the extent of making them marvellous and sometimes even fabulous. In actual life he said one would have to study several characters to create a single one in fiction; the writer had to proceed like a painter, take the hands of one model, the feet of another, the bust of a third. For instance, in creating the characters of Père Goriot and his daughters, each fact or incident taken separately was from life, though some of the actual happenings in the lives of the living models he considered too frightful and too improbable for a novel. The writer, he agreed, might or should take his facts from life, but he would have to reassemble them to suit the pattern he had in mind. For example, he might have to take the beginning of one incident, the middle of another, and the end of a third, to create a single incident in literature.

Balzac's art, as has often been said, especially by realists, was a sort of gigantization of life. What he actually did was to create a world of his own out of patterns he had picked out in the world of reality. No writer studied the mainsprings of human motives or actions as carefully as he did, and few writers in the whole course of literature had such powers of observation, such intuition as to what was happening in people's minds. His power of insight became so acutely developed that he could pierce through the exterior into the interior life of others, identifying himself with them. He tells us in memorable words how, dressed like one of themselves, he would mingle with workingmen in the streets and watch them concluding their bargains or quarreling as they left their work. Again, he tells us how he would follow a workingman and his wife as they came home from a theatre, listen to their conversation as they talked of the play, of the way they spent their money, of the price of potatoes, of the dreariness of winter, of their debts to shopkeepers, becoming angry in sympathy with them as they talked of a domineering boss. Listening to them he was able to merge his personality with theirs, and he himself considered that he had a power in all this that was strange and unique. The people he created out of this sort of observation he confused with the world of reality; he had difficulty in getting outside the world he himself made. As Sainte-Beuve said, he had created them so powerfully that, once he got them going, he and they could never part again.

Balzac's ideal of himself as the secretary of society, in the *Comédie Humaine,* gave him principles outside his purely literary ones: a writer who was something more than a mere entertainer ought to have fixed opinions in morals and politics and to be able to make a decision on human affairs; he ought to be able not only to depict life but to come to conclusions about it. He himself based his opinions and conclusions on his convictions as a Catholic in religion and as a monarchist in politics. "I write," he said, "under the ægis of two eternal truths, religion and monarchy." As a historian of manners he considered that a writer should be, not only a delineator of human types, a recorder of dramas of intimate life, but that he ought to include in his work such descriptions of professions and occupations, of towns, streets, houses, furniture, as would be a record, for the future, of the state of civilization in the epoch he was describing; in short, he considered that the novelist should get down all the accessories of existence, of whatever period he was dealing with, which might seem of importance to future readers. In addition to all this, he thought the writer should try to bring to light the reasons behind events, the motive powers behind society. Outside its task of painting society, he believed that literature should attempt to make a better world; that a writer ought to make moral comment, to accompany his revelation of the passions with instructive lessons, and point a moral by the juxtaposition of good and evil.

A realistic novelist making his work a representation of life, Balzac was not—in spite of all his passages about copying life and studying men and women as a naturalist studies animals. Every emotion, every action, every personage in the *Comédie Humaine* is, to be sure, drawn from a careful observation of the motive powers behind life and a superhuman insight into them, but Balzac enlarged everything in his work to the scale of the gigantic or the eccentric or the demoniacal. "No delineation of character or of surroundings," says Croce, "but he exaggerates to the extent of making it altogether marvellous and fantastic. . . . He gives an extraordinary aspect to what is ordinary." And Baudelaire wrote of him, "all his characters are endowed with the same vital ardor that he himself had . . . all are more eager for life, more active and wily in combat, more voracious of joy, more angelic in devotion, than the human comedy of the real world shows us."

3

But the very year before the death of Balzac, the year 1849, another step was taken towards getting the human being, as he actually existed in the real world, into literature, and it was taken by Flaubert. How strikingly literary opinion had advanced to the next step on that road is evident from the account of what led Flaubert to the writing of *Madame Bovary*. He had finished a first version of *The Temptation of St. Anthony,* on which he had spent three years, and had invited some literary associates to a reading of it. Its lyricism and romanticism belonged to an age that was passing, and to the up-to-date young men who listened to the reading, the *Temptation* seemed so old-fashioned that they thoroughly discouraged him from continuing in that vein. "Give it up," they said. "Starve out your lyricism! Take a feet-on-the-ground subject like those of Balzac, like his Cousine Bette!" This verdict was a blow to Flaubert, but it meant a turning point in his work, and when, the next day, one of his auditors suggested as a subject the story of a country doctor who had been an interne under Flaubert's father in the hospital of Rouen, whose wife after love affairs had poisoned herself, the author accepted the suggestion. The novel, thus projected, it was decided, should follow real life in its smallest details. Following a habit of his mind, Flaubert allowed the characters, the plot and the theme to develop slowly in his imagination, and the novel itself was not begun until about two years later. The writing of it took some four and a half years, during which he lived in tranquil isolation in the small town of Croisset, near Rouen, because, as he said, a complete immobility of existence was necessary for him before he could write.

Finally, in the year 1857, was published the first realistic novel, *Madame Bovary*. Balzac had given a foretaste of what it might be, so, in a measure, had Stendhal, so had Mérimée; it was left to Flaubert to accomplish it. In fact this year, 1857, saw the publication of two books of the kind that had been dreamed of since Lessing's criticism had first burst on Europe. One was Flaubert's *Madame Bovary;* the other was a book of verse, Baudelaire's *Les Fleurs du Mal*. Realism in both prose and verse, the Comédie Humaine of the actual world, long envisaged, long struggled towards, was in literature at last. Here the older symbolism was exchanged for shapes and symbols from every-day life; here, instead of the older dramatic effect, was real life in a series of pictures.

The two books were startling in every way—in outlook on life, in subject matter, in technique, in style, in language. In each, personages were presented with reality of a kind hitherto unknown in literature—their characters, their souls were revealed with complexity and subtlety; the language of both the prose writer and the poet had a sharp intensity; both showed a like concern for the absolutely correct word; with each of them the inspiration, or genius, or talent was intense and penetrating, rather than large or exuberant. The novelist was far from the loose abundance of Balzac or Walter Scott; the poet far from that of Hugo or Wordsworth or Byron. To their readers they offered the essence of their minds. The result was a grave and careful art, the fruit of labor and deliberation, and of an integral observation—an observation that represented the very height of emotional and intellectual communication with the life they were drawn to express. What they put into writing was experience, winnowed until the necessary kernel was shaken free. The poetry was as realistic, as ironic, as the novel, but with the deeper subtlety and concentration of verse. What Sainte-Beuve said of one of them is equally true of both, "a severe and pitiless verity has entered into art as the last word in experience."

The story of *Madame Bovary* is familiar to practically all seasoned novel readers, as it is to all accomplished novel writers. We are led through the life experiences of the two major characters, Charles and Emma Bovary, from their childhood until their deaths, and are brought into intense contact with a number of people who abut on the lives of these two. While Flaubert took the outlines of the plot and of the chief characters from actual happenings and personages in his own neighborhood, these really represented only the framework, and he kept making careful notes, suggested by many sources, for the events, the emotions, the characters he was going to reveal. Here, in these jottings for the character of Charles Bovary, is a sample of his note-taking: "Intimate vulgarity even in the manner in which he carefully folds his napkin . . . in which he eats his soup . . . animality of his organic functions. He wears in winter knitted waistcoats and gray woollen socks with a white border, good boots, habit of picking his teeth with the point of his knife, habit of whittling the corks of bottles so that he can put them back in the bottle."

We first meet Charles at school, a commonplace youth of the small bourgeoisie; then we see him studying for his medical examinations; then practising medicine in the small town of Yonville; then entering into a marriage, arranged for him by his parents, with an elderly widow supposed to have a dot. That Bovary was a widower who had first been married to an elderly plain wife was one of the little insignificant facts that made for the realism of his character, the ordinariness of his life. During the lifetime of his first wife he encounters Emma when, as a doctor, he is called in to visit her father. She has been educated in a convent boarding school, has graces of appearance, dress and manner which captivate him. After his wife's death he marries Emma and takes her from her father's farm to his house in the small town where he practises. Flaubert himself lived for the most part in a similar town—in fact, he lived in it all through his writing of the novel—and he had meticulously observed and documented the life around him. What had he seen there? asked Sainte-Beuve, in his study of the novel—littleness, sordidness, pretentiousness, stupidity, routine, monotony, ennui. And as for the people, they were vulgar, flat, stupidly ambitious, entirely ignorant or semi-literate, and when they loved, they were lovers without delicacy—they loved grossly. Among these people Flaubert placed Emma Bovary and her dreams of love.

There were, as has already been indicated, originals who were models to some extent for the principal characters and for the incidents of their lives, and the other personages were composites of people Flaubert was acquainted with. Nevertheless, the author said of Emma, as he also said of Frédéric, in *L'Education Sentimentale,* as perhaps every novelist can say of his chief character, "Madame Bovary c'est moi." That is, she symbolized one of the personalities of which his own personality was made up. He revealed, in her, certain potentialities of his own mind and of his own emotions. The school days, the youth, that had been his own were partly the youth, the school days, that he now gave Emma. "I believed in the poetry of life, in the plastic beauty of the passions. . . . I do not know what may be the dreams of schoolboys nowadays, but ours were superbly extravagant. . . . Those with romantic hearts sighed for dramatic scenes of love with obligatory accompaniment of gondolas, masks, and ladies swooning in post-chaises on Calabrian hills. We ruined our eyes reading novels in the dormitory." Emma, too, read novels in the dormitory of her convent school; she, too, sighed for the dramatic scenes of love; she dreamed of the romantic life and was resolved to attain it. She tried to make life correspond to these dreams, her own dreams, as well as those in the romances she had borrowed from her sewing teacher. The ennui of her life with her good, commonplace, stupid husband became unbearable; she succumbed to two lovers, and during her relations with them experienced all the gamut of emotions and temptations connected with physical love. Finally, beaten down by a series of events, she slowly disintegrates and dies a suicide.

4

Madame Bovary not only crystallized the literary genre, but fixed the novel as the primary literary form, the one most favored by writers and readers for nearly a century; it also set the pattern for novel writing in subject, theme and construction down to our time, and still shows signs that it may continue into the future, side by side with new patterns that may be brought in. It is very important to note the theme of this first realistic novel—that is, the theme as apart from the plot and the content—for we find it repeated over and over again by realistic novelists. The theme of *Madame Bovary* is the attempt to make life, every-day life, conform to one's youthful dreams, and after the vain attempt to make it conform, the renunciation of all dreams. This is not only the theme of Flaubert's other realistic novel *L'Education Sentimentale,* but is the theme of all the great realistic novels. Sometimes the renunciation of the dream comes violently as in *Madame Bovary* and *Anna Karenina,* and it is well to remember that not only the theme of Tolstoy's novel but also the plot is the same as Flaubert's. However, for Tolstoy every-day life was the life of the aristocracy, and so the personages are aristocrats, while Flaubert's are middle-class. The renunciation comes violently in Theodore Dreiser's important novels. Sometimes there is a compromise between the life of dream and reality as in George Moore's *Esther Waters,* Somerset Maugham's *Of Human Bondage,* Arnold Bennett's *The Old Wives' Tale,* Sinclair Lewis's *Main Street.*

The theme and the pattern are substantially the same with all the practitioners of the Flaubertian novel, which means that "facts," with the great realists, concern the interior life as well as the exterior. There were the "facts" of the imagination, the "fact" that life was dream as well as actuality, and they took both sides of life into consideration. This novel was the reversal of the old English themes of romance: it was almost a reversal of the Balzacian theme or subject, for Balzac, in spite of his efforts at imitating life, made his characters extraordinary, doing extraordinary and even fabulous things, whereas Flaubert's were ordinary people with only a dream of being extraordinary that passed with youth. What had happened in this book was that a writer for the first time in the history of literature had turned all his gifts, not to poetry or high romance or great drama, but to the revelation of people who might be encountered in any small town or any little suburb. The chief character, in spite of some flights of imagination beyond those of the majority of her acquaintances, in spite of expectations from life a little beyond theirs, was, at the same time, not more distinguished from the others than one woman might be among the inhabitants of the street of a small town and yet remain quite within the ordinary and the commonplace. Nothing happens to her beyond the possibility of happenings in any little community. All the personages could be duplicated in any town, village or suburb, and none of them do or say anything that had not been done or said a million times before in the world. They were created out of Flaubert's observations and experience; very completely indeed were the personages and appurtenances of romance replaced by every-day life, the gods and heroes, the kings and princesses, the lords and ladies, by the bourgeoisie—and, according to Flaubert's own definition, the bourgeoisie was now all mankind, including the people. The carefulness of his observation, his note-taking, showed itself not only in the personages, the incidents, the conversation, the habits and customs, but also in such details as the way the first Madame Bovary wore her little shawl, the details of the Agricultural Show, the stores, the pharmacy, the village church, the wedding festivities. The world in which the personages moved was not only their own world, perfectly created for them, but was, besides, the world lived in by the bulk of the reading public, who consequently understood and appreciated the book on its first appearance more rapidly than did the intelligentsia.

The personages who, whilst we are reading the novel, give the impression of being individuals become, in retrospect, types—that is, they are at once individual and typical. Emma Bovary herself, considered in turn by critics as the most complete feminine portrait in literature, as one of the most fascinating revelations of the soul of a woman, and—especially by Anglo-Saxon critics, like Percy Lubbock—as the portrait of a common, silly little person, foolishly romantic, meanly ambitious, in conflict with her environment, is in reality such an exceedingly subtle portrait that she is in some respects every woman. The portrait of Charles Bovary, good, stupid, with even a more limited expanse of consciousness than the average man, living a common, semi-animal, semi-plant life, with no desires or ambitions that his environment cannot more than satisfy, betrayed by his wife, represents the character of more men than any other type that up till then had appeared in literature. In the same way the character of Homais, the druggist, fairly intelligent, determined to get on in the world, using the environment and his adherence to all the social and tribal laws to advance himself, having some acquaintance with literature, having even a faint touch of artistry, a faint, but not too disturbing sense that there are great men in the world whom it is well to admire at a distance of both time and place, is to be found by the score in every community. It is he, observing all the laws, habits and customs, keeping all the moralities, fulfilling all the ambitions of the ordinary man, who is the one happy person in the book, a contented husband and father, a success all round in his business and in his community. The vast irony of the portrait could not have been apparent to more than a fraction of the first readers of the novel; it is, perhaps, not apparent to the bulk of readers even now. The curé, Bournasien, to whom Emma went for comfort, is also both an individual and a type. According to Flaubert's own notes, as the son of a peasant he thought only of the physical, of the sufferings of the poor, their lack of bread and fuel, and never divined the spiritual wants, the vague mystical aspirations of his fellow men. There is no portrait in *Madame Bovary* created with less irony than that of Emma herself: there is indeed less of Flaubert's well-known and often expressed contempt for humanity in his delineation of her than in that of any other character he has built up.

It has often been said of Flaubert, and he thought and said it himself, that the whole life depicted in this book was so alien to his temperament and mentality that he had to evolve an anti-self to enable him to write it and to devote himself persistently to a sort of life and to a type of humanity that he despised with a patient and all-embracing hatred. In reality, he was the first author whose mentality represented strongly and clearly the two goals that the whole modern movement in literature, beginning with Lessing, was moving towards—the romantic and the every-day, the dream and the reality. A writer could depict the reality only if he thoroughly knew the dream, and he could realize the significance of the dream only by coming into conflict with reality. Flaubert was, like the bulk of humanity, a dreamer and a realist. In addition, he was a man with a lyrical temperament and an analytic mind, part idealist, part materialist, in his philosophic outlook a scholar with a profound knowlege of literature, an artist born with the sense of form, the very type of those who create new modes of expression.

At the same time, far from being the pure lyric and romantic he sometimes thought himself, he only understood the romantic and lyrical temperament when it was well anchored on one side to common sense and every-day realism. Hence his harsh criticism of men like de Musset, lyricists without being realists, whom Flaubert liked in his lyrical moments because, as he said, his own spiritual vices of lyricism, vagabondage, and temperamental swagger were flattered by this type of work. "He never could separate poetry," Flaubert wrote of de Musset, "from the sensations it arises from;

music for him was made for serenades, painting for portraiture, and poetry for the consolation of the heart. . . . Poetry is not a debility of the spirit, and these nervous susceptibilities are. . . . This faculty of feeling beyond measure is a weakness. . . . Passion does not make poetry, and the more personal you are the weaker you are." And of Leconte de Lisle, he said, with a master craftsman's contempt for one who has not the accomplishments essential to his job, "He has not read the classics of his language sufficiently, and so has neither swiftness nor clarity." In these comments, carefully examined, will be found the basis of Flaubert's æsthetic, an æsthetic which, with that of Baudelaire, was adopted by a great portion of the modern accomplished literary world.

Working out the theories he put into practice in his realistic novels, *Madame Bovary* and *L'Education Sentimentale,* Flaubert expressed his conclusions in a series of convictions for the most part stated in his correspondence with Louise Colet, to whom he wrote half of the letters in the published correspondence; with George Sand, who had only a limited admiration for the new realistic novel and was too much immersed in her own ideals of writing for Flaubert's to be entirely sympathetic or even quite comprehensible to her. Some of the more salient of these conclusions have passed into the common stock of literary and critical ideas, not only in relation to the novel, but to poetry; for, as with all significant writers, the basic construction of Flaubert's mind was poetic. "The author in his work," he said, in a well-known sentence, in which he expressed his theories about the type of novel he had invented, "ought to be like God in the universe, present everywhere but visible nowhere. . . . Art being a second nature, the creator of this nature ought to act by analogous proceeding. I do not believe that the novelist should express his own opinions. . . . According to the ideal of art that I have, I think that an artist should not manifest anything of his own feelings, and that he should not appear any more in his work than God in nature. . . . The man is nothing, the work is everything."

In his realistic novels, Flaubert deliberately turned away from the accidental, the extraordinary and the dramatic which had so beguiled Balzac; he created neither remarkable persons nor heroes, though he did not blame anybody who did, for, as he said, "Art is what one can make it; we are not free. Each follows his own path in spite of his own desires." As for the meticulous power of observation shown in his books, he, like most men of genius, did not place too high a degree of importance on it; it was valuable, but subsidiary. "If I have arrived at some knowledge of life," he wrote, "it is by dint not of chewing a great deal of it but of having ruminated a lot on it." A little experience well pondered over—that gave him the matter for his novels. Other general theories of his have been repeated over and over again and re-created in a form that now represents the most advanced literary ideas of our age, such as are being enunciated by Valéry and T. S. Eliot. "The less one feels a thing, the more apt one is to express it as it is, as it is in itself, in its universality, freed from accidental ephemera." But he added that one must have the faculty of making oneself feel it, that is, one must have the potentiality of feeling what one expresses, even if one has never actually experienced it in life. "One does not write with one's heart, but with one's head, and no matter how well endowed one may be, one always has need of that concentration which gives vigor to the thought, luster to the expression."

That "form and matter were two subtle qualities, neither of which could exist without the other," was the first article in Flaubert's artistic creed. He weighed sentences and phrases, and he carved and filed until he got the exact words in the exact order with the sound that he felt expressed what he wanted to say. Because, as he said, the words fitted for expressing an idea have a predetermined relation to the facts that gave rise to the idea, the discovery of the inevitable word, phrase, or sentence required from him great travail. Working seven hours a day, he would manage to produce in a month about twenty pages or even less. "To write a book is for me a long voyage," he said, and for the voyage that was *Madame Bovary,* between the conception, the working-out and the writing, he took more than seven years in all. But when the voyage was ended and the completed book reached the public, it produced an excitement similar to that caused in our day by the publication of Joyce's *Ulysses,* for another milestone on the road to expressing in literature the totality of human experiences had been passed, and the ordinary man, or to use Flaubert's own phrase, "the bourgeois that is now all mankind," was to be the hero of literature for a long time to come.

Strange and even startling as was Flaubert's achievement, he was in form, even in technique, the heir of a long line not only of French writers but of the whole Latin tradition; in the psychological construction of his characters, as well as in his carefully wrought style, he showed himself of the same line as Racine: the shape of his plot, with its beginning, its crisis, its conclusion, was clearly in the classical manner. He used the old splendid tools on new material and as a new practitioner.

5

Inclined towards determinism, which was the accepted philosophy of the age, Flaubert was akin to Taine on one side of his mind, but on another he had a singular kinship with the author of the second great literary sensation of 1857, with the poet of *Les Fleurs du Mal*. Baudelaire, on his side, felt the kinship, and after the appearance of *Madame Bovary,* wrote one of the two understanding critiques of that novel, the other having been written by Sainte-Beuve.

The two books broke on a startled public, accustomed to regarding the established literary works and their subjects as representing the perpetual standards of art, with a moral shock—the novel differed from all preceding novels and romances and the volume of poems from all preceding poetry. Looking backwards, one cannot avoid the conviction that the ensuing legal prosecution of the two books, *Madame Bovary* for immorality and *Les Fleurs du Mal* for immorality and blasphemy, resulted as much from mental shock, caused by a blasting of existing conceptions of literature, as from any moral or religious scruples.

As *Madame Bovary* changed the shape and content of the narrative, so *Les Fleurs du Mal* changed the shape and content of poetry: together, the two modified, all over Europe, the attitude towards literature and literary form of the great bulk of the writers who came after them. It was not that narrative was never again to be written as it was before Flaubert, or poetry as it was before Baudelaire, but that materials and values, persons and things, whose expression had been dimly longed for, hazily struggled towards since Lessing, were now definitely emergent in literature.

The two who had accomplished this were subject to many of the same influences: what Taine would call the intellectual climate was very similar for both, with the difference in final effect that one was a prose writer and the other a poet, dowered differently in imaginative quality and nature of expression. The effect, on writing, of Flaubert's work was immediate; that of Baudelaire's was slower except in the case of a small group of the younger poets, particularly those who later were to call themselves Symbolists, the group around Verlaine and Rimbaud. At the period, the dominating trend in writing was towards the utmost care in form and style, towards an impersonal attitude to material, towards a cult of objectivity, towards keeping the personality of the author out of his work. These were the aims of a group of poets who called themselves Parnassians, with the leader of whom, Théophile Gautier, Baudelaire felt strong enough kinship, strong enough common aims, to dedicate to him *Les Fleurs du Mal*.

Flaubert's aims in prose were, in theory anyhow, the same as those of Gautier and the Parnassians in verse. The same rays of influence poured on all of them from the milieu and the moment, but each took what best suited his temperament, what best developed his own originality. Apart from the peculiar differentiation of their genius, Baudelaire's resemblance to Flaubert was sufficiently striking. To begin with, both were born in the same year, 1821; both produced their epoch-making books in the same year, 1857; both were realists in the only sense in which a man can be a realist and be a great artist, in their sharp consciousness of the struggle between the dream and the reality, between the aspiration and common happenings. The nervous structure of their personalities had much in common: a similar dread of life was manifested by both at an early age. As a child of thirteen, Flaubert could write to a friend about a story he was weaving around Queen Isabeau, "If I had not in my head and at the end of my pen a French queen of the fifteenth century, I should be totally disgusted with life and a bullet would deliver me from the buffoonery that one calls living." And Baudelaire wrote in one of his journals, "As a child I felt in my heart two contradictory sentiments, the horror of life and the ecstasy of life." Nevertheless, Baudelaire did not continually display that hatred for the folly and futility of mankind which goes like a refrain through Flaubert's correspondence, through his life, and which he made the groundwork of his art.

The attitude of both to life and art was, in great part, the result of a highly strung temperament, subtly attuned nerves, and an inherited lack of that sort of physical force and vital abundance that made Hugo and Balzac at once objects of admiration and something of ironic mockery to both. Their nervousness, their irony, their general outlook on life, gave their writing a sharpened sense of reality. This sense of reality made Baudelaire incapable of making poetry out of mere reverie or fantasy: his utmost fantasies, his strangest emotions, were well winnowed by his intellect before they were transmuted into art and were always made definite through being brought into touch with some common experience, some familiar occurrence. His attitude in this respect is characteristically revealed in that remark of his about de Musset—that he never understood the process by which a reverie became a work of art: de Musset was satisfied when he had versified the reverie.

Baudelaire expressed his passion for form and style in terms akin to Flaubert's: for both, the writing of a book was a long travail; the coupling of the right adjective with the right noun a matter for laborious experimentation. For the poet, the significant adjective or noun sometimes came from analogy, sometimes from incongruity. In their care for form and style they were not only part of a reaction against the carelessness and flamboyance of the more exuberant romantics like de Musset, Sand and Hugo, they were the heirs of the long line of masters of French literature. In addition, Baudelaire was the inheritor from Lessing, Herder, Wordsworth, Coleridge, through Sainte-Beuve, of all the innovating ideas about poetry. The strong effect on him of Sainte-Beuve's verse is one of those not uncommon instances of a poet of rare genius receiving an influx of energy and ideas from one of lesser caliber, one who, in this particular case, was supreme in a field of literature that included the intuitive perception of new poetic directions. We must keep in mind that Sainte-Beuve's *Ra-*

yons Jaunes and *The Poetry of Joseph Delorme,* of which Baudelaire described himself as an incorrigible lover, were in their day a new species of poetry and remained a new species of poetry for a generation younger than that of Baudelaire, Verlaine's.

But to get to the root of Sainte-Beuve's sway over a couple of generations of poets, we must go back to those influences that made him. He was one of the few great critics in all literature—an idea-carrier, an innovator, a shaker-up of old conventions, a man who foresaw the motive forces in literature. The new wave of poetic ideas had come from England and was to return to England in another form, in later time. Sainte-Beuve was steeped in English literature, and he brought into French not only the ideas and poetry of Wordsworth and Coleridge, but of Lamb, Kirk White and Cowper, and even of the Bowles who is so strangely praised in the *Biographia Literaria.* The hearth-and-family school represented by Cowper in England never made much headway on the Continent; it was, however, cherished by Sainte-Beuve, who conceived that if he failed in his ambition to become the French Wordsworth he might become the French Cowper. The bulk of the poetic principles that he strove to turn into terms that could be assimilated by French genius came from Wordsworth and the Lake School, especially from the powerful summons of the Preface to the *Lyrical Ballads.* "The principal object," Wordsworth had written, "proposed in these poems was to choose incidents and situations from common life and to relate or describe them throughout, as far as possible, in a selection of the language really used by men." Sainte-Beuve accordingly took on the ambition to be the French Wordsworth and proceeded to write about incidents and situations and people chosen from common life; made, in fact, a considerable effort to be a realist in verse. As he said, his muse was no brilliant odalisque, no young and vermilion peri, but a "poor girl washing clothes by a stream." So he chose themes suited to the "poor girl" and these occasionally were difficult to make poetry out of; some of the poems derived from Wordsworth had more of the famous prosiness of the master than of his high poetry. Nevertheless, there can be no doubt that Sainte-Beuve was a poet both in mind and performance, even though it is in his influence on poetry rather than in his poetic achievement that his importance lies. Wordsworth had said that he had chosen humble and rustic life for his poems "because in that condition the essential passions of the heart find a better soil in which they can attain their maturity."

The humble and rustic life that gave him the matter for his poems Wordsworth found in his daily walks. Sainte-Beuve proceeded to find subjects in his walks. The walk, in fact, became an inciter of inspiration, and "Promenade," as a title, acquired a vogue. But common life for Sainte-Beuve was not rustic life: it was such as he could find in the streets of Paris, and he describes the promenades of his "Joseph Delorme" and the sights and scenes he encountered "in that vast cemetery that is called a great city." The holes in the hedges through which could be viewed the mean little vegetable gardens, the monotonous side streets, the elm trees gray with dust, an old woman crouching on the ground with children, a belated soldier going back to barracks with tottering steps, a workman's party. His Sunday evenings in Paris he described in the poem called "Rayons Jaunes," and this poem, in spite of its touches of prosiness, had repercussions in poetry that affected not only Baudelaire, but Laforgue and Laforgue's followers in every country, and among these we can reckon many of our own contemporaries, and, outstandingly, T. S. Eliot and Ezra Pound.

Baudelaire could write to Sainte-Beuve, "I hope to be able to show one of these days a new Joseph Delorme grappling at each incident of his promenade with his rhapsodic thought and drawing a distasteful moral from everything." Sainte-Beuve himself spoke of his *Rayons Jaunes* as the *Fleurs du Mal* of the day before, and he adopted Baudelaire as his son in Apollo, addressing him as "my dear son." But in spite of all this mutual interest and admiration, this undoubted kinship, it is clear that the author of *Les Rayons Jaunes* never really became an appreciator or even a comprehender of the stronger and stranger music, the more heady wine of *Les Fleurs du Mal.* He was even a trifle nonplussed at some of the subjects exploited in that volume, and suggested that Baudelaire should have written certain of his verses in Latin. And with all his admiration for Sainte-Beuve, Baudelaire could write to him the following: "In certain places in 'Joseph Delorme' I find too many lutes, lyres, harps and Jehovahs. This is a blemish on the Parisian poems; besides, you have come to destroy all that." It was true, he had come to destroy all that. But it was Baudelaire who was really destined to accomplish the destruction. He sought for his material where Joseph Delorme had looked before him, "in that vast cemetery that is called a great city." His muse was far from being Sainte-Beuve's "poor girl washing clothes by a stream," and the life he found in Paris was other than what Joseph Delorme discovered in his daily promenades.

Baudelaire's common humanity was neither Sainte-Beuve's nor Wordsworth's; it comprised the castaways of a great city—beggars, tramps, prostitutes, assassins, drunkards, lesbians, rag-pickers, the old men and old women of the parks and the quays; his scenery was destitute of running brooks, singing birds, primroses by a river's brim; it was, instead, dawn on the Seine, fogs, rain, hospitals, cemeteries, the streets, the cafés of Paris. Parisian life, he affirmed, was full of marvellous subjects, and he took what he called "the bath of multitude," for to the poet belonged "the incomparable privilege of being both himself and others," of being able to "enter at will the personality of any man." That he deliberately chose to find poetry in subjects where nobody thought of looking for it before is clear not only from his work but from his own comments on it. For, he declared, as the great poets of the past had divided among themselves the happier provinces of the domain of poetry, he set himself to extract beauty from evil and misfortune, or, in his own words, "extraire la beauté du mal," and Sainte-Beuve wrote to him, "You, the latest comer, said to yourself, 'Well, I will find poetry where no one thought of culling it before.'"

Baudelaire could, apparently, draw poetry from anything in life that came to his attention, for there were depths of reverie and emotion and memory in his being, that could couple themselves with any experience. His daily experience, intermingled with his indestructible memories, with the nervous complexity of his emotions and the sharp power of his senses, formed the groundwork of his poetry. He expressed the conviction that art ought to be a revelation of modern life, that contemporaries were more important than the men of the past, and so he placed Balzac above Homer, Wagner above previous musicians; he considered that Manet and Delacroix were painting the modern world's pictures; the age of gods and goddesses was gone by; the great artist, he wrote, would be the one who could seize from every-day life its epic side and show us how great and poetic we were in our neckties and polished shoes. He himself, to be sure, did not always seek greatness and poetic emotions in neckties and polished shoes, but was fond of inducing other emotions and sensations by drinking strange potions, by eating hashish and opium, by means of which he entered what he called his artificial paradises. But he did seize, from every-day life, its epic side and he seized the epic side of the morbid, the exotic, the neurotic, the unwholesome, the disintegrated, the bored, the exasperated and the lonely. The Goncourts said that both language and literature had been formed by men who were too healthy and well-balanced to be really representative of humanity. They concluded that the instabilities of the ordinary man, his vagaries, his experiences, his bewilderments, his sins and his suffering, must be expressed in a different style of writing and in a language and syntax susceptible of taking on the coloring of the modern world and the shapes of the many complex human types that compose it.

The Goncourts believed that they themselves were to be the first to accomplish this in prose, for the old Titans of literature had expressed the few and not the many, the uncommon, simple emotions instead of the common, complicated ones. But their contemporary and friend, Baudelaire, was doing it in poetry in their lifetime with a complexity and completeness which no one, either in prose or verse, has since equalled. He got into poetry emotions, thoughts, spasms of the mind and senses, that people recognized to be theirs only after he had expressed them. For, as has been said of him, he modified the sensibility of generations of intellectuals; he gave voice to the complexity of sentiments and sensations embodied in one emotion; he manipulated language and language-combinations and sounds so that a single line or a couplet could convey layers and layers of experience that lay outside the realm of the older poetry.

Les morts, les pauvres morts ont de grandes douleurs.
(The dead, the poor dead, have great sorrows.)

. . . .

L'Irréparable ronge avec sa dent maudite
Notre âme.
(The Irreparable gnaws our soul with his cursed teeth.)

. . . .

La Maladie et la Mort font des cendres
De tout le feu qui pour nous flamboya.
(Illness and Death make ashes of all the fire that flamed
    for us.)

. . . .

Ma jeunesse ne fut qu'un ténébreux orage,
Traversé çà et là par de brillants soleils.
(My youth was only a tenebrous storm, traversed here and
    there by brilliant suns.)

. . . .

O douleur! O douleur! Le Temps mange la vie,

Et l'obscur Ennemi qui nous ronge le cœur,
Du sang que nous perdons croît et se fortifie!
(O sorrow, sorrow! Time eats life away, and the obscure
    Enemy that gnaws our heart, grows and is fortified by
    the blood we lose.)

. . . .

J'ai plus de souvenirs que si j'avais mille ans.
(I have more memories than if I had a thousand years.)

. . . .

           mon triste cerveau,
C'est une pyramide, un immense caveau,
Qui contient plus de morts que la fosse commune.
(My sad brain is an immense cave that contains more dead
    than the potter's field.)

. . . .

Rien n'égale en longeur les boiteuses journées,
Quand sous les lourds flocons des neigeuses années
L'Ennui, fruit de la morne incuriosité,
Prend les proportions de l'immortalité.
(Nothing equals in length the limping days, when, under
    the heavy flakes of the snowing years, Ennui, fruit of
    gloomy incuriosity, takes on the proportions of im-
    mortality.)

When he wrote the poem "La Servante au Grand
Cœur," a commemoration of the dead, of a servant who
had attended him as a child, it was not just the expression of a simple emotion accompanied with a little
philosophic reflection, as it might have been in a Wordsworth poem or even in one by any poet preceding Baudelaire; it became laden with memories, with medita-

tions on life, love and death, with visions of cold October winds shearing the leaves off the trees, the memory of his mother's jealousy, the forgetfulness of the living, the sadness of the dead in their isolation—the restlessness and loneliness of the grave.

LA SERVANTE AU GRAND CŒUR

La servante au grand cœur dont vous étiez jalouse,
Et qui dort son sommeil sous une humble pelouse,
Nous devrions pourtant lui porter quelques fleurs.
Les morts, les pauvres morts, ont de grandes douleurs,
Et quand Octobre souffle, émondeur des vieux arbres,
Son vent mélancolique à l'entour de leurs marbres,
Certe, ils doivent trouver les vivants bien ingrats,
De dormir, comme ils font, chaudement dans leurs draps,
Tandis que, dévorés de noires songeries,
Sans compagnon de lit, sans bonnes causeries,
Vieux squelettes gelés travaillés par le ver,
Ils sentent s'égoutter les neiges de l'hiver
Et le siècle couler, sans qu'amis ni famille
Remplacent les lambeaux qui pendent à leur grille.

Lorsque la bûche siffle et chante, si le soir,
Calme, dans le fauteuil je la voyais s'asseoir,
Si, par une nuit bleue et froide de décembre,
Je la trouvais tapie en un coin de ma chambre,
Grave, et venant du fond de son lit éternel
Couver l'enfant grandi de son œil maternel,
Que pourrais-je répondre à cette âme pieuse,
Voyant tomber des pleurs de sa paupière creuse!

THE SERVANT OF THE GREAT HEART

The servant of the great heart, that you were jealous of,
And who sleeps her last sleep under an humble sward,

THE COMING OF THE REALISTS

We should nevertheless bring her a few flowers—
The dead, the poor dead, have great sorrows,
And when October blows its melancholy wind—
Shearer of old trees—around their marble tombs,
Certainly they must find the living very ungrateful
To sleep as they do warmly between their sheets,
Whilst, devoured with black broodings,
Without bed-companion, without good conversation,
Old frozen skeletons wrought upon by the worm,
They hear the snows of winter dripping,
And the century go past, without friends or family
Replacing the tatters that hang on the railing.

When the log whistles and sings, if in the evening
I should see her placidly sitting in the armchair,
If, in the blue and cold night of December,
I found her crouched in a corner of my chamber,
Grave, coming from the depths of her eternal bed
To look tenderly at the child grown from her maternal eye,
What could I reply to this faithful soul,
Seeing the tears fall from her hollow eyelids!

(Literal translation by M. M. C.)

6

With Baudelaire, came into poetry the civilized man of the cities, with the sort of life experience of the man of the cities, with the nervous reactions of one whose life is complicated with happenings, with people and with sufferings, with sorrow and sin. He dowered misery, sordidness, dissolution, with a beauty shocking to the vigorous, to the happy, the optimistic, to those

185

accustomed to think that contemplating the bright side of things was alone worthy of a man. He sought for poetry in the story of the drunkard who had killed his wife, from the sight of a corpse rotting on the highway, a beggar girl, an old ragpicker livened by wine—"the people harassed with care, ground down by toil, plagued by old age." He told us their dreams when they escaped from misery through wine or sleep. He revealed death in all its shapes, the fear of death, the victory of death, the relief of death, the death of lovers, of the poor, of artists. He revealed love, if not in all its shapes, at least in more shapes than any single poet had ever done before. Assassins and damned women, beggars and vampires, and emotions and sensations, and even senses, that had never before appeared in poetry were in this single volume of his. It was indeed said of him that he had transfixed in his verse all sorts of fleeting states of mind and body, passing loves, fugitive melancholy, the fugitive loves and melancholies and joys of men and women who were not at all like the characters in the work of the older masters. In "La Passante" the poet meets a woman passing by in the street, meets her eyes for a minute, falls in love with her for a minute, and out of it he makes a poem of a moment that leaves an immortal mood. Opposite as his temperament and life were to Wordsworth's, many of his subjects are the exact city parallels of the rustic subjects that Words-

worth treated. Wordsworth has a meditation on the
country girl:

> Three years she grew in sun and shower;
> Then Nature said, "A lovelier flower
> On earth was never sown;
> This child I to myself will take;
> She shall be mine, and I will make
> A lady of my own.
>
> "Myself will to my darling be
> Both law and impulse; and with me
> The girl, in rock and plain,
> In earth and heaven, in glade and bower,
> Shall feel an overseeing power
> To kindle or restrain.
>
> "She shall be sportive as the fawn
> That wild with glee across the lawn
> Or up the mountain springs;
> And hers shall be the breathing balm,
> And hers the silence and the calm
> Of mute insensate things. . . .
>
> . . . .
>
> "The stars of midnight shall be dear
> To her; and she shall lean her ear
> In many a secret place
> Where rivulets dance their wayward round,
> And beauty born of murmuring sound
> Shall pass into her face. . . ."

Baudelaire has a meditation on a girl of the city
streets.

FROM THESE ROOTS

Blanche fille aux cheveux roux,
Dont la robe par ses trous
Laisse voir la pauvreté
    Et la beauté,

Pour moi, poète chétif,
Ton jeune corps maladif,
Plein de taches de rousseur,
    A sa douceur.

Tu portes plus galamment
Qu'une reine de roman
Ses cothurnes de velours
    Tes sabots lourds.

Au lieu d'un haillon trop court,
Qu'un superbe habit de cour
Traîne à plis bruyants et longs
    Sur tes talons;

En place de bas troués,
Que pour les yeux des roués
Sur ta jambe un poignard d'or
    Reluise encor;

Que des nœuds mal attachés
Dévoilent pour nos péchés
Tes deux beaux seins, radieux
    Comme des yeux;

Que pour te déshabiller
Tes bras se fassent prier
Et chassent à coups mutins
    Les doigts lutins

Perles de la plus belle eau,
Sonnets de maître Belleau
Par tes galants mis aux fers
    Sans cesse offerts,

Valetaille de rimeurs
Te dédiant leurs primeurs
Et contemplant ton soulier
    Sous l'escalier.

Maint page épris du hasard,
Maint seigneur et maint Ronsard
Epieraient pour le déduit
    Ton frais réduit!

Tu compterais dans tes lits
Plus de baisers que de lis
Et rangerais sous tes lois
    Plus d'un Valois!

—Cependant tu vas gueusant
Quelque vieux débris gisant
Au seuil de quelque Véfour
    De carrefour;

Tu vas lorgnant en dessous
Des bijoux de vingt-neuf sous
Dont je ne puis, oh! pardon!
    Te faire don.

Va donc, sans autre ornement,
Parfum, perles, diamant,
Que ta maigre nudité,
    O ma beauté!

FROM THESE ROOTS

To a Brown Beggar-Maid

White maiden with the russet hair,
Whose garments, through their holes, declare
That poverty is part of you,
    And beauty too,

To me, a sorry bard and mean,
Your youthful beauty, frail and lean,
With summer freckles here and there,
    Is sweet and fair.

Your sabots tread the roads of chance,
And not one queen of old romance
Carried her velvet shoes and lace
    With half your grace.

In place of tatters far too short
Let the proud garments worn at Court
Fall down with rustling fold and pleat
    About your feet;

In place of stockings, worn and old,
Let a keen dagger all of gold
Gleam in your garter for the eyes
    Of roués wise;

Let ribbons carelessly untied
Reveal to us the radiant pride
Of your white bosom purer far
    Than any star;

Let your white arms uncovered shine,
Polished and smooth and half divine;
And let your elfish fingers chase
    With riotous grace

THE COMING OF THE REALISTS

The purest pearls that softly glow,
The sweetest sonnets of Belleau,
Offered by gallants ere they fight
    For your delight;

And many fawning rhymers who
Inscribe their first thin book to you
Will contemplate upon the stair
    Your slipper fair;

And many a page who plays at cards,
And many lords and many bards,
Will watch your going forth, and burn
    For your return;

And you will count before your glass
More kisses than the lily has;
And more than one Valois will sigh
    When you pass by.

But meanwhile you are on the tramp,
Begging your living in the damp,
Wandering mean streets and alleys o'er,
    From door to door;

And shilling bangles in a shop
Cause you with eager eyes to stop,
And I, alas, have not a sou
    To give to you.

Then go, with no more ornament,
Pearl, diamond, or subtle scent,
Than your own fragile naked grace
    And lovely face.

                  (*Translation by F. P. Sturm.*)

FROM THESE ROOTS

The next quotations, where both poets write of seeing an old man on their morning's walk—Wordsworth
on a country walk in the moors, Baudelaire in the
city streets—show even more strikingly the likeness
of the theme and at the same time the opposed temperaments of the two poets.

LES SEPT VIEILLARDS

Fourmillante cité, cité pleine de rêves,
Où le spectre en plein jour raccroche le passant!
Les mystères partout coulent comme des sèves
Dans les canaux étroits du colosse puissant.

Un matin, cependant que dans la triste rue
Les maisons, dont la brume allongeait la hauteur,
Simulaient les deux quais d'une rivière accrue,
Et que, décor semblable à l'âme de l'acteur,

Un brouillard sale et jaune inondait tout l'espace,
Je suivais, roidissant mes nerfs comme un héros
Et discutant avec mon âme déjà lasse,
Le faubourg secoué par les lourds tombereaux.

Tout à coup, un vieillard dont les guenilles jaunes
Imitaient la couleur de ce ciel pluvieux,
Et dont l'aspect aurait fait pleuvoir les aumônes,
Sans la méchanceté qui luisait dans ses yeux,

M'apparut. On eût dit sa prunelle trempée
Dans le fiel; son regard aiguisait les frimas,
Et sa barbe à longs poils, roide comme une épée,
Se projetait, pareille à celle de Judas.

THE COMING OF THE REALISTS

Il n'était pas voûté, mais cassé, son échine
Faisant avec sa jambe un parfait angle droit,
Si bien que son bâton, parachevant sa mine,
Lui donnait la tournure et le pas maladroit

D'un quadrupède infirme ou d'un juif à trois pattes.
Dans la neige et la boue il allait s'empêtrant,
Comme s'il écrasait des morts sous ses savates,
Hostile à l'univers plutôt qu'indifférent.

Son pareil le suivait: barbe, œil, dos, bâton, loques,
Nul trait ne distinguait, du même enfer venu,
Ce jumeau centenaire, et ces spectres baroques
Marchaient du même pas vers un but inconnu.

A quel complot infâme étais-je donc en butte,
Ou quel méchant hasard ainsi m'humiliait?
Car je comptai sept fois, de minute en minute,
Ce sinistre vieillard qui se multipliait!

Que celui-là qui rit de mon inquiétude,
Et qui n'est pas saisi d'un frisson fraternel,
Songe bien que malgré tant de décrépitude
Ces sept monstres hideux avaient l'air éternel!

Aurais-je, sans mourir, contemplé le huitième,
Sosie inexorable, ironique et fatal,
Dégoûtant Phénix, fils et père de lui-même?
—Mais je tournai le dos au cortège infernal.

Exaspéré comme un ivrogne qui voit double,
Je rentrai, je fermai ma porte, épouvanté,
Malade et morfondu, l'esprit fiévreux et trouble,
Blessé par le mystère et par l'absurdité!

FROM THESE ROOTS

Vainement ma raison voulait prendre la barre;
La tempête en jouant déroutait ses efforts,
Et mon âme dansait, dansait, vieille gabarre
Sans mâts, sur une mer monstrueuse et sans bords!

THE SEVEN OLD MEN

Ant-hill city, city full of dreams,
Where the specter in broad daylight accosts the passer-by,
Everywhere mysteries flow like sap
In the narrow arteries of the powerful Colossus.

One morning, whilst in the sad street
The houses, whose height the fog steepened,
Were like the embankments of a river receded,
And which, a setting akin to the soul of the player,

A dirty yellow fog inundated, all the space,
I followed, steeling my nerves like a hero,
And holding speech with my soul, already wearied,
The purlieus shaken by the heavy wagons.

All at once an old man, whose yellow tatters
Imitated the hues of the rainy sky,
And whose looks would have made alms rain
Except for the villainy which gleamed in his eyes,

Appeared to me. One would have said that his eyeballs
      were steeped
In gall; his glance made keen the winter,
And his overgrown beard, stiff as a sword,
Protruded like the beard of Judas.

He was not bent but broken, his backbone
Making with his leg a right angle
So true that his stick, finishing his appearance,
Gave him the gait and awkward step

THE COMING OF THE REALISTS

Of a lamed quadruped or a three-legged Jew.
In the snow and the mud he went hobbling
As if he were stamping the dead under his old shoes,
Hostile to the universe rather than indifferent to it.

His fellow followed him—beard, eye, back, stick, tatters,
No sign made them different, come from the same hell,
These centenarian twins, these grotesque apparitions
Marched with the same step towards an unknown goal.

What infamous game was being played on me,
Or what mischievous chance thus humiliated me?
For I counted, minute to minute, seven times
This sinister old man multiplying himself.

Let any one who laughs at my uneasiness,
And who is not gripped with a sympathetic shiver,
Consider that in spite of so much decrepitude
These seven hideous monstrosities seemed immortal.

Would I have, without dying, looked on the eighth,
Inexorable, ironic, deadly counterpart,
Disgusting Phœnix, son and father of himself?
But I turned my back on the hellish procession.

Exasperated as a drunkard who sees double,
I turned home; I shut my door, affrighted,
Sick and benumbed, my spirit feverish and troubled,
Wounded by the mystery and the absurdity.

Vainly my reason strove to take the helm,
The tempest, frolicking, baffled its efforts,
And my soul danced, danced, an old hulk
Without masts, on a monstrous and shoreless sea.

(*Literal translation by M. M. C.*)

195

FROM THESE ROOTS

Wordsworth's old man is a leech-gatherer, and in his walk on a beautiful morning after a night of rain he sees the old man standing by a pool.

I thought of Chatterton, the marvellous Boy,
The sleepless Soul that perished in his pride;
Of Him who walked in glory and in joy
Following his plough, along the mountainside:
By our own spirits are we deified:
We Poets in our youth begin in gladness;
But thereof comes in the end despondency and madness.

Now, whether it were by peculiar grace,
A leading from above, a something given,
Yet it befell that, in this lonely place,
When I with these untoward thoughts had striven,
Beside a pool bare to the eye of heaven
I saw a Man before me unawares:
The oldest man he seemed that ever wore grey hairs.

As a huge stone is sometimes seen to lie
Couched on the bald top of an eminence;
Wonder to all who do the same espy,
By what means it could thither come, and whence;
So that it seems a thing endued with sense:
Like a sea-beast crawled forth, that on a shelf
Of rock or sand reposeth, there to sun itself;

Such seemed this Man, not all alive nor dead,
Nor all asleep—in his extreme old age:
His body was bent double, feet and head
Coming together in life's pilgrimage;
As if some dire constraint of pain, or rage
Of sickness felt by him in times long past,
A more than human weight upon his frame had cast.

. . . .

THE COMING OF THE REALISTS

At length, himself unsettling, he the pond
Stirred with his staff, and fixedly did look
Upon the muddy water, which he conned,
As if he had been reading in a book:
And now a stranger's privilege I took:
And drawing to his side, to him did say,
"This morning gives us promise of a glorious day."

. . . .

He told, that to these waters he had come
To gather leeches, being old and poor:
Employment hazardous and wearisome!
And he had many hardships to endure;
From pond to pond he roamed, from moor to moor;
Housing, with God's good help, by choice or chance;
And in this way he gained an honest maintenance.

The old Man still stood talking by my side;
But now his voice to me was like a stream
Scarce heard, nor word from word could I divide;
And the whole body of the Man did seem
Like one whom I had met with in a dream;
Or like a man from some far region sent,
To give inhuman strength, by apt admonishment.

. . . .

While he was talking thus, the lonely place,
The old Man's shape, and speech—all troubled me:
In my mind's eye I seemed to see him pace
About the weary moors continually,
Wandering about alone and silently.
While I these thoughts within myself pursued,
He, having made a pause, the same discourse renewed.

. . . .

These poems, while characteristic of the minds of the authors, contain some lines that are examples of the famous prosiness of which both have been accused. In Wordsworth's case that prosiness came from a commonplace streak in his mind, from a wingless literalness, from a didacticism, from the Country Curate temperament that sometimes dominated his faculties as it dominated his existence; it also came from an occasional undue application of his formula for language. In Baudelaire's case the accusation arises from a conventional attitude in the reader's mind, and this is based on the fact that some of his poems present a picture deliberately filled in with details like the details on a Dürer woodcut, for as the French critic Charles Du Bos has pointed out he executed an engraving with words.

It must be repeated that Wordsworth and Baudelaire were the oustanding poets of the nineteenth century who made poetry out of the people and spectacles that every-day life presented, so that some of their readers, used to the older content of poetry, sometimes had difficulty in believing that their work was poetry at all. As with the poet-dramatists, it was humanity itself and the souls of men and women that stirred their imagination: they were poet-psychologists, "with a greater knowledge of human nature and a more comprehensive soul than are common." Wordsworth, to be sure, like all the great English poets, sometimes made an ascent into a region where the ordinary man could get little foothold, but

when Baudelaire took flight into the upper air he peo-
pled it with the nerves and emotions of humanity; he
gave a tongue to senses, to anguishes and ennuis that
until then had been voiceless. At least one half of Wordsworth's verse is of little value as poetry and might have
been composed by a country curate with a turn for
versifying and moralizing on life. There is not a single
line of Baudelaire, with the exception of one experiment
in conversational verse, that is not sheer poetry. He was
the first of the poets who deliberately eliminated from
poetry anything that he thought might be just as well
or almost as well expressed in prose. All his work is of
such density and intensity that it seems as if a world of
concentrated thought and emotion went into every
verse, even every line. Into that one book of poetry he
put the essence of his mind: truly enough he believed
that a man could put all of himself into one or two
books; in comparison with him, as with Catullus,
other poets seem intolerably long-winded. Put within
the covers of one book, as was done by Matthew Arnold,
Wordsworth gives a more real impression of the great
poet that he was than in his collected works.

7

Almost the whole of modern poetry has sprung from
roots dug up to the common sight by these two oddly
affiliated poets, Baudelaire and Wordsworth, so apart
from each other in temperament, environment and

life experience; almost the whole of it has come out of territory explored by them, out of theories evolved by them, and from the special sort of revolt their work led to. It is well to remind those who figure them as apart from each other in time that when Baudelaire was writing *Les Fleurs du Mal,* Wordsworth was Queen Victoria's laureate. And as to the much-publicized influence of Edgar Allan Poe on Baudelaire, as far as the poetry is concerned there is not much reason to take it into serious consideration. A resemblance can be pointed out to some of Poe's poems, as for instance to "Ulalume," the poem beginning—

> The skies they were ashen and sober;
> The leaves they were crispèd and sere,
> The leaves they were withering and sere;
> It was night in the lonesome October
> Of my most immemorial year.

Or to certain lines of "Dream-Land," or of "The City in the Sea." We know that the greater part of *Les Fleurs du Mal* was written before Baudelaire had any acquaintance with the work of Poe, for the book was already announced for publication twelve years before it actually appeared, that is in 1845, and it is not till a year or two later that we have any record of Baudelaire's reading Poe. Though all the poems that finally appeared in *Les Fleurs du Mal* were not finished at that early date, yet many of the most striking were, and some had been given magazine publication.

Baudelaire has left a record of the effect on his mind of his first encounter with the work of Poe. In a letter to a friend, one Armand Fraisse, he wrote, "In 1846 or '47 I made the acquaintance of a few fragments of Poe; I experienced a strange excitement. His complete works having been collected in a single edition only after his death, I took the trouble of making myself acquainted with Americans living in Paris, so that I might be able to borrow collections of journals that had been edited by Edgar Poe. And then I found, believe me if you will, poems and tales of which I had had the thought, vague and confused and badly arranged, and which Poe had been able to combine and bring to perfection." As is well known, Baudelaire translated the *Tales* and thus brought into French literature a whole new influence. We can truly say that if Baudelaire had written tales or short stories they would have been akin to Poe's. We can also say that what might be termed the Poetic Principles of both had many points in common, though Poe's idea of the content of poetry was conventional and traditional when compared with that of Baudelaire, who had the large variety of emotions, the extensive communication with life, of the very great poets.

But Poe's æsthetic, as defined in "The Poetic Principle," might conceivably have been known in French literary circles long before his general work, and if so, it certainly influenced Baudelaire in his conception of poetry, and all the more so as his mind was already working in the same direction. Poe had come out strongly and sensationally against the long poem, maintaining definitely that the phrase "a long poem" was a contradiction in terms; the value of a poem lay in its elevating excitement, and as all excitements are, through a psychical necessity, transient, no excitement could last all through a long poem. The poem should be written for the poem's sake, regardless of how the result affected readers. This is very like what Baudelaire, who never wrote a long poem, has said about poetry. He had the same abhorrence of a didactic element, the same belief in the importance of music, for the preoccupation with the music of verse was very intense with both poets. "Music," Poe said, "in its various modes of meter, rhythm and rhyme, is of so vast a moment in poetry that he is simply silly who declines its assistance." And Baudelaire was not only concerned with the musical structure of lines, but with the interior music of words. "Any poet," he wrote, "who does not know exactly what rhymes each word allows, is incapable of expressing any idea whatever. The poetic phrase (and in this it touches the art of music) can imitate the horizontal line, the straight line ascending and the straight line descending. . . . It can express every sensation of sweetness or bitterness, of bliss or of horror, by coupling such a noun with such an adjective, analogous or opposite." And these two poets had similar notions of what constituted the beautiful: Poe believed that a certain taint of sadness is "inseparably connected with all the higher manifestations of true beauty"; and Baudelaire defined beauty as "something ardent and sad, something slightly vague, giving conjecture wing. . . . Mystery, regret, are also characteristics of beauty. . . . Mystery, and finally, let me have the courage to confess to what degree I feel myself modern in æsthetics, misfortune. . . . I can scarcely conceive a type of beauty in which there is no misfortune." Here it may be noted that the title of his book, *Les Fleurs du Mal,* might with just as much accuracy be translated "Flowers of Misfortune."

Like Poe, Baudelaire believed that the supernatural was a fundamental literary quality, but to this he added others of which Poe was incapable—irony, macabre humor, qualities few poets other than Baudelaire and Swift have ever got into poetry. On the whole, it has to be said that Poe's influence on Baudelaire's successors, especially on Verlaine and Mallarmé, was greater than ever it was on Baudelaire himself. Baudelaire's intense sympathy and admiration for Poe, a similarity in some of their experiences, in their misfortunes, their poverty, their pursuit of artificial paradises through drugs and drink, a similar breaking away from old literary and social traditions, have caused their names to be joined. But Poe made no such experiments with life as did Baudelaire, who pursued exotic experiences and emotions, whose mind and senses registered a hundred responses to the most common incidents of life, whose senses had a score of points of contact where the average man has only one, and even great poets not many more. The acuteness of his senses and his nerves, his undoubted touch of manic depressiveness, his somewhat pathological concern with remorse, with death, his ennui, his obsession with the tedium of existence, his melancholies, are responsible for the popular attitude towards what was called "la folie Baudelaire." The terrible complexities of a civilization that had grown without the control of man, and without consideration of him, as registered on the mind of one who was one of the most subtle products of that civilization, were expressed in his verse. As both the product and the victim of such a civilization, he expressed its miseries and its despairs at every point at which he touched them, the natural miseries and despairs like death and disaster and balked love, the unnatural ones like corruption and vice, and with them the escape, the search for artificial paradises.

Baudelaire's special use of the word "artificial" has been commonly and perhaps deliberately misunderstood. By it he meant simply a creation of art in contradistinction to the creations of nature. In this he was at the opposite pole from Wordsworth, for whom the artificial was something not only contrary to what was natural but inferior to it. For Baudelaire, to whom the Church's doctrine of original sin was one of the profound ideas that enabled one to understand the universe, the artificial was a discipline by which one improved on nature. He had none of the eighteenth century's belief in the natural goodness of man. Good, he thought, was always the product of art, whereas evil was done naturally without effort. "Analyze," he said, "all that is natural, all the actions and desires of the natural man, and you will find nothing but what is horrible." Virtue for him was artificial and supernatural. Out of his belief in this duality, good and evil, he wrote that sentence since adopted into the philosophy of Paul Valéry and embodied in one of his greatest poems, "Ebauche d'un Serpent": "What is the Fall? What is meant by the Fall? It is unity become duality, it is God who has fallen. In other words, is not creation the Fall of God?"

> Comme las de son pur spectacle,
> Dieu lui-même a rompu l'obstacle
> De sa parfaite éternité;
> Il se fit Celui qui dissipe
> En conséquences, son Principe,
> En étoiles, son Unité.
>
> Cieux, son erreur! Temps, sa ruine!
> Et l'abîme animal, béant! . . .
> Quelle chute dans l'origine
> Etincelle au lieu de néant! . . .

Baudelaire's philosophy, though it included belief in God and, in a bizarre fashion, belief in the Church and the Church's doctrine, was one of profound and even perverse pessimism. Yet no poet has produced a book more profoundly philosophical in the sense of being a vast meditation on life and man and man's miserable fate in the universe, none has produced a book more under the guidance of the intellect, the intellect interwoven with the senses and the emotions. In sheer modernity, expressing the modern world and modern pessimism, no book written since has gone beyond it. It was the first in that genre to which the bulk of the great modern books, whether in verse or in prose, belong— the literature of memory. It was a complete confession, in essence, of all that life, art, love, despair, ennui, had done to a modern man of the subtlest emotions and senses, who could not feel or think except in a complex manner. When he loved, his love had not only, like Catullus's, a mixture of hate, but of a score of other emotions. His concern with life was suffused with a perpetual concern with death; his love of goodness was mixed with a perpetual desire to experiment with evil. Some of his perverse opinions were undoubtedly due to a desire to *épater le bourgeoisie,* or else to that vast ironic attitude, in life and in art, which is the last gift or curse of the gods for the too subtly civilized. The title of his book, *Les Fleurs du Mal,* was adopted with a mixture of irony and of a desire to shock, while at the same time he permitted himself to believe that this provocatively titled volume would bring him and the publisher fame and fortune. Previously he had considered other titles, such as "Les Lesbiennes," "Les Limbes," which were equally calculated to disturb the average reader, and which were even more unrepresentative of the contents of the book as a whole. A friend finally suggested "Les Fleurs du Mal," but as far as the contents were concerned, "Fleurs de Beauté" would have been more accurate.

The provocative title, on a work published in the middle of the nineteenth century, in itself invited attack, though even without the label the courts would probably have prosecuted the author, on religious and moral grounds, for some of the contents. Flaubert got freed by the courts because, after all, there was really nothing in *Madame Bovary* that was uncommon or abnormal, but the sins to which some of Baudelaire's poems were devoted, like "Les Femmes Damnées: Delphine et Hippolyte," "L'Une Qui Est Trop Gaie," were abnormal, and "Le Reniement de Saint Pierre" was regarded as blasphemous. While the prosecution of *Madame Bovary* was the result of nineteenth-century Puritanism, the prosecution of *Les Fleurs du Mal,* or at least the demand for the withdrawal of certain of the poems, was based on a profound instinct of men— the desire to hold on to the slowly and painfully constructed plan of life that humanity has evolved for itself. It is but fair to realize that there can be two attitudes towards a work of art, the attitude of the artist and the attitude of the moralist. A work may be entirely justified in the eyes of the artist and the critic, yet seem unjustifiable to a large section of the people. It is these two attitudes that will be considered in the next chapter.

Chapter Seven

THE TWO CONSCIENCES

I

LITERATURE, like every other art, is produced for a minority of the human race; the masses in any country have no great direct interest in it because they have neither the time nor the vitality, apart altogether from the question as to what proportion of the people have the intellectual or emotional equipment for understanding any art. The vitality of men in the mass is engaged primarily in all the activities and organizations and labors connected with that major concern of humanity, handing life on to others. They are so busy trying to live, trying to earn the necessities, real or imaginary, connected with providing a home and the rearing of offspring, that they have little energy left over for the comprehension of life or of any art. They make the most of what forms of life or art come their way, provided these do not make too great demands on them, preferring those that either give entertainment and recreation, or are a help in the management of their lives. The mass of men, now as always, prefer forms of art related to spectacles, pageants and dramas, such as are given in theatres, or arenas. In certain periods and in certain countries, like ancient Greece or Shakespearian England, the people were better conditioned to the understanding of art, or else were less spoiled and worn out by their occupations, so that the drama produced was great literature written for a people who demanded it and understood it.

Art is the direct concern of only a minority in any country, and it is for this minority that all the books are written, all the pictures painted, and all the music made. There is nothing strange about this: all high products of the human mind, whether science or philosophy or theology, are for minorities and interest the majority only as something that will either amuse them or help them, with the difference that from science they demand some form of material help, from art or literature, as from religion or philosophy, some form of immaterial help—from the one, something for the body; from the other, something for the spirit. Sheer disinterestedness in the pursuit of these occupations is not of any great import to them, for they are engaged in "making the world go round," in the simple living of physical life or that part of it which can be lived according to anybody's potentialities and opportunities. No one can, with any conviction, set about saying whether the majority or the minority is more important in what is termed "the final scheme of things." One only asks that the labors of each be recognized in their place and importance and according to their own rules and laws.

Man, however, to whom material things have such tremendous importance, has nevertheless decided that the human achievements most worthy of remembrance come from the spirit, and these are what the race really values—indeed, it is these that set up the ideal values by which other values are measured. These spiritual achievements are attached to or spring from religion, art, philosophy. Though art and religion and art and philosophy have frequently worked hand in hand, there has never been a time when morals, which is both a branch of religion and a branch of philosophy, has not been at loggerheads with art. This is simply stating that the two main consciences of the human race, the ethical conscience and the æsthetic conscience, contemplate man from standpoints which are often completely incompatible: the ethical conscience contemplates the human passions as moral qualities, the æsthetic conscience, as an array of poetic and psychological powers. The ethical conscience evaluates man not only as a creature of abstract vices and virtues but by the manner in which he fits himself into society and obeys the rules that society has formed for the convenient and orderly arrangement of living; it summarizes man as good or bad, virtuous or vicious, as he keeps these rules and laws and codes. The æsthetic conscience summarizes man as a creature of passions and aspirations the history of which is the history of life itself. Naturally enough, more people understand the ethical conscience in its ordinary every-day manifestation than understand the æsthetic conscience in any manifestation. A man who keeps conscientiously the laws and codes may seem to the every-day ethical conscience a virtuous person, yet the same man may conceivably appear, when viewed by the æsthetic conscience, a very poor creature indeed, bereft of all psychological interest. Morals are the fruit of the ethical conscience, art of the æsthetic conscience; each has its own rules, and while in actual practice neither ethics nor art can be at all times judged exclusively by its separate laws, just as nothing in life can be so judged, it is the desire of every artist that his work should be judged by purely æsthetic laws.

Life is the subject of all the arts, but literature more than any of the others has the power to express life and to be the history of life and human relations. As no definition of literature can be fully explanatory, no apology is made for the numerous definitions or explanations or repetitions that are scattered through these pages. Literature is not, as many professors of it assume, the history of the moral laws man has evolved, or of the regulations he has invented for the control of the passions. It is not the history of the best that has been known and thought in the world: it is, as far as possible, the history of everything that has been known and thought in the world; it is the attempt of man to express all human experiences that have inherent in them sufficient emotion, imagination, vitality to make them significant. All the arts, of course, are an attempt to express human experience, everything that the race and the individual have undergone, but the other arts are limited by the nature of their medium. Brass and marble, paint and canvas limit the life of the work of art expressed in them to the life of the medium; the picture can live only as long as the canvas it is painted on; the sculpture and the monument as long as the marble or the bronze they are made of. But literature is made with words and sounds and these, once recorded, can endure to the limits of time. The artist who chooses to express himself in words has chosen, not only an everlasting medium, but the one most universally understood. Of all the arts it alone is unlimited and has in itself the potentiality of revealing the whole history of man—his emotions, his passions, his longings, ordered or disordered, tutored or untutored, good or bad.

Such a history of life is both disinterested and interested—disinterested in that it is a search for truth, as science is. Its authors are under the necessity of regarding as psychological forces and poetic powers those human passions that are the pivots around which their history moves; they do not regard them merely as moral qualities, in the manner of theologians or moralists. This history of life which is literature is, on the other hand, interested in that it is colored, re-created, re-arranged according to the personality, temperament, intellectual and emotional powers of the recorder. Every work of genius is a new creation, as every human being is, made up of elements of which the material—that is, the external life which the author had to deal with— is one element, and the other the author's individual mind.

2

Art includes both the material and the manner in which the material is worked and used. The most luminous and, at the same time, the most practical definition of art is the one abstracted from scholastic philosophy by the French philosopher Jacques Maritain—"Recta ratio factibilium," which may be freely rendered into English as the right ordering, or the right arrangement of the work to be done or the thing to be made. A book by a popular ephemeral writer might be concerned with the same material as a work by Flaubert or Tolstoy or Hardy, but would not, on that account, be comparable to the work of these great artists, for the popular writers in general have not the emotional, intellectual, or imaginative power to accomplish the right arrangement, the right revelation of the material. In addition to not having the power to produce a work of art, the bulk of the popular writers have not that aim: themselves and their work carefully looked into, it will be found that their aim is to produce a salable article which, in addition to bringing them money, may bring amusement, a sense of well-being, or even of moral uplift, to their readers. It would be difficult to think of such authors producing a work which would not be in response to the desire of a great number of people and agreeable to them in manner and treatment.

On the other hand, it may happen that an artist like Baudelaire, wishing to transmute into poetry his responses to life, to the life he felt urged to live and express, will find that, for the right revelation of the material, he may have to express emotions disagreeable or even shocking to a number of people. Similarly, an artist wishing to create a character like, for example, that of Mrs. Bloom in *Ulysses* may find that for the perfection of his creation, for the right revelation of the character, he has to give her lines of thought and a vocabulary also disagreeable, or even shocking, to a great number of people—so shocking, in fact, that the book is banned in many countries, even though it has attained that highest virtue in the work of an artist, the right revelation of the material. In the case of *Les Fleurs du Mal,* six poems were ordered to be excised by the court. With these cancelled, Baudelaire was still violently attacked for expressing emotions and sensations shared by a great number of human beings.

It can happen also that an artist, a man with a gift for producing a work of art, may, through desire for money or popularity, deliberately omit from his work qualities that are necessary for the right revelation of the material. In that case he is doing what is called prostituting his art, producing something for the greatest entertainment of the greatest number, or pandering to their prejudices.

Often a work of art needs no fight whatever against received ideas or prejudices; opposing received ideas or accepted moralities is, in itself, no sign of originality or artistry; it may in fact be a sign of weak-mindedness or neuroticism. The originality of a work of art is in the material, the ideas, and the just expression of them. The material, the arrangement, and the final form are all inseparably bound together; not the matter alone, or the form, or the style, but all together make a work of literature.

A work of literature is not destined for such or such a particular end, or for such or such a common good of humanity; it is not meant to serve the greatest good of the greatest number; it is its business simply to express the piece of life the author knows or understands, or has discovered, or can reveal. As a scientist cannot be turned away from the pursuit of truth in his discovery, let us say, of the nature of time or the nature of man because he happens to be confronted with the idea that existing knowledge will receive a dangerous shock or existing notions will be dangerously uprooted, so an artist cannot allow himself to be turned from the pursuit of truth as he sees it by the notion that the way he sees it is not for the happiness or the well-being of his fellow men. He has to make his work as sincere and as fine as he can, without allowing other provinces of human achievement to shove their laws or rules onto him. Pure literature, therefore, can never be propaganda, for propaganda is the turning aside of literature from the expression of life, which is its field, to the praise or advertisement of some policy, some endeavor, some side line of life, which may represent a public good. It is the subjection of one form of human endeavor to another, and frequently in practice is the submission of men of mind to men of action. Some great literary artists have applied themselves to propaganda of a kind and become pamphleteers, but it is not for the object of the propaganda they are remembered but for some revelation of life that they could not help but give. The right of any artist to work according to the eternal laws of his art does not at all imply that any public, if it is so moved, cannot criticize harshly, and condemn as much as it pleases, a work of art. The right of the public to condemn the work of an artist is as valid as the right of the artist to produce it, but no more valid. No public or law ought, in a civilized country, to have the right to suppress or destroy a work of art, although it has the right to censure and condemn it, or even, in cases, to limit its circulation.

In the case of *Les Fleurs du Mal,* the order of the court to excise from the next edition particular poems, six of them, might be regarded as justifiable from the point of view of the general public and its *mores.* But what really aroused hostility to the book was not these incidental poems but the whole startling newness in literature of the material that the author welded into poetry. He was attacked most frequently for expressing emotions and tendencies, nervousnesses and morbidities, transitory movements of the soul, common to at least half of mankind.

Works of art are attacked by the general public for one thing mainly—freedom or frankness in treating matters connected with sexual relations. They are commonly attacked by philosophers and theologians if they display subversive tendencies in politics or religion. Sometimes they are attacked for what is called false logic, from the idea that what is logically sound or dialectically proved must be true in life—an idea contradicted by experience. However, most of these attacks and criticisms are perfectly legitimate. The public in all periods has objected to descriptions of emotions connected with sexual relationships, and for the psychologically sound reason that for only a small proportion of the human race has the sex relation in itself been a poetical and transforming experience. The vast majority think, and have always thought, that all manifestations of sex love, except such as take place within legal or conventionally arranged bonds, represent an undignified, if not a low form of animal life, and that sex is a dignified experience only when settled down and veiled with domestic affection, with a legal relationship for the woman and children. As nudity was supposed to suggest sex, nudes have been very generally disapproved of. One must remember that Michelangelo's statue of the naked young David was as gravely attacked in the Italy of his time as any piece of frank contemporary art by Anglo-Saxon Puritans.

Man has arrived but slowly at the conception of love, as he has arrived but slowly at thought, and only a minority understands either one or the other of these, the most ecstatic and at the same time the most profoundly mournful experiences of humanity. Every one has the right to defend his own comprehension or lack of comprehension of them, the ordinary man as much as the artist or thinker. If the artist has a right to choose any material he wishes and the right to employ every means he can to make a lasting thing and to defend it, the public also has the same right to defend what it has made, its rules and regulations for the convenient conduct of life. One must remember that there are many battles to which there can be no end, which in their very nature must be perpetual. There have to be such conflicts; if there were not, the world would become static and in a static world both art and morality would lose their meaning.

Chapter Eight

THE RUSSIAN CONTRIBUTION TO
REALISM

I

IN THE MIDDLE of the nineteenth century realism was definitely in the public domain and it still had half a century or so of inspiration-giving power before it grew away from the men of genius and down to the men of talent. One must remember, however, that realism in literature was in the main limited to that comparatively new form, the novel, and to the drama: realism in poetry, what there is of it, is in descent from Wordsworth and Baudelaire; it made but limited head-way, though in our own time it has influenced several schools of poetry. Making poetry out of every-day life, making it realistic, was always destined to be a rare achievement, attainable in the isolated poems of a few poets. The literary genre that was easiest to make the vehicle of the realistic doctrine was the novel, and so it was the novelists, chiefly, who proceeded to put into practice the Taine dictum—to note facts, to choose important and significant ones, and to circumstantiate them fully. The author, in short, began to keep a notebook and to set down all his observations and experiences of every-day life, and from this notebook procedure came the bulk of our great realistic novels, short stories and plays. For a time, all other theories of art were displaced by this new one, which set out to show "real" life in literature. It was in vain that certain writers pleaded that other theories of art had at least equal validity and that which of them he gave allegiance to depended on the writer's temperament.

The doctrine of realism spread quickly from one literature to another until it took in all the literature-producing countries of Europe, with one great exception. Pure realism made little and spasmodic advance in England, where literature has always been predominantly romantic, or, to apply one of the terms that Zola used to denote a literature opposite to realism—idealistic. It would almost seem as if any other type of literature was alien to England, where the classicism of the eighteenth century was no more than an interregnum, and realism, with some few exceptions, something brought in by the outside writers of English, like the Irish or the Americans. It should be noted, however, that whereas George Moore is generally regarded as the first realistic novelist in English, actually the first realistic English novel written was Samuel Butler's *The Way of All Flesh,* which was not published until after the author's death. But the most romantic

THE RUSSIAN CONTRIBUTION TO REALISM

English literature always had enough common humanity to make a literary revolution uncalled for. In the
highest realism there has to be romanticism, for that is
natural to human life and human imagination.

Is it possible to give a definition of realism in literature? No single definition, of course, can be fully explanatory, but realism may be described as the attempt
to give a reproduction of life as actually lived by the
average person, or by what, in the author's experience,
is the average person, and it was the natural accompaniment in literature of the new scientific discoveries
that rocked the world in the nineteenth and the beginning of the twentieth century—in fact, the literary
doctrine of the new material civilization which had
been given the world by science. It was in the early
nineteenth century that it first seemed credible that
the experimental study of facts, of data, would in the
end explain everything—man, nature, God and the
universe—that it would not only explain everything but
bestow everything humanity longed for—happiness,
health, security. Facts, which began by being the matter of science, proceeded to become the matter of literature, and Taine with his doctrine of the "little facts"
became, from about 1865, the most celebrated and influential of the legislators of ideas.

The great realists and semi-realists—Balzac, Gogol,
Dickens, Thackeray, Flaubert, Turgenev, Dostoevsky,
Tolstoy, Ibsen, Zola—were all living at the same

time and were not too far apart in age; all of them, except Balzac, being born in the beginning of the nineteenth century, all of them, except Tolstoy and Zola, in the first quarter of it. It is safe to say that every one of them was influenced by Balzac, and that, in spite of differences of talents and temperaments, they have in common the desire to depict life as it presented itself to them, and men and women as they knew them. Balzac, Dickens and Gogol, the great semi-realists, had this intention, as well as the other realists, but when they sat down to write, the marvels and wonders of the world they could invent would sometimes sweep the every-day world from their minds, and the whims and oddities of the human beings with whom their imaginations teemed would overshadow the common every-day personages in their pages; they created worlds that touched the real world at points, sometimes firmly, sometimes hardly at all, but which were more fascinating to their readers than the every-day world, giving them both the desired contact with it and a desired escape from it. In point of time, the earlier of the great novelists were the semi-realists, who carried over from older literary doctrine certain conventions of structure and character but who also possessed a good deal of the abundance and extravagance of temperament characteristic of the romantic side of the movement. Balzac, Dickens and Gogol satisfied their minds and imaginations by putting things into their books in the excessive measure which it would have pleased them to find in actual life, and in this way they were related to the great romantics. Balzac's personages, their emotions and actions, were, as has been said in a previous chapter, exaggerated to the point of being larger than life. He patterned them on what he encountered in the real world, but he made them more gigantic, more marvellous. The characters of Dickens and Gogol, both writers of less tremendous genius than Balzac, were exaggerated, not in the sense of being made larger than life, but of being caricatured; they were given traits more grotesque, more humorous, more pathetic than actual people had. These three representatives of different literatures were all prodigious creators, men of indeliberate genius, not always careful in their workmanship, not always conscious of what they were doing, as were the bulk of the more thoroughgoing realists who came later. But the thorough realists, those who created people life-sized, were sometimes regretful that the Time-spirit, or their own temperament, trimmed their talents. "Some things," said Flaubert, "I can do better than Hugo; some better than Balzac; some better than Rabelais. But I lack their thrusts of power beyond the reach of conscious art."

2

Although realism spread rapidly through the literatures of Europe, there were two countries that stood out from the others in the production of the realistic novel—France and Russia. The French and the Russians, with marked differences in the type of novel they produced, became the masters of all the others; developments of the realistic novel, which might have been distinguished in many countries, were dwarfed by the achievements of the Russians, Turgenev, Dostoevsky, Tolstoy, and by the technique and the doctrines of the French. The new movement in literature, especially the realistic side of it, awoke Russia into conscious and extensive expression. The romantic side had little soil to take root in, although Byron and the German romantics had had their effect. It was about 1840 that Carlyle uttered his famous sentence, "Russia has not spoken," though, unknown to him, there had been several remarkable writers, including the great Pushkin. But when Russia finally spoke out strongly enough to make all Europe listen to her voice, it was with the tongue of realism. Turgenev, Dostoevsky, Tolstoy, with a bound, brought Russia and Russian psychology into the consciousness of Western Europe, and their names became household words and their works so widely read that people all over the world began to speak of the characters in their books, as they spoke of the characters in Dickens and in Balzac. Turgenev was a sort of half-way house to the comprehension of the others: he was half way between the French objective novel and the Russian analytical one. More Western in his outlook, he provided a halting-place for the mind before it could encompass Tolstoy and Dostoevsky, writers immensely different from those of the West. One who had read *A Nest of Gentlefolk,* or *On the Eve,* or *Smoke,* had, as it were, the necessary groundwork of Russian literature and psychology to get on with *The Brothers Karamazov,* or *War and Peace,* or *Resurrection.*

Russia, which had been regarded contemptuously as a barbarous country that could be symbolized by an English poet as "the bear that walks like a man," broke into expression, in the complacent Victorian age, in a startling manner. The Russians who were putting forth novels seemed not only men of vast imagination and intellectual powers, but the diversity and complexity of their emotions, their experience of life and humanity, the profound level at which they themselves had lived before writing at all, made the Western writers seem a little complacent, or, to use a word that was then generally coming in, bourgeois. They were, in addition, all melodramatic; none of them, not even Turgenev, had the Western objection to striking an emotion on its topmost note. Tolstoy, in *Resurrection* and *Anna Karenina,* could write scenes parallel to those in *L'Education Sentimentale,* or in *Madame Bovary,* with an intensity, with a pity mixed with moral ardor, with a high coloring, that made the Western novel seem too restrained. The Goncourts' complaint that language and literature had been made by men who were too healthy and well-balanced could never, after Dostoevsky, seem such a valid criticism as before, for the characters in his books were sick in body and mind, and a touch of madness seemed to the author to be the norm of humanity. His people felt no emotion in its singleness; they loved where they hated and hated where they loved; they were cruel and pitying, fearful and ecstatic, all at the same time. Yet whatever they felt they felt with such intensity, such diversity and complexity, that they seemed to embody all the emotions and fears of mankind.

The manner in which a modern literature began in Russia was parallel to the way it began in Germany, though the Russians had no such literary past as Germany, just as Germany had no such literary past as France, England, Spain, and Italy. The first great influence in starting a modern literature in Russia came from her great monarch Catherine, who corresponded to Frederick the Great in being one of the psychic forces that brought about the expression, in literature, of a nation. Like Frederick, Catherine wrote in French because the culture of her educated subjects, the culture of the aristocracy, was French. Like Frederick she was a great admirer of Voltaire, and like him also she encouraged pseudo-classical writing in imitation of the French, so that it was not surprising that in Russia, as in Germany before Lessing, literature and French classicism seemed almost interchangeable terms. But Catherine had a wider knowledge of Western literature than had Frederick; her mind was more open to the currents that were coming in; intellectually she belonged to a later age. She set up a corps of translators to put Western works into Russian, and she herself set about providing the Russian stage with a repertoire of plays from her own pen, imitating any playwright whose works came into her mind at the moment, Shakespeare, Molière or Voltaire. That her mind was more awake to the age that was coming in is shown by the fact that whereas Frederick had Voltaire at his court, Catherine had Diderot, to whom so many modern ideas can be traced. However, about the time of the French Revolution the Empress's ardor for things French dampened considerably, partly because of the effects of the Revolution, partly because, with all her Liberalism, she was an absolute monarch, and partly because a strong wind of ideas, ever increasing in force, was coming from Germany. The success of Lessing and Herder in ridding Germany of French classical and pseudo-classical influence, in initiating a new order of literary ideas, and in starting a German national literature, made itself felt in Russia, reinforcing the desire for a Russian national literature. Those two ideas of Lessing, then so fresh and vital, that literature was national and racial expression and that it should reflect contemporary life, quickly made headway in Russia and went in with the newborn Slavophile movement which was attracting the devotion of the young intellectuals and writers. Russian students in German universities returned with the works of the new German literature in their baggage, and, what was even more important, with the works of the philosopher Hegel.

Catherine herself lived long enough to hear of what was happening in Germany; she was a German herself. As she corresponded to Frederick, so the Russian critic, Belinsky, corresponded to Lessing, in the rôle he played in a dawning national literature. Without a knowledge of the Russian language we are in no position to appraise the importance that has been claimed for Belinsky in Russian thought and Russian progress generally. But there seems to be no doubt that his was one of the shaping minds of the nineteenth century. He held many conflicting literary theories from time to time, but the literature he understood thoroughly, by temperament, was the literature of realism. He knew that his was the age of realism in literature, and the literary form he understood and advanced was the novel. If the new national literature of Germany took shape in poetry and drama, the new national literature of Russia took shape in the realistic novel. Belinsky made no mistake in this: he knew that realism had an affinity with the Russian spirit; he had qualities by no means universal among important critics, a power of stirring up a ferment of creative activity and a sound sense of the value of the work produced in his own time. When Dostoevsky's first book, *Poor Folk,* written at the age of twenty-two, reached Belinsky's editorial desk, he saw, through all its faults, the great writer, the mighty genius, who was making his beginnings, and the enthusiasm of Belinsky's praise was said to have made the young Dostoevsky intolerably vain for a while.

Like all the men of outstanding mentality in the beginning of the nineteenth century, Belinsky's mind was roused by Hegel, and like most of them, he was able to find a backing in Hegel's philosophy for his own ideas, even when he switched from one line of thought to another. The Hegelian "concrete reality," the Hegelian "reality in experience" became for him the philosophic support of the literary doctrine of real ism. Very familiar with the literature and literary doctrines of the West, he thoroughly accepted de Staël's conception of literature as an expression of society; like hers, his understanding of poetry, in spite of, in later life, an appreciation of Pushkin, seems to have been incomplete.

Belinsky gave the writers grouped around him a philosophy, ideas that roused their creative power and afforded a focus for their work. The dominating idea of his critical work was that reality, for a writer, was to be found in the life, the problems, the events, the people of his own time. It was a program that was

bound to have the maximum influence on his contemporaries. This critic was essentially a man of his
own time, understanding really, perhaps, only the tendencies, scientific, social and literary, that were potent
in his own time. He died before the century in which
he was born was half way through, having fostered
and cherished most of the great Russians of his day.
Belinsky's mind finally hardened into something very
like the conclusion that the function of literature was
to serve society and to help solve social and political
problems. This sort of attitude is really indigenous to
the Russian mind; afterwards, it reached its most noble
as well as its most absurd expression in Tolstoy's *What
Is Art?*, where all the literature that does not propa-
gate directly the ideal of human brotherhood is considered wanting and where the bulk of the great artists
of the time are arraigned because they do not conform
to the ideals of Tolstoy's later period. Belinsky's special
conception of the social function of literature, reinforced by Tolstoy's, grew to be a sort of canon with
a later school of writers and is the basis, with some even
the total doctrine, of what has come in our day to be
called "Marxist" literary criticism.

There have not been wanting recent Russian critics
who hold that the social doctrines of Belinsky were
mainly responsible for the decline of Russian literature
that came about after the passing of the great realists.
With them, the social doctrines had been mingled with

the moral doctrines of Christianity, especially with those that had to do with atonement and expiation, the equality of souls and the brotherhood of man. On such subjects, if he is a great genius, a writer can be didactic without any deep injury to his work, because invariably his power of giving spontaneous life to his characters is in the ascendant. The urge to be preachers, not uncommon in writers, was strong in the Russians. Even in the case of a great genius like Tolstoy, whose gift might be supposed to be powerful enough to carry it along, the didacticism is too evident, so that the second part of *Resurrection* reads like a tract dealing with atonement and expiation.

All the great Russian realistic novels—the very greatest are Turgenev's *Fathers and Sons*, Dostoevsky's *The Brothers Karamazov,* Tolstoy's *War and Peace*—came after *Madame Bovary,* but not one of them equalled it in technical perfection, or in the perfectly convincing feeling that real every-day life was being depicted; we believe in Flaubert's novel completely, from start to finish, as in something that has happened since the world began and will go on happening until its end. But in details the Russians made a deeper penetration into life, even if all around they were not so convincing. They were not hampered by Western conventions of life or art, and before they wrote their greatest work they had seen forms of life, experienced forms of emotion, closed to the Western mind. Life had touched them all at so many points before they set themselves to produce their masterpieces that, in comparison with their immense human experience, the bulk of Western writers seemed to have led the existence of small-town bourgeoisie.

The life around the Russian writers was touched with the barbaric, the savage and the cruel, yet all of them, in spite of serfdom and feudalism, particularly Tolstoy, gave the impression of being intimate with all sorts and conditions of men. They were so sensitized to experience that they gave the impression of feeling with their intellects and thinking with their hearts. Of Dostoevsky it has been said that he felt ideas as others feel cold or hunger or thirst: more than this, his senses responded to ideas as those of others did to passions. In his case, we wonder, not so much that he was psychopathic and subject to fits of epilepsy, as that he ever had the strength to assume the responsibilities of existence, the fortitude and endurance to work so hard and to produce so many masterpieces after his shaking experiences. The author of the first realistic novel, Flaubert, also an epileptic, lived a carefully guarded life, away from the battle, with an assured income on which to do his books and put his literary theories in practice; as he said himself, he knew life by tasting it a little and ruminating on it a lot. It was very different with the Russians; even Turgenev, the gentlest of them, gave to his French writer-friends the impression of a man with an immense background of experience. Dostoevsky had all the harassments that make up the life of a writer who lives by the sweat of his brain on advances from editors: he had to have work in at fixed periods and had not always time to write with careful art. In addition to disturbing if illuminating love affairs and two marriages, he spent years as a political prisoner in Siberia, having been at first condemned to death only to be reprieved at the last moment as he was standing in his shirt waiting to be executed. When he was in his teens his father had been murdered by serfs: this episode may have been responsible for his interest in murder, and the marvellous intuition in depicting incentives to murder, displayed in his two great books, *The Brothers Karamazov* and *Crime and Punishment*. With all this, he himself was subject to a practically uncontrollable temptation to gamble, to satisfy which he would sometimes pledge everything he and his wife had.

Tolstoy had as wide a life experience as Dostoevsky, though it went along different paths altogether. As a young man he lived a life not unlike Byron's and went in for what he conceived to be the natural existence of a young aristocrat, satisfying all his desires, which included women, drinking, gambling, and hunting. Being both more of a sensualist and more of a puritan than Dostoevsky, every passion satisfied brought sooner or later an immense moral crisis in his life. He fought through the Crimean War, where he was able to note all the psychological motives that possess men on the battlefield, motives which he afterwards developed into his great novel, *War and Peace*. A man of great genius and great atonements, he was composed of a number of contradictory personalities, but at the same time, as a writer, a leader, a prophet and a preacher, he was the most towering personality in modern literature.

3

The impact of the Russian novel had significant effects on Western literature; it saved the realistic novel, at its greatest period, anyhow, from becoming an indictment of mankind, an attack and a denigration. The discoveries of science had diminished man's place in the universe; Taine and the whole philosophy of determinism and materialism were situating him in the animal world; the later minor realists were bent on diminishing him more and more. But the immense sympathy and dynamic emotional characterization of the Russians, their faith in mankind in spite of sins, crimes and crazinesses, gave a new scope to the realistic movement, helped, in fact, to make it one of the really great movements in literature. Raskolnikoff, in *Crime and Punishment,* might be a half-crazed, hallucinated creature; Prince Muishkine, in *The Idiot,* might be a moron and an epileptic; the brothers Karamazov might be all deranged; but nevertheless they were subtle creations of the spirit, far above the brute-beasts to which the later realists degraded men and women. Tolstoy's heroes, the most realistic men in literature, were all conceived on a high plane, caring intensely for moral perfection and struggling unceasingly towards it; they were very different from the males of almost purely physiological reactions who came to be the standard characters in the decline of realism.

But it was not only the content and personages of the Russian novel that had a vast influence: the technique played a great rôle in the evolution of the present-day novel. The Russians knew French literature and French technical developments well; they not only read Balzac, Flaubert and Hugo, who were the vogue, but we know that Tolstoy studied the work of a writer whose vogue did not come in until much later, Stendhal, whose *Le Rouge et Le Noir* and *Chartreuse de Parme* influenced his *War and Peace*. Turgenev was an intimate of the great French realists, not only of Flaubert, but of the Goncourts and Zola. They took what they needed from the discoveries of the French realists, but what they took they gave back in new combinations. One outstanding characteristic, however, of the Western novel, its narrative construction, they treated with scant respect; the Aristotelian and classical ideal, that a work should have a beginning, a crisis and a conclusion, was no appreciable part of the Russian literary canon. Instead of rising to a crisis, as in *Madame*

Bovary, the Russian novels had a way of beginning with a crisis, and very often they had no conclusion in the Western sense at all. Then, instead of being all-knowing creators making disclosures about their characters, the authors gave the impression that their knowledge of the characters was not something fixed but something unfolding; they built them up with happenings, emotions and background, so that we got to know them gradually as we get to know people in life; in any chapter the personages might surprise us with something unexpected. Instead of description, the Russians, particularly Dostoevsky, went in for evocation—that is, instead of laying out before us the scene or the character, they evoked them in the manner since made familiar to us by very modern writers. All of them, but Dostoevsky markedly, dealt with the unconscious springs of action in personality in a new way: they were all, probably, aware of contemporary psychological findings, and Tolstoy shows in his books an acquaintance with the recent discoveries of the then well-known French psychologist, Charcot. The devices by which the subconscious groundwork of a personality is suggested, the psychological exploration taking the place of narrative development, the use of characters and episodes that had not much connection with the main theme but which revealed some spring of personality, and, finally, the inconclusive ending, all played a revolutionary part, for good or for ill, in the technique of the novel as we know it in our own day. But with all this, the primary influence, and the most widespread, remained that of Flaubert; the realistic novel in general so thoroughly kept to the Flaubert model, and especially to the pattern that is in *Madame Bovary*, that the modern novel, except as written by certain recent innovators, is, and has to be thought of as, the Flaubertian novel.

In less than half a century after the publication of *Madame Bovary* all the outstanding realistic novels had been written; the movement swept through the literatures of the world bringing the novel form into great popularity, a sort of popularity that often had but little to do with literary value. It is noticeable that the movement was in its decline, and that the reaction against it had set in, before the realistic novel had made its appearance in English. It is highly probable that Samuel Butler's *The Way of All Flesh* was the first written, in point of date, at the high mark of Flaubert's influence, but the first realistic novels actually given to the public were those of George Moore, who modelled his work by turns on Flaubert, the Goncourts and Zola. In America, the first realistic novel, Dreiser's *Sister Carrie*, did not appear until 1907.

Chapter Nine

THE DECLINE

I

A LITERARY PRINCIPLE is the sharp crystallization of a number of related impulses and tendencies and gropings towards a new kind of literary expression. No literary principle is ever new in the sense that it has not appeared in literature before in some subsidiary and unchallenging way. It is only that an age comes which picks out and focuses attention on a facet of expression that is suited to its needs. The principle of realism was the sharp crystallization into one point, of the impulses, tendencies and gropings towards the expression of every-day life and modern man. Romanticism and realism represented different groupings of the same related impulses; they did not represent disparate movements but were component parts of the same modern movement. A literary principle should not be confounded with literary opinions which, of necessity, are ephemeral; a principle is something lasting, in the sense that once it is developed it will always exist even though newer and later developed principles may bring

240

about a revaluation of the older ones. Romanticism and realism, for example, which displaced in most modern literatures what was called classicism or pseudo-classicism, have implicit in them a great many of the characteristics and forms of the principles they had displaced. Romanticism, which has been defined as a form of literature in which lyricism dominates—this like every other literary definition is too limited—was merely emphasizing a tendency that was part of Greek classical literature, the lyric tendency. And the form of the bulk of the realistic novels, like the form of *Madame Bovary,* was classical; it followed the old classical formula with its beginning, its crisis, and its conclusion—the form of the old classical plays and the old tales. The plot on such lines, inherited from the older literature, started the notion that the realistic novel was not realistic enough. In the latter part of the nineteenth century the new realistic theorists declared that such a plot, that any plot, was an imposition upon the novel and the short story, and should not be used at all. The plot was actually an encumbrance, in revealing the life of an average human being. After all, it was maintained, the life of such a person has no great crises or excitements; he very seldom has a story; the story is merely a literary convention. The life of the average human being is generally only a string of banal events which have no particular consequences, none of the developments nor the coincidences which the novelist, even the realistic novelist, imposes on his characters. The real art of the novel and the short story should be to present every-day life, which is in the main mediocre, neither especially interesting nor uninteresting, more likely to be ugly than beautiful.

The matter proper to a novel should be "a slice of life," and this "slice" need not have beginning, middle or end, as ordinary careers have no real beginning, middle or end. Neither should this "slice" be about an extraordinary happening in the experiences of a character, since extraordinary happenings in life were so exceptional that to deal with them in literature would contravene the realistic effect. It would likewise be a great mistake to go in for writing about great emotions—ordinary people did not have them. The thing to do was to study scientifically the physical state which gave the impression or the illusion of an emotion. Remorse, for example, was not an emotion; remorse was a disease, and should be studied physiologically. There were a number of theorists who wanted love treated in the same way.

Some of the above theories or some facets of them were, of course, Flaubert's also, especially that concerning the avoidance in art of the extraordinary, of extraordinary people or extraordinary happenings. "I avoid," he said, "the accidental and the dramatic. . . . I try to stick to the greatest generalities; no extraordinary people, no heroes." But many of the realistic developments and the realistic theories he, as an artist, could never accept, for he looked upon them as something alien to art. Nearly twenty years after the publication of *Madame Bovary* he was roused to write: "I curse what they agree to call realism, though they make me one of its high priests. . . . The people that I see often [the Goncourts and Zola were his intimates] cultivate all that I scorn and are indifferently disturbed by what torments me. . . . I am seeking above all for beauty, which my companions pursue but languidly."

The truth was that already in the lifetime of the master the decline had set in. What was happening to the doctrine of realism is what happens to every idea once powerful in the world—it began at a high level, rose in the work of its greatest practitioners to a distinguished development; then it began to deteriorate to a type of writing that expressed only the side of people susceptible to external observation. Every new member of the realistic school—and some of them, to Flaubert, regarded as the founder of it, were not writers at all—developed a few theories of his own. The attaching to literature of scientific and medical theories went further and further. The neo-realists decided that the realism of *Madame Bovary* and *L'Education Sentimentale* was not scientific enough or physiological enough, though their author had devoured medical literature for all it could tell him of soul and body and their disorders, and though he had submitted all his characters to physiological and psychological examination. But Flaubert made no bones about saying that though he regarded accuracy in technical details, in local exactness, the precise side of things—in fact, observation—as important, yet it was only of secondary importance.

2

As the progress of the realistic novel followed the same path in every country, even in those countries where its appearance was comparatively recent, a general description of its course is applicable to every literature. The æsthetic on which the new literary doctrines were based, and which was displacing the old æsthetic of the beautiful, held that nothing human was alien to literature, and with this in the forefront of their minds the writers evolved more and more theories. The French were the most unmitigated theory-spinners and *nomenclateurs* of all. As soon as they evolved a theory they proceeded to attach a new name to it, with the result that any petty movement, in the shape of a reaction against realism or a development of it or a degradation of it, was given a new title, and new *isms* and *ists* were manufactured for every phase. "Things have to be given new names," Zola explained, "so that the public will think they are new," and this was said when he tried to replace the name Realism with the older name Naturalism. But every theory in connection with realism has had a persistent if fevered life and is in circulation all the time, for the reason that realism opened the way for a rush of people into writing who could previously have had no place at all there.

The general theorizing started with the question, What has not yet been expressed in literature? Among other things, it was obvious that, owing to the older ideals of the spiritual and emotional content of literature, the physiological side of man had not been given any great rôle, and that what were called "the lower classes" had had very little showing. After all, the neo-realists argued, one did not ordinarily meet doctors' adulterous wives or young gentlemen of independent means, any more than one met Walter Scott's heroes or heroines, or Balzac's millionaire misers. The ordinary person was none of these; the ordinary person was the working man or the working woman; the "fact," the great, the significant "fact" that the older realists were leaving out of account, was that ordinary life was the life of the greatest number; consequently, the proper subject for literature was the life of the populace, or, as we should name them in present-day parlance, the proletariat.

The Goncourts were the first experimenters in the proletarian novel, and Zola and his followers, in addition, set about revealing the physiological man, and what they called "the fœtid and palpitating sources of life." The Goncourts put forward both a literary and a social reason for tackling the working classes in literature. Living in the nineteenth century in a time of universal suffrage, of democracy, of liberalism, in a country without caste or legal aristocracy, could the people, they asked—the lower class, that world under a world—be ignored any longer by writers? Tragedy, an art form belonging to a dead society, might not in itself be dead. It might now, instead of dealing, according to the Aristotelian convention, with people above the common and with actions of magnitude—it might deal with the little miseries of the poor, in the new expanding form of the novel. The Goncourts made no pretense of thinking that their novels of the working class would be read by the working class—no, their novels of the *canaille* would let the upper classes know how the majority lived. As for themselves, they were, as they said, gentlemen, attracted—they surmised frankly enough—to lower forms of civilization as to something exotic; interested, by way of contrast to their own lives, in those of the *basses classes,* their radicalism, their working-class sympathy being, as it were, a reaction against their own genteelnesses and delicacies. As a relief from taking notes about the working classes and delving into facts, into real life, they took refuge, as another form of reaction, in the study of delicate Oriental art. They were very careful of their style, which they tried to make artistic and striking, experimenting with grammar, with phrases and sentences, to make language more suitable for expressing the sick, the miserable, the hallucinated, the debilitated people of modern life. Like all the other realists, they made perpetual appeal to science and demanded that the novel be "scientific," based on a careful study of facts and documents. They put into general circulation expressions such as "human document," "reportage," to describe the type of writing they would have take the place of the novel of romance and adventure and what they called "anodyne and consoling works."

Zola, the youngest of the first group of realists—he died at the beginning of the present century—enthusiastically attached himself to all these theories, and after stewing them around in his own mind, and adding a few more to them, put the lot forth in a form which is still popular and which we are likely to hear, in some shape, at all discussions of "proletarian" literature. He attached himself to Taine's literary doctrines, and took over Taine's particular psychological determinism; he believed that he was incorporating Taine's ideas in his practice of the novel, especially in the Rougon-Macquart series, in which he claimed to encompass "the natural and social history of a family under the Second Empire." This family was composed of the descendants of a neurotic and delinquent woman by a healthy husband and an alcoholic lover, and the volumes of the series were supposed to exhibit scientifically and clinically the effects of heredity and of "the race, milieu and moment."

More voluminously than any writer before or since, Zola filled notebooks with "the little significant facts, minutely noted and amply circumstantiated."

Taine had written a famous essay in which he had agreed with Balzac's own thesis that a novelist should deal with men and women as a naturalist with animals and plants, and he had put into currency the expression "naturalism" to describe this new practice of literature and the new literature itself. But with Zola the expression came to include things that had not gone into the Balzac *Comédie Humaine,* and especially the "physiological man." He considered himself Balzac's successor and accepted eagerly the conclusions that Balzac had extracted from Buffon, that there is only one animal, that man is a variety of it; therefore, the revelation of the human animal was the all-important affair for the new novelists, the naturalists. Given a puissant man, Zola postulated, and an unassuaged woman, the problem is to find the animal in them, even to find only the animal. Finding the animal in man soon came to be looked on as an end to be worked towards, and it was not long until the conclusion was reached that as the real man, the natural man, was the physiological man, the ultimate in naturalism was to be found, not in the lowest social and economic order, to which the great number belonged, but to the lowest moral order. To depict the lives of rudderless men and women, their miseries, their follies, their passions, "feeble but uncontrollable," to use a phrase of Doctor Carrel's, their vices, their trickery, their inability to cope with life except by ruses—this became one of the aims of the neo-realists. The more brutal, the more revolting, the facts, the more they dealt with the waifs and strays of society, the better material they were considered for literature.

The physiological man was deemed such an important subject that Zola annexed the realm of medicine to the novel, and as Balzac had attached his speculations to the discoveries in natural history and the animal realm of Buffon the naturalist, so Zola attached his speculations to the findings of the medical scientist, Claude Bernard. His gifts as a novelist entitle Zola to a place among the great realists, for when he got down to writing his talents got the better of his more extreme theories, yet in comparison with his great predecessors his intellectual and reasoning power was limited: his attempts to attach science to literature and to make literature scientific frequently resulted in fantastic conclusions, all of which, however, were swallowed eagerly by his followers. Claude Bernard had discussed experimental medicine; Zola proceeded to discourse on the experimental novel, attaching to it all the phraseology that Bernard had used about medicine, and announcing, "Since medicine, which is an art, is becoming a science, why should not literature also become a science, by means of the experimental method? . . . We naturalistic novelists submit each fact to the test of observation and experiment." The novelist experimented on dangerous sores that were poisoning society; in the same way as the "scientific" doctor he tried to find the initial causes. By pursuing this method the realists would construct in time what Zola called a "practical sociology" and their work would be an aid to political and social science; they would thus be "among the most useful and the most moral workers in the human workshop." Finally, he summed up what was to be the result of this moral work—"to regulate life, to regulate society, to solve in time all the problems of Socialism . . . when society becomes putrified, when the social machine gets out of order, the rôle of the observer and thinker is to note each new sore, each unexpected shock. . . . We are living in the ruins of a world, our duty is to study the ruins."

It was in vain, as far as Zola's followers in every country were concerned, for gentlemen in the higher courts of literature to maintain that devotion to such subjects was not likely to result in literature—his followers for the most part were not much concerned about literature, anyhow. Zola went ahead. He uttered pronunciamentoes in a style imitated from Taine's more dramatic declarations. "Finding the formula of the thing" was one of Taine's well-known approaches to the solution of difficult problems, and this, together with the observation of the "little facts," was assumed by his disciples to be a technique for solving riddles of all kinds as well as illumining obscurities. Zola cast around for a formula that would describe the new literature and make its aims clear: he said he had extracted it or evolved it from a reading of *L'Education Sentimentale*. "Naturalism," he announced, "is a formula of modern science applied to literature." This was received as an illumination and it had the advantage that it could be re-arranged, without changing it much, to fit any new notions that might come in. His German disciples were soon able to improve on the famous definition. In Germany, French influence, which Herder and Lessing had banished, came back with a rush; Flaubert, Maupassant, Zola—all the French realists —made a new conquest of German literary thought, as they did of Italian literary thought, but no writer rose out of it who could be compared with the great French or Russian realists. It was noticeable that the German trend, for the most part, was towards Zolaism and naturalism, the Italian trend towards Flaubertian realism. The manifesto of the Italian realists—they called themselves the Verists—put forward by Giovanni Verga, was completely derived from Flaubert.

In Germany, along with the influence of the new scientific discoveries, there was being developed a sort of scientific sociology and political economy, all owing much to English and French thought. The outstanding figures connected with these developments were Lasalle and Marx, and, affected by these, Zola's German followers were able to recast the formula; it became in turn a formula of modern sociology or a formula of modern politics applied to literature. Except for Gerhardt Hauptmann, whose work, however, belongs more closely to our own time, the bulk of the German realists were minor practitioners of Zola's doctrine, and their work suffered, to quote Professor J. R. Robertson, from a "too exclusive application to the lower life of the great cities and from a tendency to exploit the proletariat in the interest of radical political doctrine." That Zola himself was familiar with the Communist Manifesto and the writings of Engels and Marx on the class struggle in France, and on the new materialism, is clear from the enthusiastic if somewhat hashed version of their doctrine which he was able to attach to his conception of the naturalistic novel. He hated not only the bourgeoisie but the socially ascendant classes of all kinds; only the workingman, the proletariat, the people, had virtue, goodness and true appreciation; the upper classes were wicked, cruel, obtuse, without real understanding. As he usually did, he forgot such theories when he sat down to write, and he has left delineations of the working class and the peasants that are devastating. Nevertheless, he was for every political idea that had for aim the augmenting of the people's power.

Zola's convictions were powerful, more powerful than his reasoning powers, his sympathies warm and generous; he was for everything that he believed would tend towards the general good. His political and social passions—he was a republican, a socialist, a communist, and an anti-cleric, in the fashion of these things sixty years ago—his discourses on how writing could help society were at least as responsible for his large following as were the literary value of his novels, the lyricism and imaginative power of which were beyond the appreciation of a good portion of his public. It was the very part of his theories that flew away from him when he started to write his novels, that had the widest influence. The influence continued unabated; it passed from one country to another, becoming tied up with all the radical and socialist movements; it reached writing in English only in our own time, and it is within the last twenty-five years that these doctrines have been brought to America by European radicals.

3

The British Islands were almost immune to these particular literary doctrines, which scorned the supernatural, the mystical and the mysterious—all those hidden worlds of thought, the expression of which had been the glory of English literature. These doctrines, materialistic, physiological, sociological, had ardent welcomers, however, among the ranks of a type of writer who was coming in. With the spread of elementary education, the development of capitalism and industrial life, this type catered to the newly literate readers. The new type of writer had for the most part no interest in literature as an art; writing for him was a trade like any other trade; it was utilitarian; it served the definite purpose of amusing people or of instructing them, of conveying opinions of all kinds and propaganda for social and political doctrines. This type of writer, in fact, belonged to none of the old orders.

In the past, before the industrial age, a writer was either an artist, a scholar or a pamphleteer: a man entered writing rather as a vocation than as a means of earning a living; in fact, of all the arts, literature was the least likely to furnish a livelihood. Hence the patrons and the sinecures, if the author had no private means. It was so simply taken for granted that a living could not be made by the practice of literature that Coleridge devoted some pages of the *Biographia Literaria* to the problem of the means by which a writer might earn a living while pursuing his art, and ended by suggesting the Church as a sort of parallel vocation that would bring in a living without too great an exhaustion of energy.

From the middle nineteenth century on, especially in the industrial and capitalistic countries, there appeared the trade writer, who produced work as a commodity. Both trade writers and their readers belonged to two well-defined classes: there were those who were interested in romance and adventure, and those who were interested in "facts." In fiction, the commonest of all literary forms since the advent of realism, one class of trade writer was the bastard offspring of the old romance and adventure writer. He generally needed little for his equipment except a facility in turning a sentence and enough fancifulness of mind to give him an unrestrained power for spinning tales of love or adventure. The second class of trade writer was the off-spring of the realists, sometimes of the lower order of realists who were defective in imaginative power and who consequently made a rubric of observation and external reality in every shape and form. The creative imagination was out of it, as far as they were concerned; the novel was to be written from documents, not from imagination; the novelists were not to concern them-selves with the interior life but with movements and happenings around them.

The interpretations of what was meant by *reality* went to more and more fantastic extremes; to write nothing but what was "true," but what had happened, to copy life as it was—that became the watchword. The older realists, the artist-realists, had been tolerant of every sort of literary doctrine, but the neo-realists could not tolerate any writing that was not akin to their own. The artist-realists had been, as far as their talents went, like the great writers of the past, dowered in the same way; it was their material, their doctrine, their theories of art, that were different. They all were, to be sure, whether Flaubert, Baudelaire, or Tolstoy, intolerant of the extremer vagaries of romanticism, but now both Flaubert and Maupassant were just as intolerant of the extremer vagaries of realism. Maupassant—and if ten thousand novelists have imitated Flaubert, at least fifty thousand short-story writers have imitated Maupassant —was roused to criticism of the raw-life group, a group coming into literature for the first time in history, and to a defense and explanation of the older realists. To give an illusion of life, he declared, was the aim of the higher realists, and this illusion could not be given us by presenting a banal photograph of life, but only by giving us a picture more perfect, more striking, more convincing than reality itself. The writer must have the art of eliminating the trivial incidents of every-day life that do not serve his end, the art of setting essential events in a strong light and of using everything else as relief; having chosen his subject he must select only such characteristic details as develop it; he must pick and choose so as to give the illusion of life. Truth for the realistic novelist consists in the production of perfect illusion by following the logic of facts and not by transcribing them from life as they follow one another pell-mell. The realistic novelist must accordingly eschew any concatenation of events which might seem exceptional. The "facts" should be normal and probable.

Maupassant showed as strongly as Flaubert his disapproval of the vagaries of the extremists and their intolerance of any type of writing other than their own.

"All the literary doctrines," he maintained, "should be welcomed. . . . To blame a writer for the way he sees things is to reproach him for not being made on a standard pattern. . . . To dispute an author's right to produce a poetic or a realistic work is to try to coerce his temperament, to take exception to his originality, to forbid his using the eyes and wits bestowed on him by nature. . . . Let him be free, by all means, to conceive of things as he pleases, provided he is an artist." *Provided he is an artist!* But that was the trouble. The new type of writer just coming in, the lower realist, was not an artist; he, they, were tradesmen of letters bent on forcing literature to serve a special end, which end they decided on. The higher realists, being artists, were tolerant of other artists, of other literary principles; the lower realists, being tradesmen of letters, could hardly even afford to be tolerant; to give themselves importance they had to force literature into the service of a practical purpose, a purpose, to be sure, in the importance of which they sincerely believed. But they brought the realistic school far down the decline, and the inevitable reaction against it, and all it stood for, set in.

But, even in its decline, realism was destined to last a long while, and one of the reasons it was destined to last was connected with the development of industrialism. Before the industrial era men and women had all sorts of humble outlets for expression: they wove, they span, they carved, they embroidered, they made chairs and tables. But the machine was soon to take away these outlets and to leave men and women empty-handed, with insistent bits of their minds and emotions dammed up. Civilization was developing recklessly, without guidance, without thought as to how it was serving human beings. There was a greater and greater rush into literary expression. The realistic method of writing, in its lower forms, was not difficult; even its higher forms could be imitated without too much demand upon creative imagination or creative emotions; facts, observation, the human document, reportage (to use the Goncourts' term)—these were a stock-in-trade within reach of a great many. Realism, in fact, admitted to writing a new world of men and women who, without any special talent, if they were literate, persevering, and carried a notebook either literally or mentally, could write a passable novel or short story of the kind that begins in the manner of the American contender for a recent international prize: "Mrs. Salz was dusting the sitting-room." The notion that the accurate observation of every-day life was what made literature became so widespread that in our day it is firmly embedded in the general reader's consciousness that a book, or play, or novel, is of value if it factually renders something in life that he knows has happened or which is within reach of his experience. As a literary doctrine, realism spread all over the literature-producing world;

it became the one literary principle known to everybody; it produced the standard of criticism that dominated all others from the middle nineteenth century until our own time. Realism made fiction so popular that a book in most people's minds was a novel, and of a novel the common criterion was, Is it true to life? Is it even a copy of life? as if there were any such thing as a standardized truth to life.

Chapter Ten

THE OUTSIDE LITERATURES IN ENGLISH: THE IRISH AND THE AMERICAN

I

LITERARY doctrines when they pass from one country to another take the same, or a very similar form of development in their new abode; the human mind is given to following like patterns with but little variation. The two new literatures in English, the Irish and the American, which developed strongly in the last century or so, followed pretty closely the pattern of similar developments in other countries. In Ireland, what was called the Renaissance represented a struggle towards cultural re-nationalization, and it followed almost exactly the same lines as had the first movement of this kind, the German movement. Exactly the same methods were employed as those devised by Lessing and Herder to found a national literature. Their ideas, principles and methods were adopted by a group of young Irishmen known as "The Young Ireland" group, or as "The Nation" group from the name of the newspaper founded by them. The most far-seeing of them, Thomas Davis, began the attempt to rouse his country to expression, with words sometimes taken literally from Lessing and Herder, sometimes in paraphrase. In an address to the young men of a college society in Dublin University in 1840—he was only twenty-six at the time—we have him using the same exhortations that were used by the German literary leaders, and we find him quoting directly from Lessing a sentence that became a rallying cry in Ireland for nearly a century—"Think wrongly if you will, but think for yourselves."

For Thomas Davis the highest poetry was national poetry, and he assessed national poetry in the same terms that Herder did: "National poetry is the very flower of the soul, the greatest evidence of its health, the greatest evidence of its beauty. It binds us to the land by its condensed and gemlike history." It was an age when young men thought they could save the world, or at all events, their own countries, by literature. The methods by which a national literature was produced in Germany, and alien influence banished, were studied in Ireland. Herder's ideas about poetry—primitive poetry, ballad poetry, folk poetry—were hopefully taken over; his utterances about folk songs and traditional poetry were eagerly discussed. That recommendation of Herder's to the young Goethe was, in another country, passed around with what later proved to be potent results, "Study the superstitions and the sagas of the forefathers." This became a credo, for Ireland, like Germany, had both a folklore and a mythology, that glorious possession of some fortunate peoples, which stamps itself so subtly, not only on every form of art they produce but on the racial character.

Of the writers grouped around Davis and "The Nation," James Clarence Mangan was the most authentic poet, and he set himself to make an anthology of the new German poetry, translated into English verse by himself. This anthology included some of Herder's ballads, his renderings of the traditional heroic poetry of other countries. Another of "The Nation" poets, Samuel Ferguson, was later to delve into "the superstitions and sagas of the forefathers," and gave versions of them in English from the native Gaelic language. Herder also had touched on these very sagas—the "Ossian" and the Fianna stories—in an essay, "Ossian and the Poetry of Other Peoples," for MacPherson's flighty renderings of the Gaelic sagas had become known all over Europe. Davis wrote some rousing national ballads, "Fontenoy," "The Sack of Baltimore"; Mangan turned to more deeply native sources, and made such impressive expressions of the national spirit as "Dark Rosaleen," "Cathleen-ni-Houlihan," "The Lament for the Princes of Tyrone and Tyrconnell."

This movement was destined to be cut short in its course; for one thing, two of its founders, Davis and Mangan, died young—the one in his early thirties, the other in his forties—for another, they had not developed a technique which would make an appeal to the two races that called themselves Irish, the Gaelic and the Anglo-Irish. But the great calamity that prevented the movement from realizing itself for another half-century was the famine of 1846–47, one of the greatest disasters that ever befell a European people. Not only national creative vitality, but individual creative vitality, was starved out under the effects of the disaster. The young and the strong flew to America, from the hunger-ridden, plague-ridden country, and the old, who were the custodians of the "superstitions and sagas of the forefathers," went into their graves.

2

It was not until fifty years later that a generation was vigorous enough to take up the movement where Davis and Mangan had left off. Meanwhile, Samuel Ferguson of "The Nation" group had survived and was still living when the next poet to take up the national tradition, William Butler Yeats, reached his young manhood. Ferguson's delving into Celtic myth and legend, his creations from them, *Congal,* and his *Lays of the Western Gael,* were the work of an older contemporary of Yeats. The younger poet knew his rôle from the start, and one of his earliest poems has the lines:

> Know, that I would accounted be
> True brother of that company,
> Who sang to sweeten Ireland's wrong,

Ballad and story, rann and song;
Nor be I any less of them,
Because the red rose-bordered hem
Of her, whose history began
Before God made the angelic clan,
Trails all about the written page.

and again:

Nor may I less be counted one
With Davis, Mangan, Ferguson,
Because to him, who ponders well,
My rhymes more than their rhyming tell
Of things discovered in the deep,
Where only body's laid asleep.

Once more the manifestoes about national literature and a national culture began. Davis's writings were re-read. "Study the superstitions and the sagas of the fore-fathers" once more showed its rousing power. The sagas and the hero tales, the folk songs and the folk tales, were again brought back from obscurity. Standish O'Grady and Lady Gregory proceeded to make modern renderings of the hero tales, Douglas Hyde of the folk tales and the folk songs: Hyde became head of the great popular movement for the restoration of the native language. Yeats, not unself-consciously, occupied a position rather like Goethe's in Weimar, and made himself the head of a theatre that produced national drama in prose and verse. There was indeed in Yeats's mentality something very like Goethe's, without Goethe's comprehensiveness. As in Germany, in the beginning of its national movement, the audiences in the newly created theatre were delighted to see on the boards plays dealing with their contemporary life, as well as renderings of their sagas. The Irish people differed from the Germans in the fact that they were not homogeneous in language and race; the literature they knew and read and understood was in the language of the people whose influence the movement was trying to uproot. It was not only the upper classes who spoke English, as the upper classes in Germany and Russia had spoken French; English was the language of almost the whole population. The native Gaelic tongue was still living and was spoken and written by a minority, but English was in the ascendancy and writers who wanted to be widely read wrote in English. This was true, and has continued to be true, even of those who could have written in Gaelic, for the Celts of Ireland, like the Celts of France, adopted the language of the conqueror, and as the French Celts became part-Latin, so the Irish Celts became part Anglo-Saxon. But though they assimilated the great language and literature of the conqueror, and even became masters of it and creators in it, they had had no part in its making. The literature of their own that they made in English was written in a language colored by their native Gaelic language and idiom. This literature in English owed much of its color and sound to the old literature in Gaelic and to the influence, generally, of the movement for the restoration of the Gaelic tongue.

The product of the writers of the Renaissance was partly lyrical, partly realistic, partly poetic drama and narrative founded on the hero tales. There arose a number of distinguished poets, and among them the greatest poet of his day writing in English, perhaps the greatest contemporary poet writing in any language, William Butler Yeats. On the poetic side of the movement there was not only the Herder-Lessing influence, there were also the influences of every other movement that had arisen in Europe in the nineteenth century, and these became woven in with the native inheritance of folk and hero poetry. On drama, there was the Scandinavian influence; there was the influence of French realism, brought in by George Moore; there was a touch of the French Symbolist movement; there was a Whitman influence, and other American influences generally. But very markedly there was the influence of the Wordsworth-Baudelaire combination. Yeats re-stated Wordsworth's doctrine of the language of poetry, in a paraphrase of the words of the Preface to the *Lyrical Ballads*. "We wanted," he said, "to get rid, not only of rhetoric, but of poetic diction; we tried to strip away everything that was artificial, to get a style like speech, as simple as the simplest prose, like a cry of the heart." John Synge was also profoundly influenced by Baudelaire—not, it should be said, by the erotic side of his genius which swayed the English poets of the 'nineties, but by Baudelaire's power of creating characters at once tragic and grotesque, and by his approach to his subjects, by his whole attitude towards life and death, and by the directness of his language. Synge was not only influenced by Baudelaire but by the older French authors who themselves had affected Baudelaire—Villon, Ronsard, and mediæval writers. But then, it should be noted that a body of Irish poetry seeming to have a Baudelaire derivation is, in reality, derived from Irish mediæval literature, and the literature-producing classes in Ireland were temperamentally attracted to French literature and had, many of them, a French culture.

Among Herder's Ideas was one, age-old, to be sure, but given a new life by him—the idea that poetry should be said or sung, not read silently from a printed book. Yeats developed this and encouraged the speaking of verse with a special utterance differentiated from the speaking of prose. With his collaboration, Florence Farr invented an instrument, a sort of lyre, to the accompaniment of which she said or chanted poetry. These experiments influenced the speaking of verse in the Abbey Theatre plays, and the speaking of verse, in turn, influenced the composition of poetry. The direction of Yeats's later poetry, with its direct rhythm and colloquial vocabulary, was strongly affected by hearing his verse spoken in the theatre. The common Irish habit of saying poetry made the verse familiar to audiences before it was printed, and certainly affected the style of the whole poetic production.

The dramatic side, with its national theatre, became the most widely known, but the real glory of the Irish movement was in its poetry. There sprang up about half a dozen genuine poets: following the precedent set by Baudelaire, Verlaine and Mallarmé, they kept their poetic production down to one or two books, but if an anthology were made of the best work of these half dozen, it would with its direct expression make most of the poetry of our ultra-modern poets seem lacking in intensity and experience as well as in poetic invention and that fundamental lyricism which is an essential of all poetry. This new Irish literature lacked the abundance of the great English periods, but what it lacked in abundance it almost made up for in intensity. Though it was distinctly national poetry, it had been fed by many cultures, so that it was lifted out of provincialism. The whole product was very different in mental climate, in spiritual temperature, from English literature; in some cases there could hardly be detected a trace of English influence, although the writers wrote in the English language. The novel, as written by George Moore, was not in the English tradition at all: it was derived, partly from the French realists and partly from the traditional Irish story-tellers, the shanachies, that Moore knew in his childhood and youth in the west of Ireland. The realistic novel that came after George Moore and that is now being written in Ireland was, in addition, influenced by the Russians. There is, to be sure, in the earlier Yeats, an occasional Swinburnian line, like "Autumn is over the long leaves that love us," and in some of his verse-plays, just as in almost all the verse-plays in Europe, since the modern movement began, there is the inescapable sway of Shakespeare; but on the whole, and for a time anyhow, English influence on Irish literature was almost nil.

3

It was far different, for a long time, in the other outside literature in English, the American. The first important American writer, Washington Irving, was not only English in his mental make-up, but English in his writing models; he could have passed for an English writer. In spite of great American publishing houses, publication in England was regarded as the real crown of a writer's success, and the gaining of this was the desired goal down even to our own time, until the time of the Great War. The audience for the first American writers was preponderantly English in blood and tradition; it was a part of the English race cut away from the main branch, but in it there dominated a quality, Puritanism, which the English did not like in themselves and which was indeed at odds with their own great dominant characteristic and the outstanding characteristic of their literature, emotional power. The men and women who made English literature felt all emotions so directly and so strongly that, in emotional force, it is the greatest of all literatures, as in form and intensity the Greek is. They had indeed felt so abundantly and so romantically that they seemed unable for long to tolerate any tendency in their literature in which emotion was not the supreme quality. But the rising American literature, particularly the New England literature, was emotionally thin, and this was one of the qualities that in the end turned it to a different line of expression from the English and into a sort of psychological and social analysis that had not been in English literature at all. Besides, the Puritan temperament, undirected by strong emotions, developed an independent, rational attitude towards life that, limiting as it may have been for literature, was a constructive force in statesmanship and social advance.

The first really American piece of literature was Jefferson's Declaration of Independence, and that had about it a sort of prophetic sweep, as of something appearing out of the future; it was a premonition of a world that was coming to birth under circumstances that the old European world could never really appreciate or assess, and this though it was raised on a foundation of ideas taken over from Europe. It was nearly half a century before the next piece of influential American literature appeared: this was Emerson's "The American Scholar"; the two together gave a pattern to the American dream, gave to America a dream and a philosophy.

But any account of American literature in the nineteenth century begins of necessity with George Ticknor and Edward Everett, those two young men who, having read a glamorous book, about glamorous new poets and philosophers and scholars, called *De l'Allemagne,* decided they would cross the ocean and see the author, Madame de Staël, and as many as possible of the poets and philosophers she had written of; in short, they determined to make a pilgrimage to the men who were creating modern literature and ideas, and to the places where these were being made. In the year of the battle of Waterloo, five years after the publication of *De l'Allemagne,* they started on their pilgrimage. The author herself was still alive—she lived until 1817—and she welcomed the young men as an elder author might welcome two of the younger generation who had been stirred by her ideas and who were to spread them in another country. Goethe was still living, enthroned in Weimar, the greatest writer and the wisest man in Europe; he also welcomed them with interest and even with enthusiasm. All doors were opened to the two young pilgrims from Washington's country. They met all the important figures; they saw the very men de Staël had written about, or all of them that were alive;

they met one, or both, of the brothers Schlegel, they who had been responsible for fastening the name "Romantic" to the new movement, a nomenclature that had spread everywhere in spite of objections from the very writers who were making what came to be known as "Romantic" literature. The younger Schlegel explained that what he meant by "Romantic" was "a progressive universal poetry," which would include all kinds. While the battle about the name went on, the name itself had made an entrance into people's imaginations and stuck there. The two young Americans were destined to become professors at Harvard, and the two Schlegels were admirable models for the progressive scholar with wide interests: they had been trying to develop further the conceptions of Herder and they kept alive, by their writings and discussions, his ideas on folk poetry, on old ballads, on what he had called "wilde poesie" in mediæval romances, in Eastern literature, Homer, Greek literature, in Shakespeare, in Ossian. The elder Schlegel, Wilhelm, did what Herder had thought of doing but had not had the time for—he provided Germany with a real translation of Shakespeare in verse; he also translated Dante and Cervantes, and was an enthusiast regarding the literature of the Spanish peninsula. The younger Schlegel published the first German book on the literatures and wisdom of India.

These were the intellectual orientations, the enthusiasms and the learning that the two young pioneers brought back to New England, and that Ticknor brought to his professorship of Modern Languages at Harvard, a chair destined to have a wide influence and to be a directing force with the New England writers, for Longfellow was Ticknor's successor, and Longfellow's successor was Lowell, and they all followed in Ticknor's path. And it was Ticknor who urged Longfellow to go to Germany and make much the same pilgrimage that he and his companion had made, and to meet those of the great figures who were left, and to read their work. Starting with Lessing, Longfellow read all the writers of the movement down to his own contemporaries. He read Herder's collection of folk songs, and those lines of his, "For a boy's will is the wind's will, and the thoughts of youth are long, long thoughts," he took from Herder's rendering of a Lapland song:

> Knabenwille ist Wind'swille,
> Jüngling'sgedanken lange Gedanken.

He returned with the same enthusiasms as those of Ticknor, and brought them, in his turn, to the Harvard chair, in modernized form.

4

Emerson was a student at Harvard when Ticknor was expounding there the modern literary ideas that he had brought back from Europe, and when the other pilgrim, Edward Everett, was the Harvard professor of Greek. However, these influences might not have done more than provide a general literary culture or a general intellectual direction and might never really have produced a focus for New England literature if Emerson had not decided, in his late twenties, to go to Europe and estimate for himself what was in these ideas, especially as they were shaping in England. When he left he was a young clergyman who had just thrown up his church and his pulpit and was groping towards his path in life; when he came back he knew exactly where that path lay, and which among the ideas were his to use and to make his own.

Not a great writer, in spite of his few fine poems and essays, Emerson was destined to be a great fructifier, a leader of thought. Lowell said of him, "There are staminate plants in literature that make no fine show of fruit, but without whose pollen, quintessence of fructifying gold, the garden had been barren. Emerson's mind is emphatically one of these, and there is no man to whom our æsthetic culture owes so much." His mind really developed only after he had gone to Europe; he was thirty when he met Coleridge and Wordsworth and Carlyle, some of whose work he already knew; he became steeped in the world of their ideas and in the antecedents of these ideas. He was not, like Ticknor, to cherish disinterestedly all the seeds he gathered; he winnowed them and kept what suited his own purpose and what could best take root in the soil of his

own country as well as in his own mind. There was
not much for New England in some of these European ideas; for the moment anyway, there was no urge
towards expressing everyday life or rustic life, though
both Whittier and Lowell, later, initiated a rural New
England poetry. And attractive as all Lessing's ideas
might be, there was not much use in America for his
conception of literature as racial expression. But Lessing's demand on his people to shake off slavish foreign
influences, to use what they could as bricks but with
them to build their own structure, to be self-reliant
and independent, to think wrongly if they liked, but
to think for themselves—these were all in "The American Scholar," an address Emerson made to the Harvard students soon after his return from Europe, an
address very like in spirit to the one Thomas Davis
was to make, a couple of years later, to the students
of Dublin University. These two college addresses were
responsible for starting off the two new outside literatures in English.

Emerson soaked himself in the work of Wordsworth
and Coleridge, in Wordsworth's poetry and in his conception of nature and his contemplation of nature.
Carlyle, with whom he felt a temperamental kinship,
turned him on to Goethe and to Fichte. However, most
of what came to be called Emerson's philosophy was
built on Coleridge and Coleridge's interpretation of
the German philosophers, especially on his interpreta-

tion of Schelling, who, like all the other German philosophers of the day, had been started off by the work of Herder and Lessing. Schelling, with his two books, *Ideas Towards a Philosophy of Nature* and *A System of Transcendental Idealism,* had exerted a potent influence on certain phases of the new literature. These two books were spoken of by Coleridge as if they were divine revelations, and they became almost that to Emerson and to the newly born Transcendental Club of Boston.

Emerson's kinship with Schelling is evident: as Sainte-Beuve would say, they belong to the same family of minds. Schelling, like Emerson, was not a systematized thinker; he was an intuitive, glorifying intuition; he was indeed Emerson's own idea of a philosopher— a sort of seer or priest in a temple, listening for revelations from the oracles, which he interpreted in oracular statements. He held what he termed the philosophy of identity—the identity, in the absolute, of the subjective and the objective, of the ideal and the real, of nature and spirit. As Madame de Staël, with a feminine desire to make plain sense of things, explained, his aim was to reduce existence to a single principle: nothing was more absurd, for instance, than the expression, the philosophy of Plato and the philosophy of Aristotle—there was only one philosophy or there was none, according to Schelling. The natural consequence of this philosophy of identity was the conclusion that all wisdom was in ourselves, and that to know the world we had only to look deep into ourselves. In short, intuition was the great revealer. This suited Emerson exactly, as did Schelling's view of the divine origin of man—that man and nature were emanations from God. It also suited the Transcendental Club, and provided a philosophical backing for the Transcendental Movement.

New England Transcendentalism was a combination of every sort of American idealism, based, on one side, on a doctrine of man's divinity and, on the other, on everything that was in the Declaration of Independence and in Emerson's "The American Scholar." All the writers were Transcendentalists, and both the movement and the writers were responsible for impregnating the national character with a peculiar form of idealism and optimism—an almost eccentric idealism, at once disinterested and opportunistic, chivalrous and utilitarian, humanitarian and egoistic, philanthropic and acquisitive. The same subtly excellent components do not belong to the optimism that springs from the vague side of Transcendentalism and the more complacent side of Emerson's teachings. What Transcendentalism provided, on the whole, was a sort of Unitarian substitute for certain of the orthodox doctrines and disciplines of Christianity, which never found a foothold in America, if they ever weathered the Atlantic at all. "Christianity," Thoreau declared, "has hung its harp on the willows and cannot sing a song in a strange land." Irving Babbitt, three-quarters of a century later, was to re-discover some of these lapsed disciplines and to deliver himself of some of the more elementary teachings of Christendom with the air of a man who has fathered a new philosophy.

The Concord group of writers belonged to the Transcendental Club, and it was the Concord group that left the deepest impress on New England literature; it was they whose work provided what may be described as the overture to American literature. After his return from Europe, Emerson had also settled in Concord, and here he, Thoreau and Hawthorne lived a cloister-like life and had the characteristics of an order of monks, of which Emerson was the preaching member, Thoreau the one who retired to his cell in solitude like a desert father, so as to come face to face with spiritual reality, Hawthorne the one who meditated on the sins of men, their lusts and their vengeances, their hatreds and their remorses. Emerson was descended from seven generations of preachers, and his own preaching, given in the form of lectures and essays, related chiefly to the conduct of life or to spiritual possessions. For what he had picked from the new European ideas were those that were especially concerned with the conduct of life and with the emergence of the divine in man; to the doctrines concerned with purely literary expression he had not so much response.

In spite of the fact that he and Thoreau discussed Herder's theories of literature, of "wilde poesie," of early poetry, of ballads, sagas and epics, and his notions of history, Emerson only played with these, for they could have had but little practical influence on America at that time, and Emerson was eminently practical in his selection of the ideas that he was able to make his own.

The interest in Oriental literature, that Ticknor had taken over from the Schlegels, who had taken it over from Herder, was to open to the pantheistically-minded Emerson a world that was of importance for his poetry. From ancient Indian poetry he took the matter and the imagery of his most memorable poem:

> If the red slayer think he slays,
> Or if the slain think he is slain,
> They know not well the subtle ways
> I keep, and pass, and turn again.
>
> Far or forgot to me is near,
> Shadow and sunlight are the same;
> The vanished gods to me appear;
> And one to me are shame and fame.
>
> They reckon ill who leave me out;
> When me they fly, I am the wings;
> I am the doubter and the doubt,
> And I the hymn the Brahmin sings.
>
> The strong gods pine for my abode,
> And pine in vain the sacred Seven;
> But thou, meek lover of the good,
> Find me, and turn thy back on Heaven!

In this, and in half a dozen other poems, and in about a dozen lines and couplets, Emerson produced poetry of a kind unique in English. From Goethe he got the irregular meter that he uses in an artificial poem like "Give All to Love," and in philosophical pieces of this kind:

> The rushing metamorphosis,
> Dissolving all that fixture is,
> Melts things that be to things that seem,
> And solid nature to a dream.

> .   .   .   .

> All forms are fugitive,
> But the substances survive.
> Ever fresh the broad creation,
> A divine improvisation. . . .

His sort of poetry and prose is not unlike the literature left us by the historic saints: the sentiments and reflections of the essays are strikingly like those of Thomas à Kempis's *Imitation of Christ;* there is the same inclination towards the same sort of spiritual maxims, though à Kempis's have more of a narrow prudence and less of an independence than Emerson's. If these essays were winnowed and the most revealing passages in them arranged in an order like that of the *Imitation,* Emerson would be the gainer. In a work edited with such intention his strange lack of discipline and his peculiarly feminine reliance on instinct, the undirected nature of his thought, and his consequent inconsistencies, might pass unnoticed. He had one gift in an almost unexampled degree, a power of intuition, a richness of the sub-conscious, out of which he could draw striking revelations; he had half the outfit of a great writer, a rich inner life, but his emotions were thin, his response to life mild. He thoroughly realized his own lack, for he noted in himself "an absence of common sympathies . . . a want of sufficient bottom to my nature. . . . I have not the kind affections of a pigeon. . . . I was born cold." He noted the coldness and unresponsiveness of the people he knew, remarking on how insulated and pathetically solitary were all his friends. "I spoke of friendship," he wrote, "but my friends and I are fishes in our habits." Concord, in fact, offered a meager world. There were none of the romantic loves and friendships, the unrestrained enthusiasms, of the European literary movements; the writers all went into reveries, betook themselves inside themselves.

Emerson and Hawthorne settled down without glamour to affectionate marriage-relationships that helped rather than hindered them in living in themselves. Emerson made the best of it; he probably got out more of what was in him in that world and in that soil than he could have in any other. But with Hawthorne it was different. Of the three, his was the most varied literary endowment, and it included a talent, the fictional, that needs for its operation a warm relation with humanity. Fate and destiny, however, decreed that he should exist out of life most of the time, without close connections with other human beings. In his own family, his mother and his sisters and himself lived secluded from each other and generally ate their meals in solitude. Though he joined the Brook Farm colony for a while, this did not give him any more facility for mingling with his fellows; though he joined the Transcendental Club, he had no sympathy with the ideas that dominated that group. He himself was a Transcendentalist, in the dictionary meaning of the term. That, in the end, he died of his painful solitude, Emerson, who knew that Hawthorne had never got all his talent into his books, said of him the day of his funeral. He did not know people, so he could not create character; his writing, except in one book where he tried to get down the life of Brook Farm, is almost pure symbolism and the theme is always the effect of sin and evil. His characters are symbols by which he illustrates the sin, the remorse, the revenge that all his books are about, as a Morality Play might be about them. He was, as he himself explained, a romance-writer, not a novelist: by "novelist" he understood the type of writer who dealt with real life. What he was, really, was a narrator of tales, and one can always hear, behind his best work, his lovely, lonely book, *The Scarlet Letter,* the voice of a man telling a story, not of people so much as of the consequences of their sins. Through two of his books, anyway, *The Scarlet Letter* and *The House of the Seven Gables,* he is not only a figure in American literature, he is a figure in nineteenth-century literature. Hawthorne himself knew that he had lost out in this life, that his was a lean world, but, because of his temperament, it was the only world he could cope with.

5

In spite of the fact that Emerson could say of Thoreau, in his general remarks on the coldness of his friends, "I would as soon take the limb of an elm tree as Henry's arm," there is more warmth and ecstasy in one little book of Thoreau's, *Walden,* than in all Emerson's prose put together. Take one or two sentences from a familiar passage, "I went to the woods because I wished to live deliberately, to front only the essential facts of life, and see if I could not learn what it had to teach, and not, when I came to die, discover that I had not lived. I did not wish to live what was not life, living is so dear. . . . I wanted to live deep and suck out all the marrow of life." Here we have that nervous style that has behind it a man of blood and fire, a creature of light; these words are vascular; as Emerson said of Montaigne, cut them and they will bleed. Thoreau's words, indeed, generally walk alive across the page, something that Emerson's very rarely do. This sort of life, this sort of luminousness, makes Thoreau's *Walden* so glamorous that it is one of the great experiences of youth in the 'teens to read it, similar to the great experience of reading *Hamlet* or *Faust,* in the twenties. Youth may only half understand an immortal book, but one that has no appeal to youth at all cannot be said to belong to literature, though it may be outstanding in some other branch of expression, in science or in philosophy.

It would not be surprising if time, the last arbiter, decided that of the three most important early New England writers, Thoreau is the greatest in sheer writing power, in the power of putting life into language. What he meant by life was not, of course, physical life or material life; reality for him was interior. He had neither wife nor child, and there is no record of his ever having been in love; he never seems to have endured that distressful temptation of the desert saints— the temptation of being, in his solitude, "harried by lust," but he was one of their order, not only in the reality of his search for what was his to get out of life, but in his bliss in solitude and in the nervous passion of his writing. His philosophy was a simple one, but its depth was unsoundable; all that men have of their own is themselves, their lives, and a little gift of time, and he made a valiant effort to get what was his to get, out of that little time, and to write down what it was.

Neither Thoreau nor Hawthorne had, to any degree, the conviction that only the Puritans or their Transcendentalist descendants had the secret of the good life, the noble life, a conviction which is at the back of Emerson's writing. Hawthorne, in spite of defects of temperament, had the artist's sense of life; Thoreau, who was of Channel Island descent, had an infusion of the free critical mentality of the French: they had few complacencies, but Emerson's complacence was at times extraordinary, and it enabled him to come to self-righteous conclusions about his European contemporaries, Goethe, Coleridge, Wordsworth, Carlyle, conclusions impossible to either Thoreau or Hawthorne, and which had, like everything else that emanated from Emerson, a great influence.

6

The rest of the New England group, except Melville, who, at the moment, has an extensive reputation and whose *Moby Dick* is described as an epic by those anxious to find all forms in New England literature, have lost out with the present generation. Longfellow, whose command of modern languages and literature did so much for the fine literary culture that was New England's, has lost his once wide reputation. The very bad poetry he wrote at his worst has cast a shadow, not only over his fine poetry, but over all his services to this first American literature—the anthologies by which he made European poetry known, his translation of Dante, which in stretches has never been surpassed in English, the beauty of a large amount of his work, which, if selected in a small, expertly edited volume, would salvage his poetic reputation. Longfellow's subjects, and his virtuosity in verse-technique, fascinated poets remote in place and genius, among whom was Baudelaire, who had no objection to borrowing from him a line or a phrase and who made a sort of version or imitation of part of *Hiawatha*.

Of the critics, Margaret Fuller's services, excellent as they were, were for their day only, but Lowell has produced something that will last. There have been critics since with a more solid knowledge of literature, like Woodberry or Paul Elmer More, and of course Poe's flight was higher, but a better all-round critic than Lowell has not appeared, or one who had more of an intuition regarding what American literature should be or was going to be. He really belonged to the type of what has since been called the impressionistic critic; what he was inclined to give his readers was the adventures of his soul among books, so that his judgments are not always careful conclusions, but quick reactions to temperamental likes or dislikes. His poetic endowment was considerable, and two of his lyrics, "When I Was a Beggarly Boy" and "My Heart, I Cannot Still It," once read, are possessions for a lifetime. His *Biglow Papers* started off the whole school of humorous, satiric, bucolic verse that became rife all over America. He and Whittier together initiated that rural New England poetry from which a poet like Robert Frost stems.

Like all the early New England writers, Lowell left the stamp of his mind and character on his countrymen. Insufficient and one-sided as New England literature might be, as an expression of the New England mind it had the quality of revealing and moulding the people it expressed, and their descendants all over the country; it was like them, like the inhabitants of the village and the countryside, in a way that a great literature, such as the English, is not like the ordinary English people at all but only like a symbolic English people. As far as it went, New England literature was true to the minds of the people, and so strongly did the writers influence the developing American civilization that one can meet in any village a miniature sage who is a vulgarization of Emerson, or a miniature naturalist who is a vulgarization of Thoreau, or a popular satirist such as Lowell, or a brooder on sin such as Hawthorne.

They also passed on to their descendants their own incapacity for close human relationships; their own limited psychic and emotional energy made them incapable of leaving any profound pattern for living or for literature. No tragedy, no love-poetry, no novel of passion, says George Woodberry, came from them. Their loneliness was tremendous except in the case of Thoreau, for whom solitude was a beatitude, as it was to the Desert Fathers, and therefore capable of generating its own warmth. Emerson took refuge from his loneliness in a contemplation of the divine in his own mind and in the angelic messages that he said came to him; in a complacence and a mental irresponsibility that made him happy. Hawthorne alone was aware of the drawbacks of a retreat from the emotional complexities and conflicts of human relationships. He left behind a few pregnant sentences showing his consciousness of the predicament from which he had not the force to extricate himself. Others took refuge from their loneliness in various ways: some, in their European memories; others, in their scholarship; Longfellow, in a yearning Teutonic romanticism; Lowell, in his books. Looking back on their literary product, distinguished as it was, and fine and broad as was their literary culture, we see that they left behind them few seminal ideas such as might yield a harvest for their descendants or for the greater America that was coming in. They worked effectively and even nobly with the ideas they took over and made their own, but they really added little to them, and they produced neither literary philosophies nor speculative philosophies as did the Germans and the French of the same period. Herman Melville, the one man among them who might have come out with a speculative philosophy expressive of a country that persistent men had conquered or half conquered, tamed or half tamed from the wild, had no real contacts with the others or with the life around him; he was more alone, more undirected than any of them. His solitariness, his strange psychic energy, his restless and gloomy speculations on the forces that rule the world, found outlet in an epical and symbolic tale of the pursuit through tumultuous seas of a white whale, a creature surviving from primeval times. The whale Moby Dick was "an incarnation of all those malicious agencies, that intangible malignity, which has been from the beginning." He is pursued by the crew under the leadership of Ahab, whose leg he has torn off, and "for whose vengeful mind all the subtle demonisms of life and thought were personified" in the whale. In the end, the malign creature and the ruthless element are the conquerors. It is hardly surprising that Americans, demanding some profounder view of life out of their history than their literary men as a whole had given them, turned to this anarchical epic and perhaps overestimated its significance.

7

But there were three writers who, though they made far less of an entrance into the minds of their countrymen than did the others, were the ones who left behind them the most penetrating influences, who impregnated their epochs with a set of literary values that have been felt all over the world. These three were Edgar Allan Poe, Walt Whitman and Henry James. It is their work that gives an earnest as to what the rôle of a future American literature is likely to be if minds can spring up equal to the task of making that universal literature of which Goethe and de Staël dreamed, a universal

literature which would overshadow the national literatures which, in their turn, had overshadowed the cul-
ture-literatures that came out of Greece and Rome,
which, again, in their turn, had overshadowed the early
wild literatures, the rhapsodic literatures, the mytholo-
gies, of primeval times. There had been in America,
from the beginning, a tendency to knit in with world-
literatures and world-philosophies; this tendency, far
from expressing subordination or derivativeness, showed
itself possessed of a shaping function. It was a tendency
natural in a people who came into literary expression
after the national literatures had partly run their course,
and who could not produce a national literature in the
sense of one that came out of old racial and national
developments. The Americans were not moulding a
language or intensifying an inherited racial consciousness; they were forming a population out of different
races joined together by a metaphysical idea, given a
tangible meaning by a piece of literature, Jefferson's
Declaration of Independence, and by a geographical
area, and not by "the superstitions and sagas of the
forefathers."

The American direction was towards an internation-
alism in literature, towards a universal stream in which
theirs would be a current—even, in time, the dominating
current; they were taking up where the elder races
halted, but that was all the more reason why they should
know all the roads the elder races had traversed. For

this reason, among others, American literature could never be the almost accidental, instinctive thing the elder literatures had been during most of their course.

The contribution of Edgar Allan Poe, Walt Whitman and Henry James to this conception was salient; another half-dozen minds as originating as theirs would have made American literature a world-force. A striking characteristic of the New England literature was its symbolist quality. The outstanding original works were symbolic—Emerson's poetry, *The Scarlet Letter, Moby Dick*. This inclination towards symbolism was due to several causes: the writers were highly endowed intellectually; they had no large or fecund material to hand; they were meagerly endowed emotionally; they were a new people in an immense unsettled country over which they felt the play of mysterious psychic forces. It was almost inevitable that their literary expression should be in the order of symbolism.

8

When Edgar Allan Poe was still in his 'teens he accomplished a phenomenal thing—he wrote an original poem, in the lines that we know as "To Helen," and a poem original as this poem was is always destined to have far-reaching effects. The originality of "To Helen" was fundamental: that combination of music and imagery had not happened previously; that note of the gamut had not been struck before. The short, ecstatic, intense lyrics had been made either on a singing note or a chanting note, but this was neither singing nor chanting; it was a new mode in lyric poetry. Tennyson, a little afterwards, was also to find that mode when he wrote the lines that Poe was to praise, "Tears, idle tears, I know not what they mean." Poe's poem had other significant elements in it: the obviously logical structure is abandoned and evocation takes its place. The beauty of Helen is conveyed to us by far-brought images—"Nicæan barks," "The agate lamp within thy hand," "The glory that was Greece and the grandeur that was Rome." The poem, in fact, belongs to a type of composition that was to come in about half a century later, in which the thought and emotion were evoked and suggested rather than directly named, and were revealed by a succession of images—that is, "To Helen" was the new kind of symbolist poem. Poe wrote other strikingly original poems, original in content, in structure, in musical effects, "Ulalume," "The City in the Sea," "The Conqueror Worm," "The Raven," but "To Helen," though it has the marks of a youthful effort and may be said almost to have the weakness of a creature of a new species, nevertheless remains the most original poem of a man whose most striking characteristic naturally, as well as the one he most deliberately sought for, was originality.

Poe's other striking distinctions were in his craftsmanship and in his discipline; he is the accomplished craftsman in all his work—in his poems, his stories and his criticism. He knew "the right ordering of the thing to be made," and he was thoroughly aware that the knowledge of "the right ordering" could not come by improvisation, but only by hard training, self-discipline and the equipment of knowledge. It is an instance of the confusion between the two consciences that it is Emerson who is always regarded as disciplined and well-ordered, while Poe is looked on as undisciplined and disordered. On the plane of thought, it was Emerson who was the self-indulgent, loose-disciplined, undirected man, and on that plane Poe was disciplined, precise, reasoning, well-ordered and industrious. This is what has made him the honored master of so many modern poets, from Baudelaire on. He was against the blind furies of improvisation and the more mythological aspects of inspiration. A poet was, especially, a man who knew his job, who guided his art consciously with his mind. His analysis of the psychological conditions from which literature is produced, of the poetic principle in itself, was bound to affect profoundly that school of modern poets who were in revolt against the loose abundance in poetic product, those who believed that poetry "is literature reduced to the essential of its active principle."

Poe had found the basis of his "The Poetic Principle" in certain ideas of Herder, certain ideas of Coleridge, and in Coleridge's practice, but it was only a basis, for on it he raised some ideas of poetry that were so remote from any his age had considered, that his originality must again be acknowledged. Wordsworth, and even Coleridge, had been almost as moralizing in some of their speculations about poetry as the New England group, and so when Poe declared that "the didactic heresy, which Bostonians had developed in full . . . accomplished more corruption of our poetical literature than all others combined," and when he announced that the aim of poetry is the rhythmical creation of beauty, that poetry has only collateral relations with intellect or conscience, that there is no such thing as a long poem, for the value of a poem depends on its elevating excitement, and all excitements, through a psychic necessity, must be short, that melancholy is the most legitimate of all poetical tones, that the higher manifestations of beauty are connected with melancholy, he was saying not only something startling at the time but saying something momentous to a large audience, larger than the America of his day, more numerous than the readers of *Graham's Magazine,* in which the statement was printed: he was saying something, in fact, destined to enter into all future considerations of poetry.

Without laying any stress on the ostensible meaning addressed to the intelligence, Poe stated that a poem should have an undercurrent of meaning, however indefinite, and mocking a little at the Transcendentalist idea of meaning and at the poets who wished it understood that they composed in a species of frenzy, he let his readers into the secret of the processes by which a poem is composed. In his most detached manner he takes his own "The Raven," because he thinks it is the most generally known of his poems, and shows, step by step, how, having decided on the tone, which was to be melancholy, on the refrain, which was to be monotone and in a single word, he settled on the subject, the death of a beautiful woman; then, he explains at what point he changed from the fantastic to the serious, and how, in the last stanzas, he decided to make the raven the symbol of never-ending remembrance: he tells us in detail how he fixed on the meter. By thus making us familiar with his method of composing a poem and with what might be called his rejections, he is responsible for a new angle in criticism —that which takes into account, not only what a writer has put into his work, but what he refused to put in, and what Paul Valéry terms the nature of his refusals.

His critical theories, his lucid analyses, had the significance of a manifesto, not of a manifesto that started a new sort of literature, but of one that initiated a new critical attitude in a writer towards his own product. A considerable amount of modern poetry—that of Mallarmé, of Valéry, of Verlaine, of T. S. Eliot, can only be properly estimated in the perspective of Poe's "The Poetic Principle" and his "Philosophy of Composition."

It is not alone by his poetry or poetic principles that he has exerted an influence; he created a type of tale in which the ratiocinative imagination takes a dominating rôle. The eeriness of his stories was in itself not new; it had been in Hawthorne's tales; it was to appear again in Henry James, a sort of distinctively American eeriness that could hardly be duplicated in another literature, but it was the influence of that ratiocinative imagination that started off the modern detective story. In addition to his stories, his poems and his criticism, Poe managed to produce one of the most astonishing pieces of speculative literature ever written by a poet, that consideration of the universe which he entitled "Eureka," in which he attempts to discover the rationale of the universe, the "plot of God," as he calls it: here he tries to unriddle the universe as if it were a cryptogram. This immeasurably industrious man, with his high gifts, his supreme artistic integrity, his subtle literary knowledge, suffered from hunger and cold, and the illnesses and emotional derangements consequent on them: he died at forty.

9

Some time after Poe's death, a younger contemporary, Walt Whitman, was also to announce that the great poet "does not moralize or make applications of morals," and he claimed for the greatest poets all the magnanimities, all the wisdoms, and all the generosities. His own desire in writing, he said, was "to articulate and faithfully express in literary or poetic form, and uncompromisingly, my own physical, emotional, moral, intellectual, and æsthetic personality . . . and to exploit that personality, identified with place and date [*e.g.,* the America of his time] in a far more candid and comprehensive sense than any hitherto poem or book." His first volume of poetry, written with this aim, appeared two years before that other volume, *Les Fleurs du Mal,* in which another poet very differently but also faithfully expressed his physical, emotional, moral, intellectual, and æsthetic personality. If *Leaves of Grass* shocked as many people in its own way as did Baudelaire's volume, it brought Whitman a following all over the world, from New York to Japan, almost as if he had been the head of a religious cult and the bearer of a new gospel. What was remarkable about Whitman was that he really soaked up something of all the ideas of his age: something of all the literary doctrines, beginning with Lessing's idea of national and racial expression; and something of all the political doctrines, beginning with Jefferson's Declaration of Independence; and of all the philosophic doctrines, including Hegel.

Whitman's aim was to be an American national poet, revealing America and everything American—ideals, scenery, war, its leaders and its men and women—revealing all through what he called "a stock-personality," which was a projection of himself. More of a seer and a prophet than was Emerson, he was at once more egoistic and less so, more complacent and less so; his voice even more than Emerson's was mystical, seer-like, uttering revelations from an oracle. But he gave a realistic note to his oracular and rhapsodic interpretations of the wonders of life and the wonders of America. He was both realist and romantic, national and universal; he contained in himself all the ideas and ideals that the new literature and the new age were struggling towards. He aimed, as he wrote, at "creating an *imaginative* New World, the correspondent and counterpart of the current scientific and political New World." He evoked this imaginative world in a large, loose way, setting himself to write for the average man in a selection of the speech of the average man; he made himself what he conceived to be the pattern of the average man, what he called a composite man and woman of democracy.

With neither private prejudices nor private emotions nor private moralities, Whitman's sensitivities and convictions were those of man as a member of society, not of man as a personal lover or friend; he was sensitive to the emotions themselves, not to their personal aspects; he was sensitive to the fact of death, of love, of universal brotherhood, for the sake of these things in themselves. Where he differed most profoundly from the other poet of his time who wrote of himself was at the point where he was most American: he had no concern with, perhaps no understanding of,

the intense personal relationships, the strong complex
personal emotions, the ever-present memories, of which
Les Fleurs du Mal is composed. Baudelaire is always
talking to somebody personally, is always writing of
people as individuals, individuals about whom he felt
intensely and lastingly, while Whitman is always talking *of* people and *to* people in multitude. He is exhorting men in the mass to comradeship, to universal love
and brotherhood; he makes a sweeping gesture of
acceptance of things in the mass, whatever they are—
fatherhood, motherhood, sex, leadership, affection,
death. He makes a sweeping get-together appeal; for
that reason he speaks in orations. And, for that, he invented the one sort of vehicle suitable: free verse unchecked by rhyme, by regular rhythms, or stanza-
formation. It was, for his theme, an inevitable form.
The others, the traditional measures, were all locked
up with the purely personal experiences, the personal
emotions of men.

Whitman was the one poet who made his audience
feel that they were a necessary part, almost collaborators
in the composition. His reader never feels alone, a lone
man listening to another lone man's confidences, but
one of a congregation. That sort of poetry, that sort of appeal in poetry, had never happened before and it really,
in spite of all Whitman's imitators, has never happened
since. He was a pure original. One may easily prefer
other poets, one may admit that because he was talking

to multitude he repeated himself over and over again, even contradicted himself ("Do I contradict myself? Very well then, I contradict myself—I am large, I contain multitudes"). One must admit, too, that only once or twice in the course of a fairly long poem would he reach the high plane of memorable expression, but when he reached it, it was as memorable as that of any poet who ever lived, and in a different way. Sometimes all that was memorable was a line, but the line was pregnant as few single lines ever were:

I am the man, I suffered, I was there.

or

Agonies are one of my changes of garments.

or

Now we have met, we have looked, we are safe.

or

Whoever you are, I fear you are walking the walk of dreams.

On his highest level, his pregnancy and his lyric potency were both unsurpassable and unique:

For my enemy is dead, a man divine as myself is dead,
I look where he lies white-faced and still in the coffin—I draw near,
Bend down and touch lightly with my lips the white face in the coffin.

or

Come, I will make the continent indissoluble,
I will make the most splendid race the sun ever shone upon,
I will make divine magnetic lands,
    With the love of comrades,
        With the life-long love of comrades.

. . . .

or

When lilacs last in the dooryard bloom'd,
And the great star early droop'd in the western sky in the
    night,
I mourn'd, and yet shall mourn with ever-returning spring.

Ever-returning spring, trinity sure to me you bring,
Lilac blooming perennial and drooping star in the west,
And thought of him I love.

or

Come, said the Muse,
Sing me a song no poet yet has chanted,
Sing me the Universal!

10

Whitman and Poe had two qualities in common—vitality and originality—and it was these two that brought them into the current of world-literature in such a way as to affect that current and to continue affecting it. They were of their time, if we regard the time over a long period, and they both reflected an array of ideas to which they also contributed. Henry James was more particularly of his time in the sense of belonging definitely to some three decades of it during which the novel developed from Flaubertian realism to something else. The evolution of his later work, "made of him," said William Crary Brownell, "perhaps the most individual novelist of his day, who, at the same time, is also in the current of its tendencies."

No writer who was born in the nineteenth or the beginning of the twentieth century can help being dominated, for some part of his career, by the literary ideas of the nineteenth century, especially the ones which announced that literature is an expression of national and racial genius, that it is the expression of society, and that the powerful doctrine of realism is almost unquestionable. But if one is to consider fairly the work of Henry James one must get outside these special theories: much as he himself, like every other writer, was influenced by them, what he accomplished belongs eventually to another conception of literature altogether, a conception which, no doubt, some critic will find a name for.

He was one of the writers who frequented the gatherings of the early realists, the group composed of Flaubert, the Goncourts, Zola, Turgenev, and while, in theory, he subscribed fervently to the new doctrines of realism and learned much from its practitioners, he was never, in their sense, a realist, and when after experimentation he evolved a method peculiar to himself, this method was destined to have an effect in combating realism; it was actually a move in the direction of the reaction. As with all the others, Balzac was his first master, and throughout his work something of Balzac remains—the Balzacian sense of the importance of appurtenances and things, which made a special appeal to Henry James. In spite of his theoretic adherence to realism, he did not believe that after Flaubert any writer could do much for the further development of the realistic novel. "Realism," he declared, "seems to us, with *Madame Bovary,* to have said the last word." So, consciously or unconsciously, after his early period, he set himself to evolve a type of novel that was destined to give those in reaction against the realists a battery of new technical devices.

What James contributed that was new was his method, his material a small, detached, over-privileged, cultivated international group, and the psychological type that made up such a group. The psychological type to which he attached his powers of intuition and investigation was in itself one which, before him, had not been given any studied presentation in literature, though, of course, it had appeared. But it should be noticed that the kind of human being presented by the great European writers, whether ancient or modern, belonged, on the whole, to one or two broad psychological divisions—they were either the men and women in whom the primitive instincts of early man had evolved to the height of strong emotions, with a consequent dimming of a sense of self-preservation, or else they were people in whom the instincts remained in a crude and untutored state, though with some emotional power. There is a third type, less simple than the other two, and to this belong the men and women in whom the instincts have not been brought to the point of strong or over-mastering emotions but have simply been refined away in motive forces of immense psychological complexity, with the sense of self-preservation very active, sometimes dominatingly so. When this type was given in the older literatures, he or she was presented as a heartless schemer or a cold sensualist—an Iago, a Becky Sharp, or a Joseph Surface.

When Henry James devoted his powers to the representation of this type—and the bulk of his personages belong to it—he presented him or her at a stage of refinement, sophistication and good breeding, that occasionally became a kind of idealism. He had studied the type carefully first, in a Puritan environment—and a Puritan may be said by definition to be one in whom primitive instincts have not developed into strong emotions but have been trimmed and regulated into something else which can in time reach, not only an extreme social refinement and gentility, but even a sort of idealism. Henry James, having encountered and appraised the type early, pursued it in many countries through the same social milieu—that of well-to-do people surrounded by the luxuries of living.

In the group in Paris that he frequented, he had noticed that when he uttered them, his ideas on novel writing made small impression. Flaubert, who had accomplished the realistic revolution, was taking very little stock in the novel-writing theories of a young American who did not seem to him to know what he was talking about; his interest, as well as his disapproval, was centered on Zola, who had nominated himself his disciple; then the Goncourts were off on a line about the novel of the working class, or as they called it, the *basses classes,* which had but little interest for Henry James. But there was also associated with the group Ivan Turgenev—"Mon grand moujik," Flaubert called him—and though James learned a great deal from all the others, it was Turgenev who turned his mind to the special problems in technique that became his lifelong interest, even his obsession. "Henry James went to Paris and read Turgenev; Howells stayed in America and read Henry James," said George Moore, that other subtle technician of the novel.

"A novel, for Turgenev," Henry James told us, "almost always began with a vision of some persons who hovered before him, soliciting him . . . then he had to find out for them the right relations, those that would most bring them out . . . and the situations most useful and favorable to the sense of the creatures themselves." This way of approaching a novel, Turgenev maintained, reduced the "architecture" to a minimum, and he would rather have too little "architecture" than too much. This preference for little "architecture" meant the minimizing of plot and became one of the corner-stones of James's technique. Like Turgenev, he took characters that solicited his interest and he set them moving in their world, using only the amount of plot that would keep them going. Like Turgenev, Henry James, in his early novels, was the narrator, narrating a story in chronological order, as in *Roderick Hudson,* or *Washington Square,* or *The Portrait of a Lady.* But after he had written some twenty or twenty-five novels, and towards 1890, it is clear that he began seriously to question himself both as to his material and his methods. He was intellectually too clear-sighted, too original, not to be aware that unless he could make a contribution of his own he would be merely one more of the numerous diggers in another man's ditch. The first sign of his uneasiness was his dropping his international material for a time and devoting himself to depicting the English society around him. The next move by which he showed his feeling that his work had need of change, of renewal, was a venture into play-writing, into the world of the theatre. This was, as most literary men's are, unsuccessful. Restlessly he turned towards writing short novels; finally, *What Maisie Knew* and *The Awkward Age* showed distinctly the beginnings of his own definitive method. His incursion into the theatre had been the artist's instinctive groping towards self-renewal. George Moore, who had belonged to the same group in Paris as Henry James, had, at the very same time, felt the same need for renewal of his work: in his case, it took the shape of going back to Ireland and turning his attention to the traditional Gaelic narrative forms.

The three novels that revealed James's new manner in complete development are *The Wings of the Dove, The Ambassadors, The Golden Bowl,* and in these we find his deeper and ever deeper concern with psychological reasons. Here he throws over whatever of the objective and direct methods of the realists still remained with him, and devotes himself completely to following clues to the interior lives of his characters, to tracing their stream of consciousness. In these novels we can note definitely the results of his incursion into play-writing. They are constructed as a series of situations, "scenically," he himself says, as if he had started by drafting a scenario, as a playwright does. Probably no novelist before or since has constructed such a complete scenario for a novel as he did, step by step, scene by scene, act by act, for *The Ambassadors.* His dialogue has also changed in character: if we compare the sort of conversation that is in *The Portrait of a Lady* with the conversation in *The Wings of the Dove,* we find in the later novel a conversation directed to the revealing of character and the preparation of situations such as might be constructed by a playwright in a piece of dramatic dialogue. Now, instead of the all-knowing author, the ideal spectator, who can reveal everything in the minds of his characters, we have an indirect device; now he begins to give "not my own personal account of the affair in hand, but my account of somebody's impression of it." In short, he begins to present his characters and his story "through the opportunity and the sensibility of some more or less detached, some not strictly involved, though thoroughly interested and intelligent witness or reporter." In the first volume of *The Golden Bowl* we see the affair in hand, and all the characters, through the mind of the Prince; later, we see it and them through the mind of the Princess. As the author himself states, the Prince opens the door to half the light on Maggie (the Princess) and she opens it to half the light on the Prince. Then, in these last novels, he does not start with the characters soliciting him, as in his early books, but with a sort of metaphysical idea sometimes suggested by an anecdote half told at a dinner table. For instance, the idea that started him on *The Ambassadors* came from the report of a conversation in which somebody had remarked, "One should live all one can," and the essence of the novel is contained in Strether's outbreak, "Live all you can; it's a mistake not to. It doesn't so much matter what you do in particular so long as you have your life. If you haven't had that, what have you had? Live, live!" A similar idea is behind *The Wings of the Dove*.

As he penetrates more and more into the interior lives of his personages, he touches on motives that are barely ponderable, and in trying to carry these over to the reader, he makes the characters themselves extraordinarily analytic, almost forcing them to penetrate into their own unconscious. In this way, the narrative of his later novels becomes an interior narrative with an interior dialogue constantly going on; he has somehow succeeded in making objectivity and chronology seem no longer so important as the realists made them. It is only a step from his interior narrative and interior dialogue to the interior monologue or to the contemporary method of sur-realism. The main thing now for Henry James became the touching of the psychological rhythm at its most significant key, for which reason he frequently begins a novel or a tale or a chapter in the middle of its interest as a story but at the height of its interest as psychological tension.

To understand the twistings and turnings in the technique of the modern novel, to understand the half-notes and the semi-tones, the detectivating attitude towards the interior motives, what Henry James has accomplished must be carefully taken into account, for he was one of the great technical masters in literature, one of those who discover how human experiences can be revealed. Granted that he was one of those to whom the supreme and devastating and transforming human emotions could never happen, yet he invented a way for expressing the infra-motives, the half emotions, the subdued desires that are a motive power with so much of civilized humanity. It is idle to suppose that fundamentally he felt he had made any sort of mistake in exiling himself from his country; to write of international society was his job and to be an exile was his function to which his instinct led him. Like most of the New England writers his instinct about his own destiny was sound; he was one of those destined to lead literature across national frontiers; he did this so well and with a technique so intellectually subtle, so meticulously worked out, that he was decades ahead of his time, as was Stendhal, and like Stendhal he was one of the masters of the distinguished workers in his own art. Also he gathered into his work many of the faint stirrings of the new manners in literature that were being worked up around him; a thorough symbolist, he took in the indirect methods of the Symbolists, and he left behind him a whole armory of technical devices for those writers coming after him who were capable of using them, and among the outstanding students of his work were Marcel Proust and James Joyce.

James was, of course, thoroughly American. When Ford Madox Ford tells us that Henry James was the most American product that New England turned out, he is stating what a critic familiar with both Europe and America, and their literatures, knows to be a simple fact. Whatever the material he used, he handled it as only an American could: only an American could have grasped the international scene as he did. Then, in his mental equipment, he had a strong common likeness to the other New England writers. He was meagerly endowed emotionally; he had a remoteness from everyday life; he had a refinement that was a trifle bewildering to his European confrères. He had the American quality of high intelligence, a penetrating intelligence, and this, attached to an acute psychological curiosity, produced what Taine would call his master-faculty. In common with Hawthorne and Poe, Henry James had a peculiarly American sense of eeriness and terror; he had likewise their inclination towards symbolism. Poe's approach in his stories, and in his "Eureka," is that of an investigator towards the problem of a cryptogram for which curiosity and concentrated intelligence could eventually provide a solution. In regard to his characters and their emotions, Henry James, like Poe, turned a concentrated intelligence onto the solution of a cryptogram.

Chapter Eleven

THE REVOLT

IN THE INNER courts of literature, for over fifty years there has been a struggle against the doctrine, the technique, the content, and the language of realism. It began in France, for it was there that the doctrine and the practice had ripened fastest, and the revolt was in full blast before the original doctrine had reached some of the other literatures. The revolters made little headway as far as the novel and drama went, for it was to the interest, not only of the real writers in these forms, but especially of a large group of the new trade writers, to hold the novel and the drama bound to the fact, the document, the observation of external and everyday life. Realism had such sanction that any sort of novel or drama that people could recognize as a transcript of life at first hand was regarded as superior in literary merit to romance and adventure writing of any kind. The documentary novel, with the locale in the lowest social milieu, with the characters treated from the physiological and economic standpoint, that would be welcomed enthusiastically in Paris, say, in 1890, would reach Berlin sometime before 1900, would get to Chicago and New York in the 1930's. And the only difference that the course of time had made between one and another of them would be in the geographical situation and the day-by-day routine of living. But in actual revelation of life there would be no difference at all. All of them would be intelligent and show powers of observation, for the realistic novel of any kind can exist only on these qualities, but of imagination, of sympathetic communication with life, of real creative effort, of power in the moulding of language, there would be little or no evidence. The ideas propounded by the authors, the characters displayed, would be of exactly the same kind, in the 1890's in Paris, the 1900's in Berlin, and the 1930's in Chicago or New York: the same critical vocabulary would be rife in acclaiming them. The Goncourts' term for non-realistic literature, "anodyne," used by them in 1865, became current in America sixty years later as "escapist" literature and was used in the same disparaging sense with regard to any literature of the imagination. A poem like Lindsay's "The Chinese Nightingale," a novel like Thornton Wilder's *The Bridge of San Luis Rey,* were attacked because the authors did not come "to grips with life," and did not deal with strikes, modern industrial life, with economic struggle. A novel about prostitutes and pimps and the moral dregs of society, like Charles-Louis Philippe's

Bubu of Montparnasse, which was received as a distinct revelation in Paris in 1900, would have its American version about 1935. In America, such works were considered the expression of after-war disintegration, whereas they were really the sign of paucity in literary invention and of the belatedness with which literary fashions of the Continent arrive in English-speaking countries. As the radical middle-class intelligentsia, interested in political and social reforms, increased in every country, realistic writing became more and more popular and profitable, for it could be made to reflect the special problems of the moment, and be a sort of history of the day.

There was, as has already been noted, a school of poetry, the Parnassian, which corresponded in a manner to the higher realism in prose. The leader of this school, Théophile Gautier, who called himself "a man for whom the exterior world exists," made an effort to translate into poetry the exterior world that he observed and knew, without injecting into it his own personality. Trained in painting, he tried to reproduce in language the effects of painting; his observations he translated into precise images and words, for he prided himself on the exactitude of his imagery and his vocabulary. He and the other Parnassians tried to produce a poetry that was hard, clear and impersonal. The bulk of the Parnassian theories, mixed with a few theories from the Symbolists, was taken over between 1910 and 1920 by a short-lived school of English and American poets who called themselves "Imagists."

2

The first clear indication of a strong revolt against realism was given in poetry. Of the two who began the revolt, Paul Verlaine and Arthur Rimbaud, both were in descent from Baudelaire, though they started with a leaning towards the Parnassians. Rimbaud had such a powerful originality and was so thoroughly in revolt against objective and realistic literature that, if he had pursued the normal productive life of a writer for about ten or fifteen years, giving his mind a chance to grow and his theories to ripen, he might have been the leader of a school of poetry that, on its side, would have been as forceful as the realists were in prose. But his creative period lasted only a couple of years, and before he was twenty he had deserted literature forever. Had he worked a few years more, his extreme, his anarchical doctrines, might have been moderated, widened, left more inclusive and usable for succeeding poets. Rimbaud's ambition was to overthrow the current ideas of prose and poetry and to start a completely new literary expression based on the idea that the only reality was in the world inside man; the world of external appearances was a snare. For poetry, the dream was the only thing—*le rêve* and the Baudelarian music. Out of the past he would admit nobody to be of any literary importance except

Baudelaire, and with him he believed a new day had begun. "Before Baudelaire," he wrote, "there was no poetry at all; there was only a sort of rhymed prose, the bovine glory of innumerable generations of idiots." In such revolt was he against realism and the external world as a subject for literature, that he forced himself into a state of mind where all was vision. "I say one must be a seer. The poet must make himself a seer by a prolonged, immense, reasoned derangement of all his senses." "I accustomed myself," he wrote, "to a simple state of hallucination. I saw very plainly a mosque in the place of a mill, a drum-band of angels, carriages on the highways of the sky, a salon at the bottom of a lake. . . . Then I explained my magical sophisms with the hallucination of words. I ended by finding sacred the disorder of my spirit. . . . My weakness was leading me to the confines of the world and of Cimmeria, the fatherland of shades and whirlwinds."

By something like a reasoned derangement of his own senses, a dream or an hallucination, Rimbaud produced his astonishing "Bateau Ivre," one of the most remarkable poems in the whole of literature, a completely original poem and of a far more sustained creativeness than that other original poem, also by a young man in his teens, Poe's "To Helen." The "Bateau Ivre" is of such vigor, such thrilling and original imagery, such varied and subtle music, that it is difficult to believe that a young man who could write in such fashion abandoned literature without regret at the age of nineteen, looking back afterwards on his brief literary career as "une saison en enfer"—a term in hell. Like Poe's "To Helen," the "Bateau Ivre" had far-reaching effects, and there have been distinguished men of letters in our day, such as Paul Claudel and Jacques Rivière, who are convinced that Rimbaud was one of the greatest and most original poets who have ever existed.

Part of the "Bateau Ivre" goes back to a boy's dream of adventure, as when in the first stanza he visualizes the boat descending an impassable river in America, attacked by redskins, its haulers seized and nailed to vari-colored totem poles. The boat itself thus left to its own devices staggers down the river to the sea without guidance, like a drunken man. Then we have the dream like adventures of the boat as it is tossed about by wild storms, drifting through strange seas, touching incredible lands, encountering all the legendary spectacles of the sea, finally, wearily sinking under the waves. All is related in verse of the most marvellous and far-fetched imagery, exhibiting in the very highest degree the seer-like quality that Rimbaud insisted the poet must attain to. While freely using colloquial expressions, he does not employ them in their ordinary meaning but according to some associated meaning that the image he is projecting calls forth. For instance, when he is noting the phosphorescent lights on the tropical sea, he describes them as "des phosphores chanteurs," which means literally "singing phosphorus," suggesting the vibration of the lights through its resemblance to the vibration of a singer's voice. Words are used with the deliberate intention of suggesting more than one meaning: thus, the Indians who have seized the haulers are described as "les Peaux-Rouges criards," which means both "the yelling Red-skins" and "the Red-skins vivid with war-paint." Now and again words are shifted from their normal place in the sentence; sometimes the reader is free to construe whatever meaning his sensibility and imagination can receive from the description of the visionary adventures of the intoxicated boat. With a boy's dream of strange lands and seas there is mixed a man's desolate feeling of the meaninglessness, aimlessness and wastefulness of life. Sometimes the boat loses its identity in the poet, and it is the man who hurtles himself, masterless, rudderless, into unchecked adventures. It is as if the poet at the age of seventeen, when he wrote the "Bateau Ivre," peered into the future and saw the adventurous, exotic, rudderless life that was to be his.

Je sais les cieux crevant en éclairs, et les trombes
Et les ressacs et les courants; je sais le soir,
L'aube exaltée ainsi qu'un peuple de colombes,
Et j'ai vu quelquefois ce que l'homme a cru voir.

J'ai vu le soleil bas, taché d'horreurs mystiques,
Illuminant de longs figements violets,
Pareils à des acteurs de drames très antiques,
Les flots roulant au loin leurs frissons de volets.

THE REVOLT

J'ai rêvé la nuit verte aux neiges éblouies,
Baisers montant aux yeux des mers avec lenteur,
La circulation des sèves inouïes
Et l'éveil jaune et bleu des phosphores chanteurs.

. . . .

Or, moi, bateau perdu sous les cheveux des anses,
Jeté par l'ouragan dans l'éther sans oiseau,
Moi dont les Monitors et les voiliers des Hanses
N'auraient pas repêché la carcasse ivre d'eau.

. . . .

Mais, vrai, j'ai trop pleuré. Les aubes sont navrantes,
Toute lune est atroce et tout soleil amer.
L'acre amour m'a gonflé de torpeurs enivrantes.
Oh! que ma quille éclate! Oh! que j'aille à la mer!

. . . .

I know the skies bursting into flashes and the waterspouts,
And the waves' back-wash and the currents; I know the
    evening,
The dawn uplifted like a flock of doves,
And I have sometimes seen what men believed they saw.

I have seen the low sun, stained with mystic horrors,
Lighting up with long, violet curdlings,
Like the actors in antique plays,
The shivering clefts of the waves in the distance.

I have dreamed the green night through with its dazzle of
    snow,
Kisses tardily rising to the eyes of the sea,
The circulation of unheard-of ichors,
And the yellow-blue awakening of the vibrating phosphorus.

. . . .

Now I, a boat lost under the lianas of the creeks,
Flung by the whirlwind into the birdless air,
I, whose drunken carcass neither iron-clads nor the schooners
 of Hansa
Would have fished out of the water.

．　　．　　．　　．　　．　　．　　．　　．　　．　　．　　．　　．

But truly I have wept too much. The dawns are intolerable,
Every moon is atrocious, and every sun is galling.
Bitter love has filled me with enervating languors.
Oh, let my keel burst, let me go under the sea!
                                    (*Literal translation by M. M. C.*)

The imagery of this poem is hardly related to actual sights or sounds but has correspondences with sight, or sound, or memory, in the poet's mind, which makes an appeal, not to the surface intelligence of the reader but to his imagination, to his sensibility and his associations. And yet one can believe that this very complicated poem might have glamorous interest for seventeen-year-olds who had never read anything except boys' books of adventure.

It is hard to know whether all the creative power Rimbaud possessed, that "circulation of unheard-of ichors," came to sudden fruition and an end in a couple of years, or whether his relation with Verlaine disgusted him forever with all memories of his literary life, that life which he was to describe as "a term in hell." It was Verlaine, however, who had the haunting regret as well as the lasting attachment. While the great intellectual power, the revolutionary originality,

the transforming force, was Rimbaud's, Verlaine had
that sort of unique emotional power which can result
in expression of the most direct simplicity. Nothing can
show this better than the little poem he wrote while
in gaol for wounding Rimbaud with a revolver.

> Le ciel est, par-dessus le toit,
> Si bleu, si calme!
> Un arbre, par-dessus le toit,
> Berce sa palme.
>
> La cloche, dans le ciel qu'on voit,
> Doucement tinte.
> Un oiseau, sur l'arbre qu'on voit,
> Chante sa plainte.
>
> Mon Dieu, mon Dieu, la vie est là,
> Simple et tranquille.
> Cette paisible rumeur-là,
> Vient de la ville.
>
> Qu'as-tu fait, ô toi que voilà
> Pleurant sans cesse,
> Dis, qu'as tu fait, toi que voilà,
> De ta jeunesse?

. . . .

The sky is up above the roof,
So blue, so calm,
A tree above the roof
Rocks its branch.

The bell, in the sky we see,
Softly chimes,
A bird, on the tree we see,
Sings its lament.

O God, O God, life is there,
Simple and sweet,
That peaceful humming there
Comes from the town.

What have you done, O you there,
Weeping without ceasing—
Say, what have you done, O you there,
With your youth?

(Literal translation by M. M. C.)

This very great sincerity, this integral expression, is only to be found in a few poems, outside of folk-songs, in the whole of literature, and oftener in English literature than in any other. Both Verlaine and Rimbaud were profoundly influenced by English poetry, and sometimes what their innovations amounted to was an attempt to reproduce in French the half-said, blurred effects of English poetry.

Verlaine, before his meeting with Rimbaud, was a fine poet; after this meeting, he became a great one, for all the potentialities that were in him, of original thought, of emotion, of musical utterance, all his latent sense of revolt against the nullity towards which literature was heading, came to the surface under the influence of this prophetic and penetrating mind and this disrupting personality. All that Verlaine did not of himself understand of the necessity for renewal in literature, this young man made him aware of. Rimbaud

322

was an example of precocious intellect and poetical intuition unparalleled in literature, with perhaps the exception of Chatterton. He was a sort of elemental creative force, bursting to reform everything he touched. In his "L'Alchimie du Verbe"—"Transfiguration of the Word"—he tells us how he wanted to invent not only new poetical forms but a new world with new stars, new flowers, new flesh; he wanted especially to invent a new language, for, as he said, it was impossible to write poetry in words and sentences that had been weighed down by the leaden meanings of practical life. He wanted to reform both God and man, for this astonishing young man thought that the mind could re-create all things; he studied magic and necromancy; he imagined himself, as other poets sometimes have imagined themselves, to be a sorcerer or alchemist, and he thought that by forcing his mind outside everyday existence he might ultimately attain the talisman for changing life. To the bespelled Verlaine, ten years his elder, he taught that letting oneself be involved in the common world of eating, sleeping, begetting and providing for a family was practically the all-inclusive vice, and that the old world of everyday happenings had nothing to do with poetry or with the poet's existence.

Whatever has to be said against their relationship, it was, while it lasted, a period of intense intellectual, poetical, and emotional activity for both Rimbaud and Verlaine. Under the influence of Rimbaud, Verlaine wrote his "Art Poétique," which crystallized the new attitudes towards poetry and which later became a sort of gospel with the Mallarméan symbolists. Most of the theories of this poem were derived from Rimbaud and from English poetry. To write poetry like English poetry in a language like French, which had been developed logically with the avowed intention of becoming an instrument of expression of the greatest clarity, was immensely difficult. To express under-tones and over-tones, hidden meanings, to attain the half-said thing, to make an appeal directly from one sensibility to another, was, in the language and in the existent metres, if not exactly an impossibility, at least a perplexing task. Consequently Verlaine's "Art of Poetry," which, though written during his relation with Rimbaud, became generally known only a decade later, was accepted as a liberation; Verlaine, following Poe and Baudelaire, demanded in poetry *de la musique avant toute chose*—music above all—and he marched haughtily past the great French sign-posts demanding the *mot juste*. The latest of these, it will be remembered, had been set up by Gautier and Flaubert. Verlaine asked the poet to choose his words somewhat carelessly, unprecisely, to join the precise to the unprecise—in short, to achieve, not the exact, but the nuanced. This was

more in accordance with Rimbaud's practice than with
Verlaine's.

> Car nous voulons la nuance encor,
> Pas la couleur, rien que la nuance!
> Oh! la nuance seule fiance
> Le rêve au rêve et la flûte au cor!
>
> .   .   .   .
>
> For we want the nuance,
> Nothing of color, only the nuance!
> Oh! the nuance alone weds
> The dream to the dream and the flute to the horn.

In a succeeding stanza he tenders that since often-
quoted advice—"Prends l'éloquence et tords-lui son
cou!"—"Take eloquence and wring its neck." This
manifesto has been taken very seriously by the poets in
English since the 1890's, the line about twisting the neck
of eloquence being put forward as a poetical principle,
though, as a matter of fact, it has very little application
for an English poet, for what Verlaine meant by "eloquence" was that deliberate study of rhetoric so usual in
France and which had played such havoc with French
literature after the great classical period. But eloquence
had been a glory in English poetry, especially with the
great dramatic poets, and still remains a glory when it
does not sink to mere declamation. Verlaine recommended the break-up of the French line into unequal
lines, and after a mocking attack on rhyme and a praise

of assonance, he summed up the modern Art of Poetry in two stanzas that have passed into the literatures of the world.

> De la musique encore et toujours!
> Que tons vers soit la chose envolée,
> Qu'on sent qui fuit d'une âme en allée
> Vers d'autres cieux à d'autres amours.
>
> Que ton vers soit la bonne aventure
> Éparse au vent crispé du matin
> Qui va fleurant la menthe et le thym . . .
> Et tout le reste est littérature!

. . . .

> Music again and ever!
> Let your verse be a thing on wings,
> Which visibly came from a soul in flight
> Towards other skies and other loves.
>
> Let your verse be the gay adventure
> Scattered on the crisp wind of morning
> Which snares the scents of mint and thyme . . .
> And all the rest is literature.
>
> *(Literal translation by M. M. C.)*

Verlaine lived for twenty-three years after the separation from Rimbaud, holding deep in his mind the memory of his lost friend, his "époux infernal," and editing an edition of his poems. The "époux infernal," on his side, abandoned poetry and Europe; he wandered in Asia, in Africa, and like his own Bateau Ivre, as a trader he descended impassable rivers, sailed phosphorescent seas, until "every dawn became intolerable, every moon atrocious and every sun bitter." He died at the age of thirty-seven in a hospital in Marseilles, caring nothing at all for the reports which reached him of his increasing fame as a poet. Verlaine died even more miserably than Rimbaud, alone in a dismal room, half falling out of bed, while the trollop with whom he lived deserted him in his dying hour to drink with her cronies in a neighboring bistro. Rimbaud and Verlaine were the last great French poets; there have been distinguished poets since, but no really great ones. When Rimbaud vanished from the literary scene, leaving his small bulk of work behind him, his admirers said that he had left with Verlaine the secret of the poetry of the future.

If a writer of great genius had then appeared, who could have taken over "the secret," who was capable of making a new synthesis of the exterior and the interior life, of the dream life and the everyday life, another new creative age might have been inaugurated. But the men who took it over, the Symbolists, were not able to use it in a way to render any powerful service to literature. The turning away from the exterior and the concentration on the interior world became, in their case, as exaggerated as the concentration of the realists on the physical world. If the realists de-valuated the life of the spirit, the bulk of the Symbolists rejected physical and everyday life as matter for literature in a manner which was destined to be not only limiting but even sterilizing. They were, in the main, accomplished and subtle men of letters, with a gift for poetry, a great flair for theorizing, and an excited interest in anything that seemed to lead to literary reform, such as the verse-forms of Whitman and the poetry and criticism of Edgar Allan Poe.

3

While the Symbolists were the most interesting literary group of the late nineteenth century, interesting for their theories and for their attempts to put them into practice, their chief doctrines did not originate with them, and the ones that did, the minor doctrines, were too esoteric and even eccentric to have vigorous life. Their progenitors in French literature were, of course, Baudelaire, Rimbaud and Verlaine; then they took over many ideas from the criticism and poetry of Edgar Allan Poe. Also, they tried to invent a French verse-form that would correspond to Whitman's: this was variously called free verse, liberated verse, polymorphous verse. This last invention has been claimed by Gustave Kahn, but it may have been initiated by the two Americans who were of the group, Stuart Merrill and Vielé Griffin. What the Symbolists accomplished separately is, in the case of most of them, not of so much importance as the general influence that emanated from the group. They were deliberately in revolt against realism and Parnassianism, more deliberately than were Rimbaud and Verlaine, though the core of their ideas came from these two predecessors. They also believed that inner reality is the only reality, and that the world from which a poet draws his poetry is a transcendent world, outside the everyday world. The whole art of poetry needed to be renewed, and the poetry of the future would be different from the poetry of the past, which had been made—and especially in French—with the same language and according to the same grammatical rules as prose. For the making of *this* poetry, the poetry of the future, the common, logical language, created for practical everyday usage, was no longer suitable; the very words that made up the language were conditioned by everyday employment and were incapable of encompassing ideas from the other world, the transcendent world of dream and poetry. Mallarmé, like Rimbaud, conceived of this language as weighing down poetry with the weight of lead.

What then was to be done with language so that it could be made a fitting vehicle for poetic expression? In the past, every initiator of a literary form had, first of all, to do something with language when it had begun to lose tone and color through being used too long in a particular way. The old way of renewing the literary language was to refresh it from popular speech. This was all very well when Dante took over what he called "the illustrious vernacular," or when Luther took over the language of the housewife and the artisan, or when Wordsworth advocated the language of the common Englishman, the rustic. But in the latter part of the nineteenth century, as in our own time, the spread of popular education meant that "the illustrious vernacular" was disappearing, for the popular language was becoming merely a degeneration of the written one. Faced with the problem of language, Mallarmé advanced a number of ideas, which he himself put into practice and some of which have been upheld by poets and writers ever since. Words, he said, should be deprived of their too obvious meaning; the poet should use words in an evocative and a suggestive instead of a literal and logical sense; the mood, the idea, the emotion should be evoked instead of described. This, it will be remembered, was what Edgar Allan Poe had succeeded in doing, both in verse and prose, and Mallarmé even more than Baudelaire was under the spell of Poe. In an often-quoted sentence Mallarmé declared, "to name an object is to suppress three-quarters of the joy of the poem, which is made of the happiness of guessing, little by little—to suggest, that is to reveal the dream." To achieve this evocative and suggestive effect, words, freed from their every-day meaning, should be given another meaning corresponding chiefly to their sound and their association-value. The sound and association-value of words had been used by Rimbaud and by many other poets before him, in many languages, but this was the first time that this special practice was deliberately advanced as part of an Art of Poetry.

Actually, if we take any words in any language—*house, bridge, love; maison, pont, amour; Haus, Brücke, Liebe; casa, ponte, amore*—each of them has at least three meanings: an ordinary sense-meaning, a sound-meaning and an association-meaning. Rimbaud did not mind using common colloquial or even slang words, but he seldom used them in their ordinary meaning, but to convey a sense of association or correspondence. Mallarmé did not use colloquial words, but he believed that words devitalized by their everyday use could again be made living by giving them an unusual place in the sentence; prepositions, conjunctions and words which marked the transitions, or gave a too commonplace clarity, should be thrown out altogether; punctuation and other marks, like capital letters, which are a logical or a conventional imposition on the line, should be rejected. The poet's business was not to trim his ideas into a logical order; it was the business of the reader to give them such an order. He held that a poem was a mystery, the key to which the reader or hearer had to search for; therefore, it might easily come about that, as each reader would supply a different key, different interpretations of a poem were quite as legitimate as different interpretations of a piece of music, for in music alone was expressed the interior life without the imposition of logical development.

331

These ideas, in practically the same form, had first been put forward as far back as the time of Goethe, by that strange romantic German writer, Novalis (Von Hardenberg, the seeker after the blue rose). Novalis announced that poetry achieved its object in proportion as it approached the art of music, the most all-embracing of the arts; like the later Mallarmé, he held that there could be a poetry which had no intelligible meaning and which might be made up of musical sounds. He held other views, similar to or identical with those which became associated with the Symbolists: that poetry should express the profound and mysterious reaches of the soul, the essence of the interior life; that poetry is an interior language, the conversation of the soul with itself, therefore, it should not be shut up in too precise forms that might hinder the free flight of the mind. Novalis also declared that the art of revealing the interior life of dream demanded something higher than our common logic, which is the art of deliberate thinking. He conceived, too, of a prose literature which would not be logically joined together but where the connection would be through the association of ideas, as in dreams. When we review these conceptions we perceive that Novalis was in possession of most of the reforming theories of the Symbolists.

But what was original with the Symbolists was their attempt to unite these theories with the new philosophies of the unconscious that were then coming in, chiefly the philosophy of Hartmann, but also that of Schopenhauer, which tended to show that intelligence was a by-product of other life-forces and that reason and logic were more or less irrelevant. This gave some of the Symbolists a more metaphysical and cerebral attitude than their predecessors towards the content and structure of a poem. Mallarmé was metaphysical where Novalis was mystical, where Rimbaud was sensuous and ardent, and Verlaine emotional. With Mallarmé, a phase of the interior life of the mind, what he called the transcendent reality, would be translated into an idea, and this idea would then be transposed into a symbol, or several symbols, that would evoke or suggest it, and would contain it as "a plant contains a flower without resembling it." From this came the Symbolist formula, or one of the Symbolist formulas: a work of art is a thought inscribed in a symbol.

To show what Mallarmé meant and how he put the theory into practice, we will take the most often-quoted of his hermetic sonnets, the one entitled "Sonnet en i Majeur," which expresses a common mood of his spirit, the blankness of his mind before a white sheet of paper. In this poem, it will be observed that in spite of its difficulty, the Symbolism though deliberate is comparatively clear. Though there is undoubtedly a secondary meaning, the primary meaning is quite sufficient for a grasp of the poem. Of the virgin day that begins, the poet wonders if it is going to rend from him some expression, but like a swan frozen into the ice, he cannot shake his mind free from the sterility which holds it bound.

Le vierge, le vivace et le bel aujourd'hui,
Va-t-il nous déchirer avec un coup d'aile ivre
Ce lac dur oublié que hante sous le givre
Le transparent glacier des vols qui n'ont pas fui!

Un cygne d'autrefois se souvient que c'est lui
Magnifique, mais qui, sans espoir, se délivre
Pour n'avoir pas chanté la région où vivre
Quand du stérile hiver a resplendi l'ennui.

Tout son col secouera cette blanche agonie,
Par l'espace infligée à l'oiseau qui le nie,
Mais non l'horreur du sol où le plumage est pris.

Fantôme, qu'a ce lieu son pur éclat assigne,
Il s'immobilise au songe froid de mépris
Que vêt parmi l'exil inutile le Cygne.

. . . .

The virgin, the vibrant, the beautiful To-day,
Will it rend for us with a flash of inebriated wing,
This hard, forgotten lake where, under the glaze, abides
Transparent the congealer of wings that have not flown!

A swan of other days remembers that it is he,
Magnificent, but who, because he has not sung
The region to live in when the ennui of sterile winter
Has gleamed, without hope delivers himself.

All his neck will shake off this white agony
By space inflicted on the bird who disowns it,
But not the horror of the ground where his plumage is held.

Phantom, that to this place his pure brightness assigns,
He immobilizes himself in the cold dream of contempt
With which he vests his vain exile, the Swan.

(Literal translation by M. M. C.)

In this poem, as in all of Mallarmé's except the earlier ones which were written under the influence of Baudelaire, like "La Chair Est Triste, Hélas!" and "Las de l'Amer Repos," if you take the lines separately or the words separately, you will make nothing of them. It is essential to get the total meaning of the poem before examining the lines and the words. The "Sonnet en i Majeur," like many of his poems, contains the history of the efforts of his mind, his struggle for themes, for he was somewhat sterile, and getting a poem out of himself could only be accomplished by enormous labor. There is nothing in his writing to show that he ever came to strong grips with life or felt the fiercer forms of love, hate, anger, melancholy, despair or compassion that are in *Les Fleurs du Mal*. But in his best poems, and above all in his wonderful sonnet to Poe, he is able to achieve an expression that does really seem as if it came from some transcendent world, so noble and sweeping it is. However, his deliberate attempt to be obscure gives one a feeling as of a man trying to arrange a cross-word puzzle, and he set the example, or he or his followers gave the formula, for some of the strange verse-concoctions of our time that are considered poetry in certain writing *cénacles*.

Towards his last phase he got to the point where he conceived that poetry should actually be written as music is written, the theme orchestrated instead of developed, the words used like notes in music, grouped in some lines, isolated in others, the whole printed so as to give obscurely the effect of a sheet of music. At this stage he had fallen under the influence of Wagner and Debussy in music, and had reached that old heresy, or old illusion, that a synthesis of all the arts could be achieved and a single art evolved which would convey visual effects and sound effects, suggest plastic effects and color effects, as well as transmit a verbal meaning. The idea of inventing a language which would convey this ensemble occurred to him and to some of his followers; this notion has, in actual fact, been put into practice in our own time by James Joyce, in his strange *Work in Progress*.

4

The poet, sometimes assumed to belong to the Symbolist group, who has had the most influence on writers of our time is Jules Laforgue. While drawing on the ideas of the Symbolists, he can hardly be regarded as one of them, for he was against their favorite doctrine that the interior life represented the only reality, and he considered that they had beaten too complete a re-

treat from everyday life. He himself evolved a sophisticated realistic poetry in which the two psychic streams,
the conscious and the unconscious, were subtly revealed and intermingled. In poems, written in ordinary
conversational language, about flirtations, railway sta-
tions, pianos playing in the suburbs, the little miseries
of winter, or in poems built around the refrains of old
songs, he accomplished, in the 'eighties of the last century, almost everything in verse which we consider to be
the special expression of this modern, post-war, disintegrated age. He sunk himself in the study of philosophy, and especially in the philosophy of the sub-conscious as, in his pre-Freudian day, it was explained by
the German philosopher Hartmann. If he did not suc-
ceed in revealing it as Joyce and Proust have done,
Laforgue managed to convey, in verse arranged, not
logically but according to the association of ideas and
with a subtle use of symbolism (not the deliberate symbolism of Mallarmé but a symbolism springing naturally from the subject), the mystery that lies behind the
most trivial happenings.

Laforgue's aim was to express in poetry the *homme
moyen* of modern civilization, the man who in each
country possesses the same sort of apartment, the same
sort of piano—in our day it would be a radio—who
wears the same sort of clothes, who has fought with
the same sort of weapons in the same war. This person-

age was given by Laforgue a variety of cultivated, sophisticated emotions and ideas, and enough music, art and literature at the back of his mind to color or give a sort of refrain to his experiences of life. Laforgue's influence has been very great, and there have been choruses and choirs of Laforguians in every modern literature. In English, the most important poets who have followed his lead have been T. S. Eliot and Ezra Pound, though there are at least a score or two others in English, Irish and American literature who have tried to achieve the same effects. The following example of a Laforgue poem is an account of a banal flirtation betwen a conventional young woman trying to be profound, and a sophisticated, ironic young man who knows that this appearance of profundity is drawn from whatever little literature the young woman knows.

Elle disait, de son air vain fondamental:
"Je t'aime pour toi seul!"—Oh! là, là, grêle histoire;
Oui, comme l'art! Du calme, ô salaire illusoire
    Du capitaliste Idéal!

Elle faisait: "J'attends, me voici, je sais pas" . . .
Le regard pris de ces larges candeurs des lunes;
—Oh! là, là, ce n'est pas peut-être pour des prunes,
    Qu'on a fait ses classes ici-bas?

Mais voici qu'un beau soir, infortunée à point,
Elle meurt!—Oh! là, là; bon, changement de thème!
On sait que tu dois ressusciter le troisième
    Jour, sinon en personne, du moins

THE REVOLT

Dans l'odeur, les verdures, les eaux des beaux mois!
Et tu iras, levant encore bien plus de dupes
Vers le Zaimph de la Joconde, vers la Jupe!
    Il se pourra même que j'en sois.

.   .   .   .

She said, with her empty transcendental air:
"I love you for yourself alone." Oh, my, my! the old story;
Yes, like a book. O illusory salary of the calm,
    Of the capitalistic ideal!

She went on: "I am waiting, here I am, I don't know" . . .
Her eyes full of the large candours of moons;
Oh, my, my! it is not perhaps for nothing
    That one takes one's college courses, here below?

But, lo, one fine evening, unfortunately,
She dies. Oh, my, my! let us change the subject.
We know that you should arise the third
    Day, if not in person, at least

In the odour, in the verdure, in the waters of the fine
    months.
And you will go levying further dupes,
Towards Giaconda's guimpe, towards the gown!
    Very likely I'll be one of them.

                        (Literal translation by M. M. C.)

Even more than the official Symbolists Laforgue
broke up the logically arranged lines in verse which
were an imposition from all previous literatures. Even
in the most romantic English poetry, which at times
provided a pattern for the Symbolists, it was the poet's
design to develop his theme logically, in logically ar-

ranged lines. A well-known poem of Shelley's runs like this:

> I arise from dreams of thee
> In the first sweet sleep of night,
> When the winds are breathing low
> And the stars are shining bright.

And proceeds by a logical sequence:

> I die, I faint, I fail!
> Let thy love in kisses rain
> On my lips and eyelids pale.

But the modern poets who wanted to express hitherto unstressed complexities of emotions believed that almost anything of the multitudinous ideas associated with love was matter for a love-poem. As a lover arising from dreams of his belovèd was just as likely to associate his emotion with ideas of how to array himself as with exclaiming, "I die, I faint, I fail," T. S. Eliot, in the "Love Song of J. Alfred Prufrock," wrote:

I grow old. . . . I grow old. . . .
I shall wear the bottoms of my trousers rolled.
Shall I part my hair behind? Do I dare to eat a peach?
I shall wear white flannel trousers and walk upon the beach.
I have heard the mermaids singing each to each.

I do not think that they will sing to me.

. . . .

We have lingered in the chambers of the sea
By sea-girls wreathed with sea-weed red and brown,
Till human voices wake us and we drown.

THE REVOLT

The influence of Laforgue in breaking up the old logic, the old unity of poetry, was greater than Mallarmé's, and the content and form of his verse, in addition, exercised a considerable influence on the technique of the novel. This was true, however, of all those modern poets who broke off from the older traditions. Baudelaire's peculiar realism, in which he expressed his own personal conflicts with life and the conflict of the interior life with the exterior world, was one of the influences which made for the modern autobiographic, semi-realistic novel, with a strong strain of lyricism running through it. Another persistent and lasting influence towards this kind of fiction was Goethe's *Wilhelm Meister,* which still holds its glamour for most young men and women, and for all young writers.

Among the other forces acting on the technique of the novel was the Symbolist formula: a writer should not describe a scene or a character or an emotion—he must evoke them. This—with Henry James's "minimum of architecture" and his later device of presenting his characters and his story "through the opportunity and the sensibility of some more or less detached, some not strictly involved, though thoroughly interested and intelligent witness or reporter," his habit of dealing with barely ponderable motives—is responsible for the bulk of modern technical reforms in fiction. The idea of giving us the scene, not as Flaubert did, completely objectively, with the novelist like God in the universe the ideal spectator present everywhere, but simply as one or two persons involved see it, was first carried out by Stendhal, who, in his famous account of the battle of Waterloo, describes only so much of it as was apparent to Fabrizio; similarly, in *Ulysses,* when James Joyce is describing a funeral, his method differs fundamentally from that of Flaubert. In the account of the funeral in *Madame Bovary,* we have every significant detail realistically described—the funeral procession, the grave-clothes of Emma, the three coffins, the chanting choristers, the lighted candles, the priest, the lowering of the coffin into the open grave. Through nine or ten pages we have nothing but the funeral. James Joyce takes about thirty pages to present his funeral, but instead of Flaubert's objective description, he presents the streets of Dublin and some people passing along, as they appear, in occasional views through the shaded windows, to the occupants of one of the mourning-carriages. We have the aimless gossip, on all sorts of topics, by the men in the carriage—the half-conscious and subconscious thoughts of the chief character, Leopold Bloom. Similarly, when Virginia Woolf is presenting, in *Jacob's Room,* a party, there is no objective description; she puts the party before us by giving us the conversation of people meeting and passing each other in the ball-room, by remarks thrown out as the partners dance past each other; and the effect, in both cases, of the inconsequent actuality of the conversation is most memorable in bringing to us the funeral and the dance; the reader feels as if he were participating in the events. However, this sort of technique is sometimes bewildering to those accustomed to the realistic, semi-realistic, or romantic novel, for it is often only when the reader has got the impression of a whole chapter in his mind that he knows what is taking place, or where it is taking place.

5

But the great, the overwhelming influences on all literary transformations—on technique, on content, on language—were the new discoveries in psychology, the new knowledge of the mind, arrived at in the last quarter of the nineteenth century and the beginning of the twentieth. When all the old conventions were being shaken to pieces, it was discovered that that universally accepted figure, the conscious man, the man that all laws, governments, civilizations, had been built around, was also a convention. Man was only conscious to a limited degree: the greater part of him was unconscious. This fact had peeped in and out of philosophy for a long time, but as it was very disturbing, the bulk of mankind preferred to ignore it. Hartmann expressed the discovery first, for the Germans, and when his work was translated into French it greatly stirred the writers in reaction against realism, for it seemed then as if this new philosophy would be a pillar of support to those who believed the interior life, the life beyond everyday life, to be the only reality. In the 'eighties, Charcot and Ribot demonstrated the discoveries for the French; and in America, at about the same time, William James, experimenting in psychology, got himself employed as a census-assistant so as to have the opportunity to meet and study a wide variety of human beings. After his census experience he declared, "We all have a subliminal self—that is, a self below the threshold of consciousness, which may at any time make an eruption into our ordinary life. At its lowest, this is only a deposit of forgotten memories; at its highest, we do not know what it is at all." It was James, too, who was responsible for the famous simile of the iceberg—that the conscious mind is comparable to the smaller part that is above water, the unconscious to the greater bulk that is submerged.

Théodule Ribot showed the existence, in us, of unconscious memory. Pierre Janet, Charcot's pupil, who lectured recently at the Harvard Tercentenary, demonstrated how several personalities could exist at the same time in one individual, each now and again breaking through to the other. Freud, a while later, developed the technique by which, he said, the subconscious personality and the hidden memory could be brought to the surface, or partly to the surface. After the conscious man and the unified personality were shown to be conventions, the philosopher, Henri Bergson, came along and said that what we call time is a convention; real time was not hours as measured by a clock, or in days or weeks on a calendar; it, too, was something inward, duration experienced; every moment in life represents our entire past shaping itself into a new creative movement; nothing was fixed or finished; everything was in a state of becoming. For Bergson, also, the unconscious was the source from which flowed, in a thin stream for some, in a wider stream for others, our conscious life.

All the literary philosophies relating to the revelation of life having reached a dead end, the writers had to turn to the experimental and speculative philosophies. Such discoveries as had come through them were eagerly seized upon by that type of mind which initiates new literary modes and ideas. Now the first problem was: Could this subconscious part of man, this part that was now described as the moving force of his being, be expressed in literature? As in poetry the first attempt had been made, in the 'eighties, so now in prose the first attempt also was made, and made by a curiously talented novelist of very limited range, who was a follower of one of the Symbolist groups, Edouard Dujardin, still alive. He attempted to express the undercurrent of the mind of his character by "the interior monologue." Now, what is the interior monologue, which is being so identified with our most advanced novelists, though, like almost every other modern literary device, it dates back to the nineteenth century? I know no better definition of it than Dujardin's own: "The interior monologue is the discourse without auditor, unspoken, by which a person expresses his inmost thought, the thought nearest the unconscious, anterior to any logical organization, by means of sentences with a minimum of syntax. It is done so as to give the impression that it is poured out, and is a slice of the interior life without explanation or commentary."

Dujardin himself had not sufficient clue to the technique to be employed in rendering "the thought nearest the unconscious." But in the interim between him and the writer who took the next step forward, James Joyce, there came all the discoveries of Freud and Freud's technique for getting a patient to pour out his unconscious life. That the interior monologue, which was one of the most discussed features of *Ulysses* on its publication, was managed so successfully was because Freud had actually discovered a method of revealing the subconscious and the twilight stage between the conscious and the unconscious. Freud made the subject lie on a couch while he himself took up a position where he could not be seen, and induced the subject to talk, following step by step anything that came into his mind, one idea leading to another, one memory suggesting another, one association dragging another to the surface of the mind, until the world below consciousness was revealed either wholly or in part. This is really the process followed by Joyce in the celebrated monologue of Marion Bloom with which *Ulysses* ends.

For purposes of illustration, I give a short quotation from this monologue, which is a widely imitated device in recent novels:

> they all write about some woman in their poetry well I suppose he won't find many like me where softly sighs of love the light guitar where poetry is in the air the blue sea and the moon shining so beautifully coming back on the night-boat from Tarifa the light-house at Europa point the guitar that fellow played was so expressive will I never go back there again all new faces two glancing eyes a lattice hid I'll sing that for him they're my eyes as if he has anything of a poet two eyes as darkly bright as love's own star aren't those beautiful words as love's young star it'll be a change the Lord knows to have an intelligent person to talk to about yourself not always listening to him and Billy Prescott's ad and Keyses' ad and Tom the Divil's ad then if anything goes wrong in their business we have to suffer.

Is this actually the way the mind works anterior to consciousness? An extraordinary light was recently thrown on the authenticity of the procedure by the case of a criminal dying in New York. Detectives attached to the criminal bureaus in our large cities are, like writers and doctors, students of psychology, and one of them had the idea of taking down a stenographic report of the utterance of a gangster, Dutch Schultz, while in that state of mind, as the result of a wound, when he was incapable of imposing any logic on what he was saying. The whole stenographic report, not more than a couple of newspaper columns, was a real revelation of the content of the man's mind. Compare the quotation from the novel with the following, from this particular report. Whereas the Joyce extract runs on without punctuation marks, the stenographer has put them into this extract:

Don't put any one near this check; you might have— please do it for me. Let me get up, heh? In the olden days they waited and they waited. Please give me shot. It is from the factory. Sure, that is bad—well, oh good ahead that happens for trying. I don't want harmony. Oh, mamma, mamma! Who give it to him? Who give it to him? Let me in the district—fire—factory that he was nowhere near. It smoldered.

On the publication of *Ulysses,* it was considered by many that it was not possible in literature to carry the expression of the unconscious further and have it keep any intelligible pattern. However, Joyce's new puzzling book, *Work in Progress,* is an attempt to carry the revelation of the unconscious life many stages further than in *Ulysses* and much further than any other writer has dreamed of bringing it. Proust said of the opening chapter of *À la Recherche du Temps Perdu,* "I have tried to envelope my first chapter in the half-waking impressions of sleep." But Joyce, in this latest work, tries to depict the whole night-life of the mind, and the result, I am afraid, will be intelligible to a very limited number of readers. In *Work in Progress* he is influenced by Novalis's and Mallarmé's theories of the sounds of words, and the work has, in its best-known passage, reproduced so effectively, through the sonority of his words and sentences, the effects of falling night and fluttering river-water that, without the words being even intelligible, the reader can know what the passage is about if it is read aloud and falls on the ear as music does. There are specific points in technique in which it is difficult to believe that any writer can go beyond Joyce. One is the skill with which he evokes a scene, an atmosphere, a personage, a group, without ever once describing them or giving a hint as to who they are or where the scene takes place. He is a master of the evocative method, and if the reader compares the opening of *Ulysses* with the opening of Sinclair Lewis's *It Can't Happen Here,* he will observe immediately and inevitably the difference between the two methods, the evocative and the descriptive. Joyce's mastery of the interior monologue is the second point in his technique in which he is likely to remain unsurpassed, and for this mastery he undoubtedly owes a great deal to Freud.

6

There are a few points in common between James Joyce and the other outstanding modern innovator, Marcel Proust. For Proust, also, the great reality is in the unconscious; he also has an interest in sleep as its great manifestation; for both writers no happening, no event is complete, everything is in a state of becoming.

The work of both represents a reaction against realism, and is at the same time a development of it. Again it should be noted that, in literature, the age that is coming to birth is not only a reaction against the age that is dying but also an outgrowth of it. Both Joyce and Proust subscribe to the fundamental dogma of realism —that literature should be about everyday life; the work of each illustrates certain of the realistic doctrines. Joyce began definitely under the influence of Flaubert, which is patent in the stories in *Dubliners,* and though in the meantime, as can be seen in *Portrait of the Artist,* he was affected by the technique of Henry James, the influence of Flaubert is still traceable in *Ulysses,* especially the pre-realistic Flaubert of *La Tentation de Saint Antoine.* His characters are on the same level as Flaubert's and he has always held to the Flaubertian veto as to the author's commenting on his personages. He has, however, a whole battery of technical devices to reveal what is passing in their minds and what rises up in their memories, of which the interior monologue is but one. Others are the use of scenes parallel with scenes from the Odyssey, of paraphrases of myths and legends, and of parodies of writing representing stages in the development of language. The technique is infinitely more complex than Proust's, the interior life revealed very much less so; in fact, it is comparatively simple, comparatively ordinary, and does not embrace a wide variety of experiences.

THE REVOLT

The formative periods of the lives of the two writers were totally different. As a student, Joyce lived in Dublin during the most exciting years of the Irish revival and shared the interest of that period in myths, legends, symbolism—not only the particular form of symbolism called the Symbolist Movement, which had a romantic rather than an influential interest, but in all the symbolism of the literature of the past, the symbolism and philosophy of the Catholic Church and the compelling mystery of history. Then, later but still as a very young man, he went to live in Austria, where he encountered the latest manifestations of the philosophy of the unconscious. Proust, a Frenchman, lived in Paris, was influenced by the ideas of French philosophers and psychologists, and also by Freud. He appears to have passed through intense and varied emotional and intellectual experiences, to have sunk himself in music, painting and literature, making a study of the English novelists and of Henry James. The great developing influence on him was that of Bergson. He moulded his work deliberately on the Bergsonian conceptions of Time and Memory; in fact, Time may be called the hero of Proust's *À la Recherche du Temps Perdu.* "This invisible substance of Time," he said, "I have tried to isolate, but to do this the experience had to last." This meant that he had to deal with personages whose lives merged and flowed into each other over a long period, so that every little happening, as he said himself, would indicate the passing of time. Time walks through his book like a personage, transforming things, people, actions, ideas, opinions, social and political groups, from day to day, from year to year. As Time passes, the same personage takes on different aspects in the eyes of others, as, to use Proust's own image, we see different sides of a town from the windows of a train winding through it. Thus, he joined his conception of psychology to his conception of Time, for, as he himself said, "As there is a plane geometry and a geometry in space, so for me the novel is not only plane psychology but psychology in time."

As for Time, real Time, memory is its deposit, but what type of memory? It is what he calls "unconscious memory," as opposed to the memory of the intelligence, to voluntary memory. An odor, a savor, experienced in circumstances quite different, bring back, after the lapse of years, people and things that seem to have been forgotten: this is the unconscious memory, the involuntary memory. For in our lives the Past is that which has ceased to act but has not ceased to exist. It survives in our unconscious and has the potentiality of rising again to consciousness. Marcel Proust produced his work out of this conception of Time and Memory. He called his work in many volumes *À la Recherche du Temps Perdu,* familiar in its English title as *Remembrance of Things Past,* but which, it seems to me, would have been more revealingly translated as *The Search for Lost Time*.

This work unrolls itself as memory brought back to consciousness, Time experienced inwardly, Time made perceptible to the heart. An exact rendering of Bergson's conception of Time is to be found in the final pages of this novel. It is, in fact, probably the first time that there has been put into literature in a moving and imaginative way the central thought, the metaphysics, of a philosopher, during his own lifetime. A sound recalls to the middle-aged man, to Proust himself, the tinkle of the bell which he had heard as a child when his parents were showing their guest, Swann, to the door:

Then, thinking over all the events that necessarily ranged themselves between the moment when I heard those sounds and the Guermantes' reception, I was startled at the thought that it was, indeed, this bell which was still tinkling within me and that I could in no wise change its sharp janglings, since, having forgotten how they died away, to recapture it and hear it distinctly I was forced to close my ears to the sound of the conversations the masks were carrying on around me. . . .

When the bell tinkled I was already in existence and, since that night, for me to have been able to hear the sounds again, there must have been no break of continuity, not a moment of rest for me, no cessation of existence, of thought, of consciousness of myself, since the distant moment still clung to me and I could recapture it, go back to it, merely by descending more deeply into myself. *It was this conception of Time as incarnate, of past years as still close held within us, which I was now determined to bring out into such bold relief in my book*. And it is because they thus contain all the hours of days gone by that human bodies can do such injury to those who love them, because they contain so many past memories, joys and desires, already effaced for them but so cruel for one who contemplates and carries back in the domain of Time the cherished body of which he is jealous, jealous even to the point of desiring its destruction. For, after death, Time withdraws from the body, and the memories—so pale and insignificant—are effaced from her who no longer exists, and soon will be from him whom they still torture, and the memories themselves will perish in the end when the desire of a living body is no longer there to keep them alive.

The novel is an unrolling of life, revealing no crisis, no plot, only the poignant effects of Time on people who, day by day, are inevitably touched by Time, changed by Time, not only in themselves, but in their relation to each other. There is a rendering of an interior life that is not under the control of the intelligence, of an emotional life driven by a mechanism deep in the subconscious and not amenable to laws imposed by logic or rational ethics. "My book," asserted Proust, "is in no manner a work of the reason; the smallest elements of it have been furnished by my sensibility; I first perceived them deep in myself without understanding them, having as much difficulty in converting them into something intelligible as if they had been as foreign to the world of intelligence as, say, a motif in music. What we have not had to clarify for ourselves, what was clear before, as, for example, logical ideas, is not ours at all; we do not know if it is real." This sentence shows that Proust did something for himself that the other modern experimenters did not really do, he passed the speculative philosophies, the philosophy of Bergson and the psychology of Freud, through the medium of his sensibility, through all the furnishings of his own mind, before he used them in his work; that is, he performed the critical task of making a speculative philosophy into a literary philosophy, through first making it usable for himself. If all the modern writers had taken the same pains, or had a like equipment for making speculative philosophies into literary material, we should have much less unintelligibility in modern writing.

This disclaiming of the reason, of the conscious intelligence, this denial of logical ideas as being really our own, is the antithesis of the realist intelligence and objectivity. With its stress on everything that happens in the mind, in the interior life, *À la Recherche du Temps Perdu* is the opposite of a typical realistic work. At the same time, it must not be assumed that because Proust declares his book is not a work of the reason it is not a work of the intellect. It is a highly intellectual book, the work of a comprehensive intellect made luminous by strong emotions and an all-encompassing memory.

Both Joyce and Proust give the same impression, that they have penetrated into reaches of the inner life of men and presented them with far more actuality than has been done before. Yet we feel that this very same impression was given in their day by the creators of Emma Bovary and Anna Karenina, and it is probably the impression given by all innovators in literature. In both *Ulysses* and *À la Recherche du Temps Perdu,* the author is a character in his own work; this is perhaps always necessary in the literature which may be described as the literature of memory, in which the author invokes Time lived through.

This is true of the American writer whose work, likewise, might be described as Remembrance of Things Past and is also made up of Time, myths, legends, history, language—Thomas Wolfe too introduces Time into his titles, and has named one of his books *Of Time and the River.* Like Proust he tells us of his struggles with Time-elements, and has, in addition to the two Time-elements of Proust, the Present and the Past, brought in a third which he calls Time Immutable, the time of rivers, mountains, oceans and the earth. Like Proust he discourses on the powers of his memory to bring back odors, sounds, colors, shapes; like Joyce he has struggled with the mystery of myths and legends; like many modern writers, Aldous Huxley and D. H. Lawrence, he has expressed the conviction that all serious creative work must at bottom be autobiographical, a conviction with which it is not necessary to agree, but which is undoubtedly true of all those forms of literature in which Time and Memory are the sources of inspiration.

7

Like all modern theories of literature, these theories about the novel are complex and intellectual. A great deal of modern poetry, also, is dominated by complex philosophical ideas. Poetry, for the distinguished French poet, Paul Valéry, as for the later Yeats, is a luminous revelation of ideas or spiritual perceptions. Poetry, for Paul Valéry, who is a direct descendant of the Symbolists, and like them somewhat sterile in his inspiration and deliberate in his attitude towards composition, is an art in which it is legitimate to use all the effects of the other arts—the sound of music, the composition of painting. In the world from which he draws his ideas, logic is of no more importance than it is in the world of Proust and Joyce, or than it was in the world of Rimbaud and Verlaine. Like theirs, Valéry's is an endeavor, but a far more deliberate endeavor, to get away from the domination of the old literary conceptions, the old literary effects. A few lines from one of his well-known poems will throw a little light, not only on his method but on the method of some other mod-

ern poets. Here is the opening of his "Cimetière
Marin":

> Ce toit tranquille, où marchent des colombes,
> Entre les pins palpite, entre les tombes;
> Midi le juste y compose de feux
> La mer, la mer, toujours recommencée!
> O récompense après une pensée
> Qu'un long regard sur le calme des dieux!

> . . . .

> This quiet roof where the doves walk
> Palpitates between the pines, between the tombs;
> Midday appeases with its fires
> The sea, the sea always beginning again!
> O recompense after thought—
> A long gaze on the calm of the gods!

Of course, in this bare rendering, all the beauty of
sound of the original is lost. To get at its meaning,
poetry of this kind, like the poetry of Mallarmé or the
poetry of Rimbaud, demands from the reader an exercise of the intellect and the imagination. The poet takes
no trouble to make it easy for the reader; Valéry puts
into these lines only the essential points of the scene
on which he gazes—the cemetery, the pines, the sea,
and the poet's thought brooding on them. The effect
of the sun on the sea, of the sails of the boat on the
water, is one of pictorial composition—it makes a picture like doves walking on a roof. What a writer out
of the older literary tradition would have written
would be something of this kind: "The quiet sea, where

the sails of the fishermen's boats move, is like a flat roof where doves are walking": all that Valéry gives us is the "quiet roof where the doves walk," and this is an inheritance from those theories of writing that Rimbaud and Verlaine worked out together.

And here is a passage from the middle:

> Ils ont fondu dans une absence épaisse,
> L'argile rouge a bu la blanche espèce,
> Le don de vivre a passé dans les fleurs!
> Où sont des morts les phrases familières,
> L'art personnel, les âmes singulières?
> La larve file où se formaient des pleurs.
>
> Les cris aigus des filles chatouillées,
> Les yeux, les dents, les paupières mouillées,
> Le sein charmant qui joue avec le feu,
> Le sang qui brille aux lèvres qui se rendent,
> Les derniers dons, les doigts qui les défendent,
> Tout va sous terre et rentre dans le jeu!
>
> . . . .
>
> They have vanished into a dense absence,
> The red earth has drunk the white generations,
> The gift of living has passed to the flowers!
> Where are the familiar phrases, the personal manner,
> The separate souls of the dead?
> The grub crawls where the tears once formed.
>
> The shrill cries of fondled girls,
> The eyes, the teeth, the moist eyelids,
> The charming bosom playing with fire,
> The blood glowing on lips that surrender,
> The last gifts, the defending hands—
> All go down into earth and back into the game.

(Literal translation by M. M. C.)

"Game" here means nature's vast game of life and death.

To eyes used to taking in the meaning of lines and sentences in a flash, as one passes, in an automobile, hoardings advertising soaps and toothpastes, this sort of writing will on first encounter be unintelligible. It demands not only a glance of the eyes, but an exercise of the intelligence, the imagination, the memory, and a power of meditation that is in itself an attainment; it demands more from a reader than a mere visual exercise. The accustomed combinations of words are not there; adjectives are employed, not for their power of description but for their power of evoking a thought.

Chapter Twelve

WHERE WE ARE

I

THE TRUTH of it is that, in spite of some interesting writers and their technical innovations, we are still living on the ideas, the literary doctrines, the programs of the nineteenth century. We write biography, history, poetry, novels, dramas, as the great critics and writers of the nineteenth century have taught us to write them. All the literary doctrines of whatever nature, whether Lessing's, that literature is the expression of national and racial genius, or de Staël's, that it is an expression of society, or the total trend of the literary ideas of the nineteenth century, that realism was the ultimate goal of literary expression, or the ideas of the later realists, that social reforms were the concern of writers and of writing, all these ideas and all the others—Sainte-Beuve's and Taine's and Wordsworth's and Baudelaire's—all were true, but they represented only a part of the truth, and none of them were meant to be assumed to stand for a dominating regulation of literature at any time. All these ideas, some more than others, have played a great and transforming rôle in literature down to the present day. Some of them have had followers as fanatical as the devotees of religious dogmas. These ideas—because, like all real ideas, they remain alive—might still play some sort of vivifying rôle if vitalized by a transforming mind that could mould them into a new shape and add its own original contribution to them. But the truth is, in their original form they have reached a dead end, and most of them, in the hands of uncreative writers, have become tyrannical platitudes. Writing is no longer re-creating itself; it is simply repeating itself, however this repetition may be masked by the use of adroit technical devices.

What we have added that is new is very slight: the material used by Joyce and Proust was developed in the nineteenth century, though an effective way of using it in literature was not attained to until the present century. The most accomplished mind in literature that we have had in this century has probably been that of Proust; he is unique among modern writers in that he made the first successful effort to translate into literary material and into a literary philosophy the formal philosophies he made use of. The inclination of all other writers who made use of psychological discoveries or social ideas or philosophic speculations was to use them in the raw without transforming them by passing them through the medium of their own sensibility or through the artistic imagination. This lack of transforming power is partly responsible for the unintelligibility of a certain type of modern literary expression: the writers have not known how to mould their material, or the critics have not assisted them to mould it. If enough disinterested and competent minds had devoted themselves to the development of new ideas in art, as has been the case in science, it would not have been possible for literature to have got itself into the rut that it is in at the present time. Nor would it have been possible, laying aside for the moment all consideration of literature as an art, for writing to have been one of the few remaining trades or professions where a man who knows nothing about the job can make an entrance and sometimes even a success. A man nowadays can produce a book that corresponds in content and construction to an early or elementary type of automobile, and yet get it published and even praised. Books that are dead as soon as they are published are turned out as fast as the printing-presses can work; the forests are denuded of trees to make paper to print works of which the world had no need, which were useless from the start, which lived only a feeble life and died without leaving a trace.

This state of affairs is due either to the paucity of first-rate critical minds or to the fact that, owing to economic necessity, such minds may be locked up in remote colleges instructing youth in the elements of literature, or are wasting their powers in the literary reviews trying to decide which third-rate trade-writer has produced a book a trifle better than some other third-rate trade-writer. It is, of course, entirely possible, that we have no first-rate critical minds at all at present. "An age that has no criticism," said Oscar Wilde, "is either an age in which art is immobile, hieratic, and confined to the reproduction of formal forms, or an age that possesses no art at all . . . it is the critical faculty that invents fresh forms . . . it is to the critical instinct that we owe each new mould that art finds ready to its hand. . . . There has never been a creative age that has not been critical also."

2

There are two great problems before the critical intellect at the present time; one is to achieve some liberating ideas that will stir minds to new expression and bring literature out of the dead-end it has reached and once more into the rôle of creation instead of reproduction—to stir minds to new expression as the great critics dealt with in this book stirred them. The other problem is to make some clear and recognizable boundaries between the various kinds of writing, for the critical mind has allowed itself to become overwhelmed by the eruption into writing, during the last fifty years, of a vast mob. Whereas, in the old days, the divisions in which writers could be placed were few—

there were perhaps two of them—we now have many.

In the modern world, writing is both an art and a trade, an art or a trade. As a trade, it came in with the development of capitalism and industrial life and with the spread of elementary education, which brought into existence an audience of the newly literate who demanded reading-matter of their own. Consequently, as a trade, writing is followed by a number of workers to whom all art, including the art of literature, is an unrevealed mystery. It is also followed as a trade, or perhaps as a profession, by writers who, on occasion, can rise to the production of a work of art. Sometimes a man writing what he thinks is a piece of trade-writing, produced for a definite market, consciously or unconsciously achieves a work of art; the other way round may be equally true, and a man aiming at producing a work of art may turn out a piece of trade-writing or merely a piece of literate writing. The line has to be drawn, and it is the critic's immediate responsibility to draw it, not so much between writers themselves as between their products, for the same writer can produce work varying between high literature and the commonest type of trade-writing. As trade-writing came in with the development of capitalism and industrialism, so in the non-capitalistic or industrially backward countries the trade-writer, except as a newspaper writer, is an uncommon figure. In the highly developed capitalistic countries he is common; in a great capitalist country like America, he is very much to the fore, and sometimes makes as large an income as any other sort of manufacturer—a coat and suit manufacturer or a toothpaste manufacturer. The smaller trade-writer is like the small trader of any kind—the house-painter, the carpenter, the small storekeeper—sometimes he makes a decent living, sometimes a starvation wage.

Writing, as a trade, in the hands of competent and talented practitioners is a high-class trade, demanding greater intelligence and broader experience of life than most others, but it should not be confused with literature, the production of a number of rare minds in every generation, a number of minds whose work is, according to Hegel's definition, the production of truth or spiritual reality in sensuous form. Trade-writing has a number of uses, some invaluable, some of little consequence; some trade-writing—and this includes a large slice of fiction-writing—serves the purpose of recreation or escape from ennui; another type conveys instruction, information, opinions, propaganda or advertisement. In a modern magazine, the part which contains the fiction and the formal articles is described as the literary section, and is published in a different way from the advertising section, but in actual fact, in an up-to-date publication, there is hardly a pin's difference between the content, language, and recreation-value of the advertising pages, and the content, language, and recreation-value of the literary section. I will give, as examples, a story from the advertising section of *Harper's Bazaar,* and a story, by a well-known author, in the literary section; no reader unfamiliar beforehand with the matter would be able to recognize, I am sure, which is meant to be the literature and which the paid advertisement.

Quotation I:

Cap'n Sam paused for a dreamy moment. "And now I'll be telling you about the Parsee princes in Bombay," he went on, ". . . and the lovely little folk that live in Bali. Peaceful people, like your mother said." Mrs. Milford looked at her husband, and he returned her smile. They both remembered that day, three months before, when Captain Sam had appeared at the back door of their country home. He had been impressive even in his threadbare clothes, patched with a sailmaker's undisguised stitches. "I'm Captain Sam Johnson," he had introduced himself simply; "and I'm eager to do anything, from gardening to a bit of seafaring." So a gardener he was, now, and a painter of porches that he somehow made to look trim and smooth like the decks of a ship.

And here is Quotation II:

Steven first met Matilda at a friend's coming-of-age party. She was nineteen then, very pretty and eager and determined; and he, of the same age, was a shy, rather sulky-looking youth with red hair and green-blue eyes. They danced together once, but he was not very good at the new steps, so they sat out a second dance and talked about books. He was a medical student and wanted to lend her a new novel he had just been reading. . . .Two days later the novel arrived, and when she wrote thanking him for it he asked her to tea at a restaurant. . . . After a few more meetings they discovered themselves to be in love and became engaged. Steven was working hard for his examinations, and it would have been a pity if Matilda had been the wrong sort of girl for him, and some people thought she might be. "They don't seem to get on very well together," people said.

The author of the advertising story is anonymous, but I really believe it is the better written and shows the more inventive power of the two. The author of what is meant to be the literary story is James Hilton, author of *Goodbye, Mr. Chips.* Both the fiction writer and the advertising writer are trade-writers, producing work to meet a market-demand and using language as a stereotyped, almost algebraicised vehicle of expression. Trade-writing is a commodity produced for a known market in exchange for cash; the market fluctuates, but in the main, in a capitalist country, if a writer produces a piece of work, say, for the market covered by the largely circulated magazines, we can tell its money value beforehand, varying a little according to the product and to the status of its producer.

So much for writing as a trade. Now we come to writing as an art, writing which is literature, the production of truth, the production of new truth in every age, in sensuous form, the sort of writing that this book is concerned with. High literature has no market value of the kind that can be assessed in money; nobody can tell what the cash value of a masterpiece might be in its author's lifetime. Some people can estimate what its value as art is, that is they can tell, roughly speaking, if it has enduring reality, though they may not be able to tell how long it will endure, for a piece of writing can be a work of art—a minor work of art— and have a fleeting life; a great work of art is, of course, one that lasts, one of the realities that forgetful mankind finds worthy of remembrance. A good piece of trade-writing can last for some years, too, but what is a long life for a piece of trade-writing would be a short life for a work of art.

When we say that a great work of art is a work of such revelation, such reality, that it is considered of lasting value by generations of men, we again have to make another distinction, for if the *Divine Comedy* has shown itself possessed of lasting reality so also has Euclid's *Elements* or Darwin's *Origin of Species* or Harvey's *Motion of the Heart and Blood*. What distinguishes a work of art from any of these, what distinguishes the reality that is *Hamlet* from the reality that is Euclid's *Elements,* is that one is spiritual truth in sensuous form and the other is factual truth in logical form; what distinguishes *Hamlet* again from Locke's *Concerning Human Understanding* is the difference between truth in sensuous form and truth in abstract form. A work of philosophy can, of course, be a work of literature as well, when the sensuous imagination enters in an organic way into its creation, as it does in the works of Nietzsche or Schopenhauer. There is, of course, imagination shown in the *Elements* of Euclid, there may even be emotion, but these are of a totally different kind from those that enter into a work of art. Even the types of imagination that enter into the composition of various forms of art differ, the one from the other. The type of imagination that is in lyric poetry differs from the type of imagination that is in a narrative poem, or a novel, or a biography, or a piece of criticism. The sort of intelligence that is displayed in Euclid's *Elements* is dominatingly the reasoning intelligence; the intelligence in *Hamlet* is an emotionalized intelligence, what Coleridge called "the heart in the head." The imagination in Euclid is a formal imagination; the imagination in *Hamlet* is the rhapsodic imagination, a type of imagination that can be uncontrolled vision, as it sometimes is in the work of William Blake, and as Rimbaud aimed at making it. A work of history, also, can be simple information, or, like Gibbon's *Decline and Fall of the Roman Empire,* it may, because of its range of emotion, the nature of its imagination, its acute sensitivity to historical experience, the manner in which it is thought out into language, belong to the category of literature.

The confusion that exists at present between literature and all other sorts of writing is partly due to the uncritical manner in which literary history has been written, in which pure literature is considered in the same volume, and even in the same chapter, with historical works, with political works, which sometimes are literature and sometimes only information, or sometimes mere opinion, and with works of science, which are almost never literature, with oratory and pamphleteering, which commonly are forms outside literature. Sometimes, naturally, out of the ruck of oratory and pamphleteering there comes a speech or a pamphlet so informed by the imagination, so quickened by a passion of indignation, so thought out into language, and illuminated by some wisdom or emotion, that it does reach the region of art; it can last even when, as in the case of *Drapier's Letters,* the object of the propaganda is difficult to recall.

Commonly speaking, when groups of critics or writers belonging to writers' Unions talk about literature what they mean is trade-writing, and, naturally enough, for to writing as a trade belongs the bulk of everyday writers: the journalists, the ordinary fiction-writers, the ordinary contributors to magazines. Writers in our time can be divided into four groups: the real writers—that is the artist-writers; the trade-writers; the citizen-writers; the amateur writers. Properly speaking, the only sort of writers deserving publication and consideration are the artist-writers and the trade-writers. The citizen-writer is a citizen speaking to fellow-citizens on matters of common interest; he need not have any writing ability at all. The amateur writer is one who can reproduce with moderate competence a type of work that has already been done many times. In America such a writer can achieve publication, with verse or fiction, five or six times, and the level of his work corresponds about to that of the sketching, or performances on the piano, of Victorian amateurs.

When the leaders of Soviet Russia, or any other modern totalitarian state, talk about literature and writers, what they have in mind is trade-writing and trade-writers; they certainly do not mean, by writing, Hegel's presentation of truth or spiritual reality in sensuous form; they do not mean the "Ode to a Nightingale," or Shakespeare's Sonnets, or *Hamlet,* or "Kubla Khan," or *Phèdre,* or the "Bateau Ivre," or any product of the interior life or the creative imagination; all such works seem to be outside their survey of the issues they have in view. When Lenin made the declaration that "literature must become part of the general proletarian movement, a cog in that vast, unified, socialized mechanism which is set in motion by the conscious advance guard of the entire working-class. . . . Literature must become a component part of the organized plan for unified socialist party work," what he had in mind was trade-writing, which can very suitably concern itself with a market or goal of any kind, and which can be turned on to the furtherance of any end. But literature cannot be conscripted in such a way; it is made of no such components as Lenin believed, and when he gave out as a slogan, "Down with the supermen litterateurs; the leadership of literature belongs to the working-class as a whole," he showed himself in a state of invincible ignorance as to the nature of literature, great genius though he was in another field. Nor can what Trotsky called mysteriously "the mastery of culture" mean that any one with such a mastery, whatever it may be, can either create or understand art. As Clive Bell has pointed out, a man may have an intellect as keen as a drill, with the best education in the world, he may even have an interest in art, literature and æsthetics, and yet not know a work of art from a handsaw. The late Irving Babbitt was, as far as information about literature is concerned, probably the most highly instructed man in America; however, the nearest his mind came to an understanding of the art of literature was in his appreciation of spiritual truths and intellectual integrity; of spiritual truth as expressed in literature in sensuous form, as apart from ethical doctrine, he was highly suspicious and frequently contemptuous, even when it was the product of the highest type of mind that humanity has attained.

3

A work of art may be totally incomprehensible to the Babbitts and Lenins and Rockefellers, and entirely comprehensible to an itinerant umbrella-mender or a fiddler or a flute-player, or an Irish or a Mexican peasant who has had leisure and strength to cultivate his emotions and spiritual forces. Art can be created by vagabonds like Villon or Gorki, sinners like Saint Augustine, Baudelaire and Verlaine, saints like John of the Cross, by a half-crazy man like William Blake, by semi-barbaric nobles like Michelangelo, or Byron, or Tolstoy, or by solid members of the bourgeoisie like Robert Browning. Art is, and always has been, the property of those who create it and of those who understand it, and they, no matter how unpalatable the statement may be to literal believers in democratic or communistic dogmas, are a minority in every state and in every class. The average reader, the average concert-goer, the average art-gallery frequenter, is not the average man but the exceptional man, the man in the minority.

The attempt to reduce all superiority to the level of mediocrity is one of the moving forces behind the desire to make all literature appear a trade that can be pursued by any intelligent man, even by any educated man. One of the difficulties in the way of progress of any kind is this resentment of all superiority, a resentment that can be so easily aroused, and more easily at some periods of the world's history than at others. Whether in this age it suits us to face the fact or not, there has always been a spiritual and intellectual leadership, persons who are not productive in the material

or economic order, but who are productive in the
spiritual and intellectual order. It is not suggested that
in what is called the total ordering of things the functioning of this class is more important than that of
any other, but if its free functioning is prohibited, civilization will arrive at the ant-heap. And its free functioning can be prohibited by other things than the ukases of
individual dictators; at present its free functioning in
free countries is partly prohibited by the domination
in writing of an uncreative majority the consideration
of whose works takes up most of the space in literary
journals, and by the tactics of a group who wish to
subordinate literature to social and political interests.
The members of an intellectual or spiritual order cannot, on penalty of being destroyed and having spiritual
values destroyed with them, become servants of any
economic or class interest; an artist ought not to let
himself be deluded in this matter by his natural sympathies.

All the classes, all the dominant interests, at one time
or another, have been in hostility to the free functioning of an intellectual aristocracy, for they have ex-
pected it to serve their own interests, or at least, not to
oppose them. Socrates, Dante, Galileo, Victor Hugo,
Dostoevsky, Unamuno, Thomas Mann, were all persecuted because they did not serve the interests or the
ideologies of the powerful classes of their day. The
number of lesser men and the names of those in our

day who have been persecuted for opposing the classes in power, from Russia to Spain, would make a very long list. Those who wish to preserve literature have to set about preserving it from assaults from all sides. It seems as if there has hardly been a period in history when writers were less independent, less devoted to their own vocation, than they are at present. There are, in our time, even among members of writers' groups, a number of people with a hatred of all spiritual values and with an impassioned desire to destroy literature and every expression of the interior life and of the life of dream. Even the most meanly gifted human beings have a life of dream, though it be the narrowest, most limited dream, a dream of marrying the boss's daughter or being the head of the office. But whatever it may be, while it lasts it takes up a great deal of each life, sometimes to the extent of nearly obliterating the life of external reality.

It is one of the objects of art to mould this life of dream, to shape it into forms that will enable men and women to achieve a greater consciousness, a profounder communication with life, stronger feelings, subtler intelligences, more noble imaginations. Why so many writers should disparage the existence of a dream-life and why a certain type of critic should regard it as having less dimension than the exterior life, is hard to understand. But the widespread development of an uninspired and decadent realism and a flat, impoverished materialist philosophy has brought about a concentration on exterior life, and the routine of exterior life, to the discrediting of all forms of interior life. A great many facets of modern art, and especially of modern literature, that the public find difficult to understand, represent an attempt at a restoration of a part of life that is powerfully existent and, with this, a restoration of myths and legends to their necessary place in the domain of human expression. The combination of materialist and positivist philosophies with literal and sordid realism in literature and the denial that we have any spiritual inheritance has given that minority, that always existing minority which since the beginning of history has had a contempt for spiritual truths and for that side of man immersed in dream, a chance to get into a dominating position.

Yet just as surely as time is composed of night and day, life is composed of dream and external reality, and the advancement and happiness of man depend not only on the elevation of his everyday life, but on the elevation of his dream-life. The displacement and the disowning of the dream-life, the lack of recognition of the fact that it, too, needs vitalizing nutriment, are responsible for a great deal of the despair of the modern world. The tendency has been to concentrate on one half of life, and this has forced men further and further back to the conviction that life and creation are not only mysteries, but dismal mysteries, and that the cosmos, instead of implying beauty and order, implies unintelligibility and anarchism. There are now engaged in writing a number of men who appear to live from day to day in the hope that some obscure disaster will overhelm art and humanity. Any sort of writing, no matter how platitudinous or derivative, that seems to portend this disaster, is greeted by them with fervour. Even from a genuine artist like Paul Valéry comes that lonely, incredibly sad solution: that nothingness is better than life, that the earth, the sun, the moon, the stars, humanity itself, are but an error of the Creator, that the universe is God's fall, a defect in chaos, the original sin. The despair of modern philosophies would be intolerable if one did not know with Proust that Time touches everything, that Time changes everything, that spring succeeds winter, and summer, spring, and that the words of another living poet, William Butler Yeats, are prophetic and true:

> O silver trumpets, be you lifted up,
> And cry to the great race that is to come!
> Long-throated swans upon the waves of time,
> Sing loudly, for beyond the wall of the world
> That race may hear our music and awake.

INDEX

INDEX

INDEX

INDEX

INDEX

INDEX